FORMAL LOGIC

FORMAL LOGIC

By
JACQUES MARITAIN

TRANSLATED BY
IMELDA CHOQUETTE

NEW YORK
SHEED & WARD

TRANSLATOR'S PREFACE

In doing this translation I have tried to keep in mind that its purpose is simply to make M. Maritain's *Petite Logique* available to the English-reading public. Therefore I have been faithful to the precision and compactness of the original at the expense of fluency and the niceties of literary expression. The eighth French edition was used and all available notes re-checked.

I am quite unable to express my appreciation to Dr. Gerald B. Phelan, President of the Institute of Mediæval Studies, Toronto, for his unfailing patience and care in reading the manuscript, and for the numerous corrections which he made. I wish also to acknowledge my sincere gratitude to Dr. Daniel C. Walsh, for his kind assistance and valuable suggestions, to Rev. John J. Hartigan and all my friends at Manhattanville, without whose help and encouragement this translation would neither have been completed nor even begun.

I. C.

MANHATTANVILLE,
April, 1937.

PRINTED IN THE UNITED STATES OF AMERICA

FOREWORD

I

In composing these elements of Logic we have endeavoured to distinguish carefully between what belongs to Logic itself, which has for its object a *being of reason*, the second intentions of the mind (*intentiones secundae*), and what belongs to Critique, which is a part of Metaphysics and has for its object real being itself in its relation to the knowing mind. This distinction is an extremely delicate one, for many problems overlap both disciplines, and nevertheless very necessary, for it is of foremost importance that the sciences be kept within the strict limits of their formal object.

We have thus been led to reserve for Critique several questions which are generally studied in treatises on Logic, particularly in *Logica Major*, for example the (metaphysical) discussion of nominalism and realism, the controversies concerning the nature of science and of ordinary knowledge, the value of first principles and the manner in which they are known by us, etc., and finally the question of the *classification of the sciences* (for we must first know what science is, and what its value, before classifying the sciences, and it *belongs to the sage*, that is to the Metaphysician, *to order* the sciences). Therefore the question of the *methods* of the different sciences, which cannot suitably be studied until the object and value of the sciences have first been determined, shall also be reserved for the treatise on Critique.

Having thus relieved Greater Logic (*Logica Major*) of a good deal of extraneous material, we have been able to restore to it many questions with which it is really concerned and which needlessly burden Lesser Logic (*Logica Minor*, formal Logic) in most scholastic manuals. By means of this general redistribution, wherein we have tried to remain faithful to the spirit of Aristotle and the ancient scholastics, we hope to have obtained certain pedagogical advantages of clarity and precision, and to be enabled to present the problems of Logic and Critique in a sufficiently natural order of increasing complexity and difficulty.

As these problems are in themselves difficult because of their high degree of abstraction, some professors may perhaps find it more convenient in teaching (in introducing students to philosophy in a single scholastic year) to depart from the *normal* order indicated in our *Introduction to Philosophy*,[1] (1 Minor and Major Logic, 2 Cosmology and Psychology, 3 Criticism as the first part of Metaphysics) and to replace it *in practice* by the following order which reaches Major Logic only when the students are already familiar with philosophical abstraction and have sufficiently studied the scientific part of the curriculum to have some experience of deductive and inductive reasoning and some understanding of the allusions and examples which the Logician must use.

1 Minor Logic (shortened and made easier by the plan which we have adopted).

2 Cosmology and Psychology.

3 Major Logic.

4 Critique.

Therefore we have decided to divide the second fascicle (The Order of Concepts, or Logic) and the fifth fascicle (Being as being, or Metaphysics) of our manual into two parts, which will appear separately. Thus the Minor Logic, Major Logic and Criticism will be published in three separate sections so as to permit each instructor to group the matter of the course in the order most convenient for him.

This *Logic* may perhaps find readers outside of the schools (as our *Introduction to Philosophy* has done). "The abandonment of logical studies in France," wrote Renouvier in 1859, "has been pushed to such a point that the theory of judgment is studied no more than that of the syllogism, and were it not that the study of mathematics and, in part, the study of law, somewhat alleviates this evil, we would find but few educated people who knew how to handle reciprocals for example, and who were not in the habit of sprinkling their conversation with crude paralogisms." (1) Since the time when this all-too-justified complaint was

[1] J. Maritain, *Introduction to Philosophy*, Sheed and Ward, 1937.

made, the number of those who understand the necessity of a return to the study of Logic for the restoration of the intelligence has been greatly increased. We would be happy if this modest work could contribute its part to this beneficial return. Concerning Logic, Stuart Mill has said (2): "I am persuaded that nothing in modern education tends so much, when properly used, to form exact thinkers, who attach a precise meaning to words and propositions and are not imposed on by vague, loose or ambiguous terms. The boasted influence of mathematical studies is nothing to it, for in a mathematical process none of the real difficulties of correct ratiocination occur (mathematical propositions, for example, are but universal affirmatives; furthermore the two terms are united by the sign, hence the immediate possibility of pure and simple conversion, etc.). For want of some such discipline many otherwise able men are altogether incapable of disentangling the intricacies of confused and self-contradictory thought. . . ."

II

May we be permitted two more observations. First, as we have remarked in the foreword to the *Introduction to Philosophy*, but as we may well repeat in order to avoid all misunderstandings, this present work is intended for beginners, especially for students in the latter half of their regular university course. For this reason it remains elementary, and does not pretend to be complete, particularly in the matter of documentary references and cited texts. Nevertheless, as it must preserve the scientific character necessary to philosophic exposition, it will form a real treatise which consequently contains *more* than is required by the official programme. But all explanations which entail some difficulty or which do nothing other than expand some point, shall be printed inset.[1]

[1] The Foreword to the French edition contains the following, which refers to the baccalaureate course in France: "Furthermore those paragraphs, the study of which is not strictly necessary towards the baccalaureate degree, shall be marked with an asterisk. This text may therefore be used by students who are preparing the second part of their baccalaureate under ordinary conditions (that is, in one year) as well as those who, by reason of exceptional circumstances, devote two years to the study of philosophy."

Secondly, there is a point upon which we had thought to have made ourselves sufficiently clear, but which we undoubtedly did not explain fully enough, since as well-informed a critic as Rev. Fr. Ramirez (3) completely mistook the true meaning of our method of procedure. We are convinced (and in this we are in accord with Father Ramirez himself and with the Aristotelian tradition) that, in any treatment which respects the order of the philosophic disciplines, the study of the nature of Philosophy, its division and value, should be undertaken only in Metaphysics. For Metaphysics alone, in its *rôle* of wisdom, may judge both itself and its proper principles, as well as the other sciences. This is indeed the procedure we mean to take in our present work. In our *Introduction* we touched upon the questions mentioned above (and upon many others) only because, to our mind, that work is in no way a *part* of the course in philosophy itself, and consequently no question is properly reserved to it. As is clearly indicated by its title, it precedes and paves the way for the course, but it remains *exterior* to it. We planned it as we did solely with a pedagogical concern for beginners, and to furnish them with a general propædeutic account wherein certain important results of knowledge might be put within their grasp from the point of view of common sense, before being proved in a deeper and more scientific manner later on. For this reason the questions treated therein should be taken up again in their proper place in the different sections of the Course, particularly in Critique.

III

The nature of this work did not permit us to discuss at length the different modern theories about Logic, with all the explanations necessary to such dicussions. However, we hope to have sufficiently treated the most important of these theories without prejudice to the complementary treatments to be given in Major Logic, and to have sufficiently clarified the essential principles governing these discussions. We shall be content indeed if we have succeeded in showing that the best way to bring new life to many problems is to go back to the thought of the ancients in its original sources.

We are not unaware of the imperfections that creep almost inevitably into a general didactic work of this type. If, despite the care with which it has been edited, certain errors remain, we shall be grateful to those of our readers who may be kind enough to bring them to our attention.

J. M.

NOTES TO FOREWORD

(1) CH. RENOUVIER, *Essais de Critique Générale*, 1st edition, 1859, *Logique*, vol. II, p. 126.

(2) STUART MILL, *Autobiography*, p. 14 (Columbia Univ. Press, 1924).

(3) *Ciencia Tomista*, July-August, 1922.

TABLE OF CONTENTS

CHAPTER III.—REASONING

APPENDIX

INTRODUCTION

(THE ORDER OF CONCEPTS)

PRELIMINARIES

1. PRELIMINARY NOTIONS. Logic [1] studies the reason itself as an *instrument* of knowledge, or a means of acquiring and possessing the true. It may be defined as : the art WHICH DIRECTS THE VERY ACT OF REASON, that is *which enables us to advance with order, ease and correctness in the act of reason itself.*[2]

Logic is the art which enables us to proceed with order, ease, and correctness in the act of reason itself.

(*a*) Thus Logic not only proceeds in conformity with reason, as do all the sciences, but bears upon the act of reason itself, whence its name, the science of reason, or of the *logos* (λογικὴ ἐπιστήμη).[3]

(*b*) The *reason* is not another faculty than the *intellect* (the *understanding*, the *intellect*) ; but, from the point of view of the functioning of this faculty, it is called more especially the intellect when it sees, grasps, or "apprehends," and more specially the *reason* when it proceeds through discourse from the apprehension of one thing known to another.

2. THE THREE OPERATIONS OF THE MIND. What act is proper to the reason as such ?

REASONING

We reason when we think for instance :

the spiritual is incorruptible,
but the human soul is spiritual,
therefore it is incorruptible.

[1] Cf. J. Maritain, *An Introduction to Philosophy*, p. 152, New York, Sheed and Ward, 1934.

[2] "Ars directiva ipsius actus rationis, per quam scilicet homo in ipso actu rationis ORDINATE et FACILITER et SINE ERRORE procedat" (St. Thomas, *in Anal. Post.*, lib. 1, lect. 1, n° 1).

[3] Logica vocatur *rationalis* non solum "ex eo quod est secundum rationem, sed etiam ex eo quod est circa ipsum actum rationis, sicut circa propriam materiam" (St. Thomas, *ibid.*).

Reasoning. Reasoning is the most complex operation of our mind; it is by reasoning that we go from what we know already to what we do not yet know, that we discover, that we demonstrate, that we make *progress in knowledge*. Since Logic studies the reason as a means of acquiring knowledge, it must consider *first* and *foremost* among the operations of the mind, *reasoning*.

There are other operations of the mind which Logic must also consider. It will consider them in relation to reasoning, as factors in it.

an act undivided yet complex. The act of reason is *one* or *undivided*, like the act of taking three steps towards a goal. One, two, three, we have reached the goal: we have taken three steps, but we moved without stopping, with an undivided movement. We reason likewise with an undivided movement; but we do not reason for the mere pleasure of running, or "discursing," from idea to idea, but indeed to *conclude*, to render evident to ourselves some truth in which we stop.

Yet the act of reason is a *complex act*; it is one or undivided but it is not *simple* or *indivisible*; on the contrary it is composed of several distinct acts in orderly sequence, each of which bears upon an enunciation similar to the three enunciations in the example given above and which we call *propositions*. Each of these acts taken in itself is called a

JUDGMENT.

This is another operation of the mind which is anterior to the reasoning and is presupposed by it. To judge is to affirm or deny; it is to think for example,

Judging. *Caution is the mother of safety*,

or again,

Formal dress is not a slight nuisance.

In the first judgment we affirm of the term "caution" this other term "mother of safety," that is, we *identify* these two terms saying: there exists one same thing (a same *subject*) to which both the name "caution" and the name "mother of safety" belong at the same time. In the second judgment we deny to the term, "formal dress," this other term "a slight nuisance."

By judging we declare ourselves to be in possession of the truth on this or that point. A wise man is a man who judges well.

The act of judging is *one* or *undivided*, as the act of taking a step ; it is even, strictly speaking, a *simple* or *indivisible* act.[1] Thus, in the example given above, the judgment does not consist in the juxtaposition of three different acts of thought—an act of thought for " caution," another for " is " and a third for " mother of safety," but indeed in a single act of thought. It bears nevertheless upon a *complex object* (a proposition constructed by the mind), and just as a step is a *movement* between two terms, between a point of departure and a point of arrival, so the act of judging is a movement of thought, translated by the word " is," which unites two different notions, expressed by the word-subject and the word-attribute or predicate.

a simple act but bearing on a complex object.

Each of these notions corresponds to a certain act of the mind called *conception*,[2] *perception*, or

SIMPLE APPREHENSION.

This is another operation of the mind, anterior to judgment and presupposed by it.

To conceive is to form in the mind an idea in which one sees, grasps or " apprehends " something. It is to think, *e.g.*,

To conceive or to make an act of apprehension about a simple object,

" man "
or " caution "
or " unfortunate."

This act is evidently at the very root of all our intellectual knowledge, and that is why it is of the first importance. For by this act *an object of thought* is offered to the sight or grasp of our intellect.

This act of perception or apprehension is, however, so imperfect that although it does indeed present to us an object of thought discernible in a thing, it does not at the same time present to us the other objects of thought which

[1] See No. 37.

[2] The word *conception* ordinarily designates only *the formation of the idea* (in which sense we are using it here) although it may also designate the formation of the *proposition* on which the judgment bears.

are united to this one in the thing as it exists (its existence being either actual or possible). Consequently our mind, remaining in a state of suspense, has nothing as yet to *affirm* or *deny*. It is clear for example that if we think :

" man "
" snow "
" delicate people "

we have but the beginning of a truth in our mind, our mind makes as yet no declaration of conformity with the real ; this declaration is not made, nor is there a completed truth in our mind, unless we think for example (in a judgment) :

" man is mortal "
or " snow is white "
or " delicate people are unfortunate "

or the like.

In the same way we do not advance by simply lifting our foot off the ground, we advance only if we take a step.

We may say then that in making an act of simple apprehension our mind merely grasps *a thing without affirming or denying anything about it.*

This act is not only *one* or *undivided*, but also *simple* or *indivisible :* the act of thinking " man " or " snow " is obviously an act which admits of no parts. Furthermore [1] it bears upon an *object* which is either *indivisible* itself (as an object of thought, *e.g.*, " man ") or at least is apprehended *in the same way as indivisible objects*, that is, without involving any *construction* erected by the mind. Hence it is called an act of *simple apprehension.*

a simple act having a simple object.

The act of conception or simple apprehension is thus a *primary* operation which presupposes no other intellectual operation. Undoubtedly it does not constitute our first act of knowledge (for it presupposes the operations of the senses), but it constitutes our first INTELLECTUAL *operation*, it is the *first operation of the mind.*

The three operations of the human mind are simple apprehension, judgment and *reasoning.*

***3. THE OPERATIONS OF THE MIND AND ITS PRODUCTS.**

[1] See below No. 7.

The study of the nature of the operations of the mind and of their inmost mechanism belongs to Psychology. But we may note here the distinction between

The *operation* itself or act of the mind, and the product which the mind produces thereby within itself.[1]

The act of *judging*, for example, is an operation of the mind involving the production or construction in the mind of a certain group of concepts, which we call an *enunciation* or *proposition.* There is as much difference between the action of assembling concepts and judging, and the constructed group itself, as there is between the action of building a house and the house when built.

The thought-proposition (the group of concepts) is distinguished in turn from the *verbal* proposition which explains it in words and is its oral sign. There is as much difference between the one and the other as between the house itself and some representation of it.

By *verbal* propositions we understand those that are actually spoken—groups of words spoken aloud—as well as those which are spoken only in the mind—groups of words formed in the imagination.

When we *think*, for example, " man is mortal," we affirm that which is presented to us by the idea of mortal, of that which is presented to us by the idea of man. But at the same time in which we form this proposition in the mind, we *imagine* the verbal proposition by which it is expressed (and sometimes we really form its phonetic equivalents with our lips).

The thought-proposition (the group of concepts) evidently differs as much from the *mentally spoken* proposition (the group of auditory or muscular images of articulate sounds), as it does from the *actually spoken* proposition.

To make more precise the meaning of the terms we shall

[1] " Sicut in actibus exterioribus est considerare operationem, et operatum, puta aedificationem et aedificatum ; ita in operibus rationis est considerare ipsum actum rationis, qui est intelligere et ratiocinari, et aliquid per hujusmodi actum constitutum : quod quidem in speculativa ratione *primo* quidem est *definitio, secundo enuntiatio, tertio vero syllogismus, vel argumentatio* " (St. Thomas, *Sum. Theol.*, I–II, q. 90, a. 1, ad 2).

use we may construct the following table of the operations of the mind :

THE OPERATIONS OF THE MIND AND ITS PRODUCTS

	THE OPERATION	THE PRODUCT (immaterial)	THE SIGN (oral and material)
The mental concept, product of the intelligence.	I. Determined by a likeness of the object received through the senses—by means of abstraction — the mind forms or " says " within itself	an idea (or MENTAL CONCEPT) in which	
First operation of the mind. The objective concept, or object of a concept.	it sees, grasps or apprehends (SIMPLE APPREHENSION) a certain essence or *object of a concept* (which logicians also call an OBJECTIVE CONCEPT) . . .	. . . .	
Oral sign of the concept.			and it designates this idea by a word (TERM) which is itself signifiable by a graphic sign (a written word) : *man.*
First product of the reason.[1]	Having thus seen or apprehended, the mind may now produce within itself . .	a complex concept relating in detail what it has seen. This is the DEFINITION of the thing	
Its oral sign.			of which the oral sign is a verbal DEFINITION (a group of words) : *rational animal.*
The second operation of the mind.	II. The mind constructs (COMPOSITION AND DIVISION)	a group of two concepts (*Subject* and *Predicate*) whose	
	agreement or disagreement it apprehends and which it affirms or denies one of the other by a simple act (a JUDGMENT) bearing upon .		
Second product of the reason.		this group of concepts or PROPOSITION. This has	
Its oral sign.		mental statement	for its oral sign a spoken PROPOSITION (a group of words) : *man is a rational animal.*

[1] " First " should be understood, here, in the logical order and not in the chronological order (see below *No.* 29*a*.) We say that the definition is the first product of the *reason* because it is the first product of the intellect *uniting* concepts.

THE OPERATION	THE PRODUCT	THE SIGN	
III. The mind sees or apprehends	a grouping of propositions (*antecedent*)		Third operation of the mind.
as "inferring" or rendering necessarily true	another proposition (*consequent*)		
which it "concludes" from the preceding propositions. This is the REASONING which constructs . . .	a group of propositions called ARGUMENTATION, whose . . .	oral sign is the verbal ARGUMENTATION (group of spoken propositions): *man is a rational animal; but every philosopher is a man; therefore every philosopher is a rational animal.*	Its oral sign.

In the first column of the table we have written that which concerns the *acts* or *operations* of the mind, in the second that which concerns the *products* that are formed in the mind, and in the third the *oral* and material *signs* of these mental products. Everyday language ordinarily confuses these three orders of things, because in many cases what is said of the product may also be said of the operation, and because it is natural for man to call things which are signified by the same name by their sign only, for this is more familiar to him. Nevertheless to take examples, a judgment is a vital act, a (thought) proposition is an immaterial organism composed of several concepts, a verbal proposition is an inert composite of material parts (words) in juxtaposition in time (oral proposition) or in space (written proposition). These distinctions are highly important if Logic is to be rightly understood.

(*a*) As we shall see later on, Leibnitz and certain logicians in his tradition tend to neglect the *operation* for the *product*, and the immaterial product of the mind for its *material sign*.

(*b*) On the other hand, in its critique of the intellect, the Anti-Intellectualist school (James, Bergson, Le Roy) often confuse the operations and products of the intelligence with the *material signs* by which they are expressed.

(*c*) No one has anywhere made clearer the distinction

between the thought and the material signs which express it than Aristotle. The object of his Logic is precisely the immaterial products of the mind, and not the spoken or written words, which he treats only in so far as they are the external signs of these products. Cf. Ammonius, *in Periherm.*, f. 19a and 20a : τά τε ἐκφωνούμενα σύμβολα εἶναι τίθεται τῶν νοουμένων καὶ τὰ γραφόμενα τῶν ἐκφωνουμένων.

To avoid confusion we shall restrict the usual meaning of the word " judgment " here, and use it only to designate the operation of the mind which consists in giving assent ; we shall use the word *proposition* to signify the *product* formed in the mind and to which this assent is given. This restriction will not obtain for the word *reasoning*, however, which we shall use in its ordinary sense, now to designate only the operation of the mind, now to designate its product or the argumentation, now to designate both at the same time. In each case the sense will be obvious from the context.

4. THE DIVISION OF LOGIC. Since Logic considers the reasoning primarily, it is in relation to the reasoning that it should be divided. But are there not in reasoning, as in every structure or work of art, two things to be considered? In a house, for instance, one must distinguish between the materials and the disposition given them by the architect ; if this disposition is bad the house will not stand because it is badly constructed. If the materials are bad (even though the disposition be good) the house will not stand, because it is built of bad material. In the same way, in reasoning we must distinguish between :

1. the ideal materials with which we reason, which are called

The matter and form of reasoning.

the MATTER of the reasoning

and 2. the disposition according to which these materials are assembled in the mind in order that the conclusion obtain, this is called

the FORM of the reasoning.

Reasoning is *correct* or *incorrect* in virtue of its *form*, and it attains to the *true* or the *false* in virtue of its *matter;* thus the reasoning—

Man can do no evil, (I)
but this criminal is a man, (II)
therefore this criminal can do no evil (III)

is *correct*, the *form* is valid, and the conclusion follows—but nevertheless it concludes to the *false* because the first proposition is untrue.

Since Logic is the art which enables us to proceed with ease, order and correctness in the act of reason itself, it must treat of both the *form* and the *matter* of our reasonings. Hence its division into *Minor* or *formal* Logic (*Logica minor*) and *Major* or *material* Logic (*Logica major*).

Minor Logic. Minor Logic studies the *formal conditions* of knowledge and *analyses* or, as we say, " *resolves* " the reasoning into the principles upon which it depends from the point of view of its *form* or disposition[1]; it sets forth the rules which must be observed if the reasoning is to be *correct* or *well constructed*, and the conclusion valid in relation to the *disposition* of materials. The mind that does not conform to these formal laws of thought is inconsistent and, as the Port-Royal *Logic* says, an inconsistent mind " has no talons " with which to hold fast to the truth.

Major Logic. Major Logic studies the *material conditions* of knowledge, and *analyzes* or " *resolves* " the reasoning into the principles on which it depends as to its *matter* or *content* [2]; it explains what conditions the materials of reasoning must satisfy if we would have a conclusion that is *firm on every side*, not only on the side of form but also on the side of matter; in other words, a *true* and *certain* conclusion.[3]

[1] This analysis or " resolution " of the reasoning into its formal principles is the object of Aristotle's *Prior Analytics*. For this reason the scholastics called it *resolutio prioristica*.

[2] This analysis or " resolution " of the reasoning into its material principles is the object of Aristotle's *Posterior Analytics*. For this reason the scholastics called it *resolutio posterioristica*.

[3] In order to obviate possible confusion it would be well to specify here that when we say that Minor Logic resolves reasoning into its *formal principles* (in which case the principles and laws in question are those which govern the *form* or disposition of the intelligible material used in reasoning) we are using the word *formal* in another sense than when we say that philosophy is resolved *formally* into the first principles of reason, and *materially* into sense experience (cf. J. Maritain, *Introd. to Phil.*, p. 140). In the latter case we mean that the

In the *Prior Analytics*, Aristotle treats of reasoning in its most general aspect, and rises therefrom to the consideration of the most formal aspect of discursive activity. This part of Logic, which studies what reasoning is, and how it must proceed whatever *its content* or the use which the mind makes of it (investigation or demonstration), should therefore be called *formal Logic* even at the risk of ambiguity. For, since the time of Kant and Hamilton, many modern authors have used the term *formal Logic* in a totally different sense.[1] In the *Posterior Analytics*, Aristotle treats of the different kinds of reasoning due to the diversity of objects or " matters " upon which discourse may bear. This part of Logic, being concerned with the different kinds of reasoning, *in virtue of their content*, should then be called *material Logic*. Formal Logic is, in truth, more abstract and therefore more difficult than material Logic. However, since formal Logic is presupposed by material Logic, it is advisable to begin our study with it, at the price of being content with a relatively summary treatment (this is what the scholastics called the *Summulae*). In this way, for pedagogical reasons, we are led to make of formal Logic a " lesser Logic " and to reserve for the second part of the treatise the more difficult questions concerning the foundations of Logic. Material Logic thus becomes " *greater Logic*."[2] We have seen fit to conform to this procedure because of its great pedagogical advantages. Further, we have found it advisable to emphasize in

first principles that are self-evident are those which constitute philosophy *formally* or *in its essence* and give it its proper light, while sense experience furnishes the materials from which intellectual knowledge actually comes materials on which philosophy depends.

So, although the first principles of reason may come into the consideration of Major or *Material* Logic, which treats of the content of our reasonings and not of their " form " or disposition alone, these first principles of reason are none the less, in another function, the *formal* principles of intellectual knowledge and philosophy, just as the soul is the form which gives life to the body.

[1] This point and the problems concerning the nature of Logic will be considered in Major Logic.

[2] Some modern treatises prefer the name *applied Logic*, but this runs the risk of ambiguity and might lead one to think that this part of Logic does nothing but apply the truths established by formal Logic, whereas it is in reality a part of Logic which treats of an aspect of things that formal Logic does not consider. The term *applied Logic* belongs rather to what the Ancients called *Logica utens*. The distinction between *Logica docens* (pure Logic) and *Logica utens* (applied Logic) will be studied in Major Logic.

the first two operations of the mind—which Logic always considers in sequence to the third—the division between formal and material analysis, which originally concerned the reasoning alone.

Subdivisions of Major and Minor Logic.

Minor and Major Logic are subdivided naturally according to the three operations of the mind; the study of the third operation which is the foremost object of Logic necessarily presupposes the study of the first two.

In addition to this, Major Logic treats especially of Definition, Division, and Argumentation as *instruments of knowledge*. It concludes fittingly with the study of the object and nature of Logic itself, a question which actually belongs to the domain proper to Critique and which Logic borrows from this science.

THE DIVISION OF LOGIC

MINOR LOGIC or Logic of correct reasoning.		1. *The Concept* . . .	1st operation of the mind	considered in relation to the rules for the construction of the reasoning.
		2. *The Proposition* . .	2nd operation	
		3. *The Reasoning* . .	3rd operation	analysed from the point of view of its formal principles.
MAJOR LOGIC or Logic of true Reasoning.	I Prolegomena	1. *The Universal.*	1st operation of the mind	considered from the point of view of the matter of the reasoning.
		2. *The Judgment.*	2nd operation of the mind	
		3. *The Three Instruments of knowledge (Definition, Division, Argumentation.)*		
	II The Logic of Demonstration	1. *False Demonstration* (Sophism)	3rd operation	analysed from the point of view of its material principles.
		2. *Imperfect Demonstration* (The Probable)		
		3. *Demonstration properly so-called* (The Necessarily true).		

CHAPTER I

THE CONCEPT AND THE FIRST OPERATION OF THE MIND

SECTION 1. SIMPLE APPREHENSION

By simple apprehension we perceive something without affirming or denying anything about it.

5. DEFINITION. What is simple apprehension? As we have seen above [1] it is

The act by which the intellect grasps or perceives something without affirming or denying anything about it.[2]

We make an act of simple apprehension when we think, for example, " man," " rational animal," " white," " intelligent," etc.

A nature or essence.

6. The *material object* of simple apprehension is the thing apprehended by thought, whatever it may be. The *formal object* of simple apprehension,[3] that which it attains first and directly, *per se primo*, is this same thing, *inasmuch as it comes directly into intellectual knowledge* or, in other words, it is that part of the thing which the intellect seizes immediately for its object. Since the essence or nature of a thing is, by definition,[4] that part of it which presents itself first to the intellect (*id quod per se primo intelligitur in aliqua re*) we may say that

THE FORMAL OBJECT

of simple apprehension is always

SOME ESSENCE, NATURE, OR " QUIDDITY."

(*a*) Here we may take the words " essence," " nature," and " quiddity " in their broadest sense [5] as meaning *what something is* (some object which I attain in pronouncing a name), or again *what this idea or this name sets before me*. I grasp *a certain essence*, in this sense, when-

[1] See pp. 4, 5.

[2] " Operatio, qua intellectus aliquam quidditatem intelligit, quin quidquam de ea affirmet vel neget."

[3] See J. Maritain, *Introduction to Philosophy*, pp. 105–106.

[4] See p. 191, *ibid.*

[5] See p. 191, *ibid.*

ever I think—*e.g.*, "living body," "animal," "French," "Peter."[1] Thus everything grasped by means of simple apprehension is, as such, ONE *essence.*

(*b*) But these words, "essence," "nature," and "quiddity" are understood *par excellence* in the narrowest and proper sense of "essence,"[2] as meaning *what a certain thing is primarily and necessarily for the intellect*, or again *what this thing is primarily and necessarily as the first principle of intelligibility.* In this sense I grasp THE complete essence OF Peter (confusedly or distinctly) in thinking "man," or "rational animal." When I think "living body" or "animal" I grasp this essence in only a part of its determinations, and when I think "French" or "Peter" I grasp (in a confused manner) this essence in all its determinations but with certain notes proceeding from the individual matter.

Thus simple apprehension is ordained *par excellence* to the perception of the *essences of things* as the formal object *quod* (this perception may be either distinct or confused, clear or obscure), and to the placing of this intelligible foundation before the mind. It is by reason of the essences

[1] The same is true if I think "white" (a concrete quality), whiteness (an abstract quality), "paternity" or "sonship" (a relation), etc., etc. The only exceptions are *beings of reason*, which, since they are creations of the mind and not *something* capable of existing in reality, may only be improperly called essences or quiddities.

[2] See J. Maritain, *Introduction to Philosophy*, pp. 197–201. Certain modern authors have misunderstood this term "the apprehension of essences" to mean that, by the power of abstraction, the mind may at once perceive the inmost constitution of a thing. The scholastics never held any such doctrine. For them, abstraction transports us from the sensible to the intelligible plane, and introduces us into the order of essences and their necessary laws. But the intelligible objects, the "natures" or "essences" perceived in simple apprehension, far from putting us in possession of the innermost constitution of things. are, at first, but the simplest and most common intelligible aspects, which are grasped in the things themselves (first of all and at the very outset, "being," as an object of thought). Thus the concept of "fire" which I derive from sense experience does not unfold to me the innermost nature and mysteries of "*ignition*"; at first it is simply a concept of *something with a determinate nature* (as yet unknown to me) which appears under certain sensible aspects. Only later do I penetrate this nature somewhat and know it as the combination of a body in its gaseous state with the oxygen of the air. Undoubtedly it was this very thing that the concept of fire revealed to me, but in a hidden way.

And even if we do succeed in attaining an explicit knowledge of the essences or the inmost constitution of some few things, nevertheless, in a great many cases (especially in the inductive sciences) we have to be content with imperfect knowledge through external signs.

of things considered as the principal object to be known, that simple apprehension grasps whatever it grasps.

In short, it is always *under this or that intelligible aspect* (under this or that "characteristic," "determination," or "formality") that simple apprehension attains natures and things. Thus in grasping one and the same nature, Peter's, for example, our mind may grasp it as "man," "animal," "rational animal," or as "every man," "this man," etc. There are as many distinct objects as there are particular acts of simple apprehension.

When the object of simple apprehension is one essence ("man or rational animal") it is *incomplex*.

7. COMPLEX and INCOMPLEX OBJECTS. Let us now consider the objects of simple apprehension as they are in themselves. To do this must we not distinguish between two kinds of objects of thought?

1—the objects of thought which are in themselves *simple* and *indivisible*, as the examples given above ("man," "rational animal," "whiteness," etc.); these are indivisible because each one is *an essence*; to add or subtract anything from its intrinsic constituents would be to destroy it, to set *something else*, another essence, before the mind.

When it is several essences combined, it is *complex*.

2—certain objects of thought which are in themselves *complex* and *divisible*, *e.g.*, "a man in sumptuous apparel," "the long-beaked heron helved with a slender neck," "an evil spreading terror in its wake," each of these contains *several essences*, or objects of the intellect. In the first case the object of simple apprehension is, in itself,

INCOMPLEX

In the second it is, in itself,

COMPLEX.

In this division we are considering the objects of simple apprehension *as they are in themselves*, as objects of the intellect. In this case they are *incomplex* or *complex* IN THEMSELVES (or, as to the thing, *re*, the ancients used to say).[1] If, on the contrary, we consider them *as to the manner in which they are attained*, *or conceived*, *in such and such*

[1] This is the only meaning that is ascribed to the word "complex" (complexe *re*) in the language of St. Thomas. He uses it to designate an *accidental* compound or *one by accident*. "*Ostensum est in VII Metaph.* says St. Thomas, *quod complexa non definiuntur*" (*In Anal. Post.* 1, lect. 2, n. 3)—Cf. Zigliara's commentary (Leonine edition, Vol. I, p. 142), *complexa non definiuntur*, etc.

a particular intellectual act, we would say that they were incomplex or complex AS TO THE MANNER OF CONCEPTION (as to the sign, *voce*), depending upon whether they present themselves explicitly under one, or several, intelligible aspects; in the first case they are expressed by a single term,[1] in the second, by several. In this sense, "man" is an incomplex object of thought, "rational animal," a complex object of thought.

In order, therefore, to divide the objects of thought from both of these points of view at the same time (considering them both *in themselves* and *as to the manner in which they are conceived*), we would have to divide them as:

INCOMPLEX *in themselves* and *as to the manner in which they are conceived* (incomplex *re et voce*), *e.g.*, "man" is one essence presented to the mind by means of a single intellectual grasp.

INCOMPLEX *in themselves* and COMPLEX *as to the manner in which they are conceived* (incomplex *re non voce*), *e.g.*, "rational animal," a single essence presented to the mind by means of two intellectual grasps.

COMPLEX *in themselves* and INCOMPLEX *as to the manner in which they are conceived* (complex *re non voce*), *e.g.*, "philosopher," two essences (philosophy and the man possessing the science) presented to the mind by means of one intellectual grasp.

COMPLEX *in themselves and as to the manner in which they are conceived* (complex *re et voce*), *e.g.*, "a man skilled in philosophy": several essences presented to the mind by means of several intellectual grasps.

Thus when we think, "the long-beaked heron helved with a slender neck," or "an evil spreading terror in its wake, evil that heaven in its wrath invented to punish earthly sins," or any such series of ideas (the length does not matter) that do not form a completed logical whole, we are making an act of simple apprehension, just as when we think "man" or "triangle." Simple apprehension may have a complex object.

Nevertheless, it remains *simple apprehension.*

[1] By a single "significative" or "categorematic" term (see below, No. 22b). For example in "all man" the "all" is not a "categorematic" term, for it does nothing but determine the term "man."

1. because it is primarily ordained to the perception of essences or quiddities which are *indivisible* in the sense explained above (wherefore the ancients called the first operation of the mind *indivisibilium intelligentia*),[1] and

2. because it grasps groups of essences, or objects which are in themselves complex, *in the same way that it grasps indivisible objects or isolated essences*; that is, it grasps them without producing any complete *structure* in the mind.

In the expression "simple apprehension" "*simple*" is understood as being contrasted with the constructive activity proper to the second and third operations of the mind.

In other words, in the expression "*simple apprehension*," the word *simple* is understood *as being contrasted with the constructive activity* manifested in the other operations of the mind by which we form within ourselves lasting structures, as it were, and works of art, so that we may reach the truth. All knowledge that does not arise from this constructive function of the mind, or that does not constitute a constructed *whole*, or a finished structure properly so-called, but constitutes only *a part* of such a whole, arises from simple apprehension. This is the case in definitions such as "rational animal," or in complex terms such as "the man who is approaching." These definitions and complex terms are to a complete product of the mind (*e.g.*, "man is a rational animal," or "I do not fear the man who is approaching") as a simple member, an arm or leg (a compound in itself, but only as a part, not as a whole), is to the organism.[2]

How then does a complete mental structure, or whole, differ from a complex part? Since the constructive activity of the mind is ordained to the attainment of truth, that is to putting thought into conformity *with what exists* (actually or "possibly") the constructions in question are not complete and finished until they signify the (actual or possible) *existence* of a subject with such and such predicates—that is until they constitute *enunciations* or *propositions* concerning which an act of assent or dissent may be made.

[1] "ἡ τῶν ἀδιαιρέτων νόησις," Aristotle, *De An.*, III, 6, 430 a, 26 (St. Thomas, lect. 11). Cf. *Periherm.*, lib. I, St. Thomas, lect. 3, n. 3: "Oportet intelligere, quod una duarum operationum intellectus est indivisibilium *intelligentia*, in quantum scilicet intellectus intelligit absolute cujusque rei *quidditatem* sive *essentiam* per seipsam, puta *quid* est homo, vel *quid* album, vel *quid* hujusmodi. Alia vero operatio intellectus est, secundum quod hujusmodi simplicia concepta simul *componit* et *dividit*." Cf. also *Metaph.*, lib. IX, St. Thomas, lect. 11.

[2] Cf. John of St. Thomas, *Curs. Phil.*, t. III, p. 514 (*Phil. Nat.*, III P., q. XI, a. 3).

SECTION 2. THE CONCEPT

A. NOTION OF THE CONCEPT

8. DEFINITION. As we shall see later in Psychology the intellectual act of perceiving taken in itself and inasmuch as it is a purely " immanent " action (that is, inasmuch as it is simply the faculty's qualitative completion) should be distinguished from the action of forming an idea, which is an action *productive* of a term or interior fruit. Nevertheless, in reality these two actions are but one, for the immanent act of intellection is in itself *virtually* productive,[1] and we may apprehend a thing only on the condition that we form an idea of this thing in ourselves : on condition that we *conceive* the thing within ourselves. A *concept* (or idea) is, therefore,

> *that which* the mind produces or expresses within itself—and
> *in which* it grasps or apprehends a thing.

The concept or mental word answers to : 1. a necessity of human intellectual knowledge ; for *to be perceived the intelligible object* must be brought in the concept to the ultimate degree of immateriality required by intellection in act. 2. the *fecundity*, *proper to the intellect*, which seeks naturally to manifest or to " tell itself " what it has just perceived. (Cf. John of St. Thomas, *Logica*, q. 22, a. 2.)

This is a concept, in the ordinary sense of the word, an " image " [2] or a spiritual likeness of a thing within us, and it is a pure *means*,

THAT IN WHICH

we attain the thing or object, " *id* IN QUO *intelligimus rem*." It may also be called an *idea*, *notion*, or *mental word*,[3] and more precisely a MENTAL CONCEPT, or " formal " concept.

A mental or "formal" concept is that *in which* we attain the thing.

[1] This thesis is proper to the Thomistic school, upheld on the one hand against Suarez, who distinguishes too little, and on the other against Scotus, who distinguishes too much, between the act of knowing as such and the *production of the word*. Cf. Cajetan, *in Sum. Theol.*, I, 27, 1 ; 34, 1, ad 2, ; 79, 2. Ferrariensis, *in II Cont. Gent.*, c. 9 and 82; John of St. Thomas, *Curs. Phil.*, *de Anima*, q. xl, a. 1. *Curs. Theol.*, t. IV, disp. XII, a. 5 and 6.

[2] In the broad sense of the word. See J. Maritain, *Introd. to Philosophy*, pp. 154–157.

[3] The concept is called an *idea* from "εἴδω," to see, because the object is *seen* by it and in it ; *notion* from " nosco," to know, because the object is known

The formal object of a concept is also called an "objective concept."

9. THE MENTAL CONCEPT and the OBJECTIVE CONCEPT.[1] The mental concept makes us know or grasp something; it has a particular object which is the very object of simple apprehension: an essence, nature, or quiddity, presented under some intelligible aspect or "formality." This formal object of the concept may be called simply the *object of a concept*, or the

OBJECTIVE CONCEPT

content of thought

The objective concept is *that which* we know by means of the mental concept.

because it is what we conceive of the object presented to the mind by the mental concept. *But it is essential to distinguish between these two accepted meanings of the word concept,*[2] *and to remember that the "objective concept" is not that by which or in which we know but, on the contrary, it is*

THAT WHICH

we know, that to which we immediately attain through the intellect (id QUOD per se primo intelligitur) *the thing itself, inasmuch as it comes immediately into intellectual knowledge, or the object known, inasmuch as it is an object.*[3]

by it and in it; and a *mental word* (*verbum mentis*) because the mind utters it within itself.

The concept is also called a *representation* because it is a likeness of the object by which it (the object) is made present to the mind, an *intention* (*intentio*) because it is that by which the mind tends toward the object, and finally a *species*, taken in the sense of a "representation" or "image" (in accord with the original meaning of *species*, cf. *aspect*, *aspicere*, *specio*, *speculum*, etc., Greek, σκέπτω). The concept is called "*species expressa*" (an expressed representation) as opposed to the "*species impressa*" (the representative impression) which determines the intellect to the production of the concept. See. J. Maritain, *Introd. to Philos.*, p. 178. St. Thomas calls this representative impression the *species* or *forma intelligibilis*, and calls the concept *verbum mentis*, *conceptus* or *intentio*.

In the strict scholastic vocabulary, the word "idea" is reserved for the concept which the artist imitates in his works, the creative idea.

[1] The distinction between the objective concept and the mental concept is being emphasized here in order to anticipate any confusion, for this distinction plays an essential *rôle* in Critique. No sane logic can be constructed without presupposing a certain metaphysic of knowledge which is, moreover, the metaphysic of common sense; indeed it could not be otherwise. Inversely, all the errors or deviations which we will have occasion to comment upon in Logic ultimately proceed from some avowed or unavowed metaphysical error.

[2] The word "intentio" also has these two different meanings: "*intentio formalis*" and "*intentio objectiva*."

[3] Although an objective concept is something other than the mental concept, yet in many cases what may be said of one may also be said of the other. Thus when we "compose" and "divide" we compose and divide both objective and mental concepts simultaneously and in one act.

It may be said of the objective concept as of the mental concept—but in an entirely different sense—that the thing is seized *by it*.

The mental concept is expressly known (*in actu signato*) [1] only by the intellect reflecting upon itself; it is the first to be considered by the *psychologist* in his study of concepts. The *logician*, on the contrary, treats of objective concepts first, although mental concepts come simultaneously into his consideration: for example, when we speak, in Logic, of the agreement or disagreement of two concepts, or of their "composition" and "division," and so forth, our primary concern is with objective concepts, with the object of thought which the mind sets before itself and which it skilfully manipulates, compares, and disposes, so that it may come to the truth.

In order to understand the notion "objective concept" as well as the notion "simple apprehension," we must note that since our ideas are the result of abstraction,[2] and are not impressed directly upon us by things, the object which we lay hold of in them is always presented as *abstracted* from ACTUAL EXISTENCE. Even if this object does ACTUALLY EXIST in reality (a fact revealed to us only through sense perception or the reasonings founded on it), yet, *inasmuch as it is the object of a concept*, it is not presented as an *actually existing being*, but only as a *possible being*, as a being that CAN EXIST (either in reality as a thing, or simply in the mind as an object of thought). Thus—

Since the formal object (the objective concept) is *that which* is immediately attained (*per se primo*), the material object is attained mediately, and "by" the formal object. In this sense we may say that we grasp a thing "*by*" the objective concept (by that in the thing which comes first and directly into intellectual vision).

We lay hold of a thing "by" our *mental concepts* just as we lay hold of an animal by our hands or see a monument by our eyes. We seize it *by* such and such an *objective concept* as we seize an animal by the paws or the ears, or as we see a monument by the façade or the apse.

By playing in the same way upon the word "to present" we may say that both the mental concept and the objective concept "presents" the thing to knowledge; the mental concept being something of ourselves by which we know the object, and the objective concept being something of the object by which it is known to us.

It is also to be remarked that the objective concept being the thing *as it is known*, *conceived*, or *presented to the intelligence*, may have a mode or state of being (state of universality) given it by the mind itself, and which the thing does not have in its extra-mental (individual) existence. Cf. J. Maritain, *Introd. to Philosophy*, pp. 159–161.

[1] *Ibid.*, p. 255.

[2] *Ibid.*, pp. 170–172.

(I)
- Blindness
- Nothingness
- Affirmation
- The species, man
- An irrational number (a surd)

(II)
- A geometric point
- A circumference
- An even number

(III)
- A better world than this one
- A tree with phosphorescent fruit
- A tower ten thousand metres high

are objects of a concept, or " objective concepts "[1] just as much as

(IV)
- Man
- An oak
- Substance
- This colour, etc.

From the point of view of simple apprehension all of these concepts abstract equally from actual existence.

(*a*) To be classified correctly the preceding examples would have to be distributed as shown in table on p. 21.

(*b*) The concept is also called a "mental term" because the resolution or analysis of the proposition *terminates* in it. From the strictly logical point of view the expression " mental term " should really be preferred to all others, for Logic considers the reasoning primarily, and therefore sees propositions as the elements into which the reasoning is resolved, and concepts as the elements into which propositions are resolved.

B. EXTENSION AND COMPREHENSION OF CONCEPTS

10. DEFINITION. Let us examine the concept " man." We can discern in this concept, a certain number of characteristics and intelligible aspects which, when united, dis-

[1] All these objective concepts are properly so-called *essences* presented to the mind, except beings of reason (Blindness, Nonentity, etc.) which may only be improperly so-called essences or quiddities. The question of beings of reason will be fully treated in Major Logic.

REAL BEING AND BEING OF REASON, ACTUAL AND POSSIBLE BEING			
Being of REASON (or being that *cannot exist* except in the mind).	Negation or privation . " blindness, nothingness " Logical being . . " affirmation, the species man " Mathematical being . " An irrational number "		(I)
REAL *being* (or being that *can exist* in reality).	Merely POSSIBLE (considered in possible existence as opposed to actual existence)	*De jure:* " A geometric point" (II)	The *mind expressly considers* the thing under *conditions* in which it cannot actually exist.
		De facto: " A better world " (III)	The *mind does not expressly consider* the thing under conditions in which it cannot actually exist.
	ACTUAL (or existing in actual as well as in possible existence).	" man " " substance " " oak " (IV)	

tinguish it from all others ; *e.g.*, *substance, living body, sentient, rational.* In the same way, in the concept " animal " we can discern the intelligible elements, *substance, living body, sentient.* Intelligible aspects or elements, which necessarily constitute an (objective) concept, and are discernible in it by the mind, are called the *notes* of the concept.

The comprehension of a concept is measured by the sum of its notes.

The COMPREHENSION

of a concept is its breadth in relation to its characteristic notes.

The EXTENSION

of a concept is its breadth in relation to the individuals (or more generally to the objects of thought) in which it is realized, and which it groups in its unity. Thus the concept " Aryan " *extends* to all Indo-Europeans, the concept " man " to all individuals with a rational soul, the concept " animal "

Its extension is measured by the sum of objects to which it applies.

to all sentient beings. The concept "square" has less extension than the concept "quadrilateral," which in turn has less extension than the concept "polygon."

The consideration of the extension and comprehension of concepts plays an important *rôle* in the theory of reasoning.

Some modern logicians, particularly English logicians, use the word *denotation* as synonymous with *extension*, and the word *connotation* (or *intension*) as synonymous with *comprehension.*[1]

The greater the comprehension of a concept the less its extension and conversely.

11. GENERAL RULE. Since the *comprehension* of the concept "animal" is *smaller* than that of the concept "man" (for the concept "animal" lacks the "rational" note and the properties derived from it), this first concept is applicable to individuals (irrational animals) to which the concept man cannot be applied, therefore its *extension* is *greater* than that of the concept "man" (there are more animals than men). Likewise the concept "polygon" has greater extension than the concept "quadrilateral" but less comprehension. Generally speaking

the extension and comprehension of concepts are in inverse ratio to each other.

The *extension* of a concept is merely a *property* that presupposes the *comprehension* or sum of the constitutive notes of the essence presented to the mind.

* 12. THE EXTENSION AND COMPREHENSION OF CONCEPTS IS TO BE UNDERSTOOD IN RELATION TO UNIVERSAL ESSENCES. It is important that the notion of extension and comprehension be firmly established from the very beginning, for any taint of nominalism[2] will prevent it from being rightly understood. In nominalism the concept has no reality other than that of the individuals which it represents.

[1] It may be said, as Goblot puts it (*Log.*, Chap. III), that the *extension* of a concept is measured by the number of possible propositions of which it is the *predicate* (Peter is a *man*, Paul is a *man*, etc.) and its *comprehension* by the number of possible propositions of which it is the *subject* (*man* is a substance, *man* is living, *man* is rational . . .). But this is only a *sign following from* the definitions of the extension and comprehension of concepts—it could never be said to *constitute* the definition itself.

Moreover, it holds good only on the supposition that the propositions in question are in *necessary matter* (in other words, that the attribution takes place *per se*, not *per accidens*). If I say "the man weighs 150 pounds" (that is, this man weighs 150 pounds) and "some man is here," the concepts "weighing 150 pounds" and "here" are not a part of the comprehension of the concept "man," nor is the concept "man" a part of the *extension* of the concepts "here" or "weighing 150 pounds." Goblot's innovation really amounts to putting the cart before the horse.

[2] See J. Maritain, *Introd.*, pp. 159–162.

Its essential and original character as a concept is accordingly derived from its extension, that is from the extent of its universality, or its applicability to a greater or lesser group of individuals. However, if it is true that a concept presents an *essence*, *nature*, or *quiddity* immediately to the mind, and that this essence is something real,[1] then it must be said that the concept as such is essentially and originally characterized by its *comprehension*, that is to say by the sum of the constitutive notes of the nature that it presents to the mind. Thus the extension of the concept is nothing more than a property following inevitably upon abstraction, and presupposing the comprehension of the concept ; in other words, the concept is *universal* only because it reveals (clearly or obscurely) the *necessary constitution* of some essence.

The comprehension of a concept is the sum of the notes which constitute the concept as it is *in itself* not only as it is *for us*.

According to the nominalist theory, concepts contain only what we put into them, for according to this hypothesis we do not attain through our concepts essences or natures which are what they are in themselves, independent of the manner in which we apprehend them. Consequently the comprehension of a concept may be understood only in a subjective sense ; it is merely a group of notes which we have explicitly collected and which, *given our present state of knowledge*, constitute the concept FOR US. But, on the contrary, if it be true that there really are essences or natures, and that our concepts attain them, then their comprehension must be understood in an *objective* sense. In other words, the comprehension of a concept is the sum of the notes that constitute the concept IN ITSELF : first and foremost, notes that constitute the very ESSENCE that is presented by this concept (*e.g.*, *rationality* and *animality* in the concept man), secondarily, the notes that are necessarily derived from this essence and fundamentally contained in its constitutive notes (*properties*, such as " risibility," " gifted with articulate speech," etc., which are brought to light by the reasoning, and are contained virtually in the concept, although as yet unknown to us).

(*a*) It follows that the comprehension of a concept finds

[1] *Ibid.* It exists in the real, but there it loses the universality it had in the mind.

its first and foremost expression in the *essential definition* of that concept (definition of man as a rational animal, or of a triangle as a three-sided polygon).

Nevertheless, it may happen (and it usually does in the inductive sciences) that we should never succeed in knowing the notes that constitute an essence presented to our mind by some concept. The comprehension of such a concept still equals the sum of its constitutive notes and, secondarily, those which are necessarily derived from them, but since these constitutive notes are as yet unknown to us, we have to determine the comprehension by extrinsic signs, by properties empirically recognized as characteristic. For want of an *essential definition* we have to be satisfied with a *descriptive definition* and with gathering by induction the other properties necessarily bound up with those we have empirically recognized. Thus, without being able to deduce the fact, we know from observation that the comprehension of the concept *ruminant* includes the characteristic *cloven-footed.* In such a case our concepts really do reveal the necessary constitution of an essence, but obscurely, and in such a manner that we *cannot use* it in our knowledge.

(*b*) *Connotation and Comprehension according to Keynes.* The English logican, Keynes, followed by Goblot, distinguishes in what is generally called the comprehension of a concept "*connotation*" and "*comprehension stricto sensu.*" He reserves the word *connotation* to signify those notes which *serve to define* the object of the concept (*e.g.*, an equilateral triangle defined as a triangle whose sides are equal, or a ruminant as an animal that chews the cud). He uses the word *comprehension* merely to designate an object's recognizable properties (*equal angles* in an equilateral triangle, and *cloven-feet* in a ruminant).

This distinction [1] has no meaning except in the nominalist hypothesis wherein our concepts do not attain to

[1] Furthermore, this distinction is defective on another account, for it does not oppose the *properties* to the *essence* or to the characteristics which define the object of a concept *in itself*, but rather does it oppose these properties to the characteristics which define it *for us*, which are of use to us in defining it, and which, in the case of descriptive definitions, are not constitutive elements of the essence, but are precisely *properties*.

essences which are in themselves rich in properties (whether they be attained intrinsically by an essential definition as in the case of the equilateral triangle, or extrinsically by a descriptive definition as in the case of the ruminant). Although the characteristic " cloven-footed " cannot be deduced from the definition of a ruminant, this characteristic—granted that it is truly a property—is none the less contained virtually in the essence presented to our mind by the concept ruminant. Therefore both " connotation " and " comprehension " really have the same object.

The English logicians' notion of " connotation " definitively supposes that a concept may be reduced to what we are *actually* and *explicitly* thinking about the several notes or characteristics which we use to define it. The concept man, for instance, contains only what actually and explicitly I am thinking of, *hic et nunc*, in saying " animal " and " rational " (instead of the vast intelligible content virtually contained in these two notes). It is not surprising that those who so misinterpret its nature should look upon the concept as something " poor " and " empty."

(*c*) *Comprehension according to Goblot.*[1] Goblot is not content with Keynes' distinction between the *connotation* [2] and the *comprehension* of concepts. His definition of comprehension includes not only the properties necessarily derived from an essence,[3] but *all the concepts* [4] *contained therein as species or sub-species*, and all the properties they in turn imply. That is, he makes extension (the sum of the concept's inferiors) a part of the comprehension of the concept. From this he naturally concludes that, if the " connotation " of concepts is in inverse ratio to their extension, their " comprehension," on the contrary, increases and decreases along with their extension. Reserving the use of the word *concept* for those elements

[1] Cf. Goblot, *Traité de Logique*, Chap. III : " Le Concept et l'Idée," *Scientia*, t. XI, 1912.

[2] For example, an animal as a " sentient living organism."

[3] As " mortal," " capable of locomotion," etc.

[4] As " man " (Aryan, Semite, etc., down to Peter and Paul), " beast " (vertebrate, invertebrate, etc., down to this dog and this oyster).

explicitly contained in "connotation," he opposes to the concept, "poor" and "abstract" notion that it is,[1] the Idea, which—to him—is the "rich" notion whose "comprehension" includes the totality of determinations, even to the individual determinations, that may be contained in a genus.[2]

Goblot errs here in treating the specific and individual differences, contained as "undetermined variables" in a genus, as if they were contained in the genus *in act* (or at least *virtually*). But their undetermined state in the pure and simple unity of the genus clearly indicates that they exist in it only *potentially*.[3]

These specific differences could not be included in the *comprehension* of the genus, for the very notion of comprehension enters into logic for the sole purpose of designating the notes that are attributed to an essence, NECESSARILY (*per se*), and not *per accidens*, and which are consequently contained in the essence *determinately*, either *actually* (as "rational animal" is in "man"), or *virtually* (as *risibility* in the same concept). But Goblot's innovation, on the contrary, would bring into comprehension accidental attributes which the concept contains only *potentially*,[4] and

[1] "Animal" reduced to what I am explicitly thinking when I say "sentient living organism."

[2] "Animal" as including in itself

man — beast

Aryan — Semite — vertebrate — invertebrate

etc., down to Peter and Paul. — etc., down to this dog and this oyster.

[3] "A vertebrate," as Goblot says (*Log.*, n. 71, p. 113) "is not an animal with neither fur, feathers nor scales, but an animal whose tegumentary appendages *may have* the forms, fur, feathers, or scales." That is, these differences are contained *potentially*, and *only* potentially, in the generic notion of vertebrate. Therefore the genus is only *potentially* richer than the species. It is poorer *in act*, and the specific difference really adds a determination to the generic characteristics.

[4] *Animal* is accidentally "rational," "irrational," "barking," or "ruminant" (differentiating notes of species included under the genus "animal"). Goblot includes, in the comprehension of a genus, not only these differentiating notes, but all the accidental attributes which may be said of it *per accidens*. "If by the comprehension of the idea," he says (*Log.*, n. 127), "we understand all that may truthfully be affirmed of this idea, then *all true judgments are analytic*." If this were the case, then, because it is true that this man is a philosopher and that man a robber, that this man was born in Athens and that one in Pekin, that this one is standing and that one is sitting down,

would thus do nothing but confuse and pervert the notion of comprehension as a logical property of our ideas.

The distinction he makes between the concept and the Idea [1] is equally illegitimate ; for in reality what he calls an " idea " really contains its ulterior differences only in potency and not in act, and what he calls a *concept* is not reducible to what is actually and explicitly thought of in the definition but, like the " Idea," contains its properties virtually, and its ulterior differences potentially, so that these notions are not really two—but identical. Goblot is too nominalistic in his notion of the concept, and too realistic in his notion of the " Idea," undoubtedly because he has been unable to achieve balance in his logic through a sane theory of abstraction and the universal. Nevertheless, some of his remarks about ideas are very accurate if their Platonism be judiciously diluted : but these remarks (there is, in a sense, more in ideas than there is in things, they are logical necessities which the mind cannot arrange according to any whim, etc.) are equally applicable to *concepts* rightly understood.

(*d*) *The Extension of a Concept is a Logical Property that* A NATURE *has in our mind.* The extension of a concept includes both the individuals and the objective concepts (universal but of less extension than itself) in which it is realized. For example, both the concept " man " and the concept " beast," are contained in the extension of the concept " animal," and consequently, " this man, that man, this horse, this butterfly, etc.," are also and by that very fact contained in the extension of the concept. A concept's extension includes an *infinite multitude* of *individuals* (for there is an infinity of possible human beings and beasts). Therefore extension is measured not by the greater or lesser *number*, but rather by the greater or lesser (infinite) *multitude* of individuals to which a concept applies. This alone suffices to show that a universal

this one pleasant and that one an idiot, this one a miser and that a spendthrift, all these attributes, " philosopher," " robber," " born in Athens," etc., etc., would be contained in the comprehension of the genus Man.

[1] Our concepts and ideas should be considered as opposed to Plato's " separate Ideas " and " man in himself "—but in another sense, as we shall see later on.

concept is anything but a collection of individuals: It applies to an infinite multitude because it is *originally one* (in the mind). That which it presents immediately to the mind is not a collection or series of individuals, but the nature realized in each one of them.

We have said that the extension of a concept presupposes its comprehension. Therefore, to consider a concept as to its "extension" does not mean to abstract from its comprehension, nor to look upon it as a mere collection of individuals—that would simply amount to destroying it as a concept. To consider "man" as to its extension is to consider this object of thought in *relation* to the multitude of individuals to which it applies, but it is also to consider it *as having* a certain characteristic comprehension and *as being one* in the mind, that is, as being something other than the multitude of individuals in which it is realized.

Nominalism tends to confound the *extension* of the concept with *its resolution into a simple collection* of individuals, and thus completely vitiates the notion of extension. This dangerous confusion, which really results in making logic impossible, is not at all foreign to the idea of the syllogism propounded by many modern logicians, particularly by several "extensivists,"[1] nor does it seem to be far removed from the systematic aversion to extension manifested by certain logicians (especially Hamelin) who are contaminated by nominalism in spite of themselves.

13. "SUPERIOR" AND "INFERIOR" CONCEPTS. Whatever is *man* is also *animal*, but whatever is *animal* is not *man*. The concept animal is implied in, or "*inferred*" from, the concept *man* (it is part of its constitutive notes), but the concept man is not implied in or "*inferred*" from the concept *animal* (it is not part of its constitutive notes). The implied or "*inferred*" concept is said to be

The "inferiors" of a concept are those concepts which "infer" it, but which it does not itself "infer," and which *it includes* from the point of view of extension.

superior

to the concept that implies or *infers* because it has a

greater EXTENSION

than the latter and includes it.

[1] See below, Nos. 70, 81.

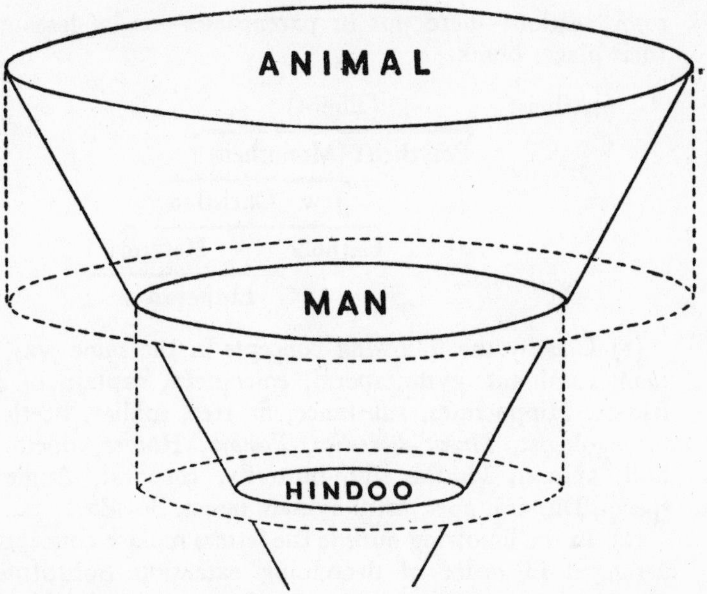

A superior concept is to its inferiors as the whole is to its parts: thus "animal" and "vegetal" are parts of "living body," "man" and "beast" parts of "animal," "Peter," "Paul," "Jack" and "John" parts of "man." Inasmuch as it contains its inferiors, the superior concept is called a *potential* whole,[1] or *logical whole* by logicians. Since, from the point of view of "predication" (the attribution of a predicate to a subject by means of the verb *to be*), these inferiors are *subjects* of which the superior concept is affirmed (as "an animal is a living body," "a plant is a living body," "Peter is a man," etc.) they are called *subjective parts* of this concept.

The inferiors of a concept are called its *subjective parts.*

Exercises. Were the following concepts: Christian, Jew, Heretic, Atheist, Catholic, Lutheran, Polytheist—produced for classification by arranging the inferior concept beneath its superior, we should classify them as below, either by mentioning the concepts missing from

[1] A logical whole is said to be *potential* because it contains its parts only in potency. "Man" and "Beast" are only potentially contained in the concept "Animal."

some sections—here put in parentheses—or by leaving their places blank.

Atheist (Theist)

Polytheist (Monotheist)

Jew Christian

Catholic Heretic

Lutheran . . .

(1) Classify the following concepts in the same way: man, ruminant, gymnosperm, coleoptera, captain of a frigate, Hippocrates, substance, fir tree, soldier, beetle, laryngologist, *Musca domestica*, *Bombyx*, Homer, doctor, bull, animal, Phidias, fly, butterfly, corporal, Angiosperm, Diptera, poet, artilleryman, insect, Bovidæ.

(2) In the following outline the letters replace concepts arranged in order of decreasing extension. Substitute for these letters any concepts answering to the same logical conditions.

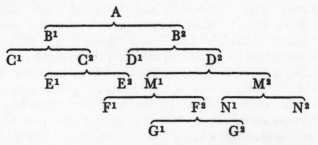

A

B^1 B^2

C^1 C^2 D^1 D^2

E^1 E^2 M^1 M^2

F^1 F^2 N^1 N^2

G^1 G^2

(3) What are the subjective parts of the following concepts, conic section, quadrilateral, art, vertebrate, virtue?

C. THE DIFFERENT KINDS OF CONCEPTS

14. Concepts may be divided or classified from many points of view. Psychology considers them in relation to their origin, distinguishing for example between *direct* concepts, by which we know something without reflecting upon our act of knowing (" the man," " the stone ") and

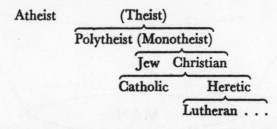

the *reflex concept* by which, returning upon our act of knowledge, we take as object either this act itself, or our mental concepts, or the faculty from which they proceed.

Major Logic considers concepts from the standpoint of the manner in which the diverse sorts of content, or objects of thought, which they present to the mind, affect their order within the mind (this is the basis for the division of concepts into Predicables and Predicaments).

Minor Logic considers concepts simply *as to the manner in which they present their content* (*whatever it may be*) to be dealt with by the reason and to be arranged in discourse.

From this point of view concepts may be divided: 1. In relation to the act of simple apprehension itself. 2. According to their comprehension. 3. According to their extension. **Different headings of division.**

1. *Incomplex and Complex Concepts*

15. IN RELATION TO THE ACT OF SIMPLE APPREHENSION ITSELF, concepts may be divided into

Complex and Incomplex Concepts.

INCOMPLEX

or

COMPLEX

a division already met with in simple apprehension, the *objective concept* being none other than the *formal object* of *simple apprehension*.

(*a*) As we said above,[1] if for the purpose of dividing concepts they are considered both *in themselves* and *as to the manner in which they are conceived*, division would be as follows:

INCOMPLEX *as to the manner in which they are conceived and in themselves* (incomplex *voce et re*): "man."

COMPLEX *as to the manner in which they are conceived* but not *in themselves* (complex *voce non re*): "rational animal."

INCOMPLEX *as to the manner in which they are conceived* but not *in themselves* (incomplex *voce non re*): "philosopher," "Batrachiomyomachia."

COMPLEX both *as to the manner in which they are conceived* and *in themselves* (complex *voce et re*): "an expert in

[1] See above, Section 1, n° 7.

philosophy," "the battle of the frogs and the mice," [1] "a long-beaked heron helved with a slender neck."

However, the expression, "*object of understanding*" refers more naturally to objects of concepts considered *in themselves*, whereas the expression (objective) *concept* refers more naturally to objects of concepts *considered as to the manner in which they are conceived*. The same concepts which are said to be incomplex or complex *in themselves* (*re*) when called "objects of understanding" will, on the contrary, be said to be incomplex or complex *as to the manner in which they are conceived* (*voce*) when called "objective concepts." Therefore, because Minor Logic envisages the manner in which its object is conceived, whether a concept is complex or incomplex depends on whether it is presented under one, or several intelligible aspects, and whether it is expressed by a single term or by several, thus we shall say that the definition "rational animal" is a complex concept although it is in itself (*re*) incomplex.

(*b*) In relation to the act of simple apprehension, the concept is also divided into the *conceptus ultimatus* (concept of the thing) and *conceptus non ultimatus* (concept of the sign), depending upon whether the concept considers the THING itself (*e.g.*, a concept of *stone*), or the written or spoken WORD—the sign (the instrumental sign, as we shall explain in Major Logic)—which, being known the first, leads to the knowledge of the thing itself, *e.g.*, the concept of the *word* "*the stone*."

2. *Concrete and Abstract Concepts*

16. By REASON OF THEIR COMPREHENSION concepts may be divided into two classes, for from this aspect they may present things to us in two ways: either by a concept such as

man

or by a concept such as

humanity.

[1] Between "Heautontimoroumenos," an incomplex concept *voce non re*, and "the self-torturer," or between "batrachiomyomachia" and "the battle of the frogs and the mice," or between "Glarnerkrauterkaesefabrikanstochter" and "the daughter of a Glaronese cheese manufacturer," there is a difference not only in words, but in the manner of conception (which is signified by the word).

When we call Socrates *man* rather than *Athenian* or *philosopher*, we consider him under a certain intelligible aspect, a certain determination which, when considered apart, we call " *humanity.*" A man is one who has humanity. Whether I think *man*, or whether I think *humanity*, in both cases a certain determination—humanity—is presented to my mind. But in the first case, it is presented *in the subject*, which it determines, and in the second it is presented *without this subject.*

Logicians call a determination affecting a subject " form " or " formality " in the broad sense, by analogy with the form that determines the matter in works of art. Thus we shall say that a concept such as " man," " white," " philosopher " presents to the mind a form *in the subject which it determines*, whereas a concept such as " humanity," " whiteness " or " philosophy " presents a form *without the subject* it determines, or prescinding from this subject. How then shall we designate these two categories of concepts? We may call the first

CONCRETE form in subject

and the second

ABSTRACT form is apart from subj.

As a matter of fact, both the one and the other are abstract in that they are both derived from sensible experience by means of the intellectual operation called abstraction, and in that both abstract from the *individual notes* of the intuitively perceived sense objects [1]; nevertheless, concepts of the second type are really *abstract to the second power*, because they disengage a *form* from the *subject* it determines in order to consider it by itself. Only in contrast with *this sort* of abstraction are concepts such as *man* or *philosopher* called: " concrete."

The concrete concept presents to the mind *what* such and such a thing is (*id* QUOD *est*); an abstract concept presents that *by which* the thing is such and such a thing (*id* QUO *est aliquid*).

(*a*) Abstraction will be fully treated in Major Logic, Psychology and Critique. We shall simply note here

[1] See J. Maritain, *Introduction to Philosophy*, pp. 154–159.

that, in distinguishing between the " form " and the " subject," which it determines, logicians make no effort whatsoever to discover whether this distinction is a *real* distinction or simply a distinction *of reason.* It is the task of the metaphysician to discern that *humanity* (human nature) is really distinct from the person of *Peter*, whereas Divinity is not really distinct from God, or that the property of *risibility* is really distinct from the substance of the human soul, whereas the property of being *spiritual* is not.

(*b*) The terms *concrete* and *individual* must not be confused. *Man* is a *concrete* concept because it presents the form *humanity in a subject*, but the subject in question is not an individual but a common subject that abstracts from all individuating characteristics.

(*c*) Abstract concepts are always

ABSOLUTE

that is, the thing they present to the mind is always presented as *a substance*, *per modum per se stantis* (" whiteness," " humanity ").

Concrete concepts are either

ABSOLUTE

when the thing they present to the mind is presented *after the manner of a substance* (man, this tree), or else they are

CONNOTATIVE

when the thing presented to the mind is presented *as an accident* determining or " connoting "[1] a subject, *per modum alteri adjacentis* (" white," " blind "). That which a connotative concept *primarily* and *principally* presents to the mind is the same thing (" form " or " determination ") which is presented by the corresponding abstract concept ; that which it presents *secondarily* (*per posterius*, or *ex consequenti*) is the subject (substance) affected by this determination or by this accidental " form ".[2] *Absolute* concrete concepts also present the form signified by the

[1] That is, *making it known simultaneously with itself.*
[2] Cf. St. Thomas, in *Metaph. Aristot.*, lib. V, lect. 9, n. 894 (ed. Cathala).

corresponding abstract concept, but they present it *with* and *in* the subject which it determines. Thus the concept " man " immediately presents human nature as present in a (universal) subject, and as constituting a universal object of thought communicable to singular subjects—to individual human beings.

§3. *Collective and Divisive Concepts*

17. Considered as to the multitude included IN THEIR EXTENSION, concepts such as " army," " family " and " syndicate " are said to be

COLLECTIVE

in the sense that they are realized, not in a multitude of individuals, but in a multitude of *groups* of individuals *taken as a whole* or " collectively."

It is a multitude of *collections* of individuals, each of which is called an army, that—by reason of the intelligible nature which they signify—constitutes the extension of the concept *army*.

Concepts, such as " man," " philosopher " and " soldier," on the contrary, are called

DIVISIVE

Collective and Divisive Concepts.

because they are realized in individuals themselves taken one by one (" divisively," *divisim*).[1]

The distinction between the *collective sense* and the *divisive* (or *distributive*) *sense* is important in the theory of reasoning. It is evident that, taking the concept " man " in the divisive or distributive sense, we may say

Men are mortal,
But Peter is a man,
Therefore Peter is mortal.

but that, taking the concept " senator " in the collective sense, we cannot say

The senators are a chosen body,
Peter is a senator,
Therefore Peter is a chosen body.

[1] The word " *distributive* " is often used in the sense of *divisive*, but its proper meaning (see No. 18) does not really coincide with that of divisive.

nor taking the concept " man " collectively, can we say

> The men (in this hall) are twelve,
> Peter is a man,
> Therefore Peter is twelve.

4. *Extension of the Subject-Concept*

18. DIVISION OF THE SUBJECT-CONCEPT AS TO EXTENSION

(1) A concept may not only be considered in itself, simply as a concept—as was done in the preceding division—but it may also be considered *as the subject of a proposition*, and in relation to the logical use we make of it in virtue of its function as the subject of a proposition. In the first division the concept was considered *statically*: it was thus we compared the extension of the concept *man* with that of *animal* and *Hindoo*; in the second the concept is considered *dynamically*, *i.e.*, in its function as subject. Therefore, the same concept, *man*, for example, may vary in relation to extension, and the word extension no longer designates only the breadth of the concept in relation to the individuals in which it is realized, but also designates the breadth of the concept in relation to the individual *to which it is communicable* in its function of Subject, *i.e.*, inasmuch as it receives a predicate. The division of the concept to which we are led by the consideration of extension from this new point of view (the point of view of the concept-subject of a proposition) is of the greatest importance in the theory of the proposition and the syllogism.[1]

We know [2] that in itself the object directly presented to the mind by every concept is universal, but according to the usage we make of it we may consider this object either in all its universality, or in a part of it merely, or again as individualized in this or that singular subject in which it is realized.

(2) Let us consider a concept-subject of a proposition. We shall have to distinguish between the case in which its extension *is restricted to one individual determinate subject*—

[1] This division belongs to the theory of the *suppositio* of the term and the concept (see below No. 27).

[2] Cf. J. Maritain, *Introduction to Philosophy*, pp. 159–172.

as "*this* man," "this philosopher" (or again "Cæsar," "Leibnitz") and the case in which its extension is not limited to one single individual determinate subject. In the first case the concept is *individual* or

SINGULAR,

in the second it is

COMMON.

Furthermore, the extension of a (common) concept may be restricted (in the sense that it is not considered as communicable to all the individuals contained under it), without, however, being limited to a single, individual and determinate subject, as "some man," "some philosopher." In this event the concept is called

PARTICULAR.

On the contrary, when the extension of a concept is absolutely unrestricted (that is when it is taken as communicable to all the individuals contained under it), as "every man," "every philosopher," the concept is

The concept-subject of a proposition is *singular*, *particular*, or *distributive* (*universal*).

DISTRIBUTIVE OR UNIVERSAL.

In this case it is universally "*distributed*" to all individuals having the nature *man* or *philosopher*. This universal nature derived by abstraction from sense experience and placed by the mind before itself is not, so to speak, "touched up" by the mind from the point of view of extension, but is considered *in all its universality* independent of all modality or individual status.

"A predicate," says St. Thomas Aquinas,[1] "may be attributed to a universal subject (1) by reason of the universal nature itself, *e.g.*, when the thing attributed is related to the subject's essence, or follows from its essential principles : *homo est animal* or *homo est risibilis*, or (2) by reason of some singular thing in which the predicate is found, *e.g.*, when the thing attributed is related to the action of the individual : *homo ambulat*. . . .

"In the first case the predicate is universally attri-

[1] *In Perihermeneias*, lib. I, cap. VII, lect. 10, Nos. 9 and 13.

buted to the universal subject, *praedicatur de eo universaliter*, because it belongs to it through the whole multitude in which this universal is actualized, *quia scilicet ei convenit secundam totam multitudinem in qua invenitur*. To show this we use the word 'all' [or 'every'] (*omnis*) signifying that the predicate is attributed to the universal subject according to all that is contained under this subject, *quantum ad totum quo sub subjecto continetur*. . . .

"In the second case we use the word 'some' (*aliquis vel quidam*) to show that the predicate is attributed to the universal subject by reason of a thing that is singular but which is designated under a certain indetermination. . . ."

We might add that this division into *taken universally* and *taken particularly* (or into *distributive* and *particular*) affects the universals considered as existing in particular things, *secundum quod est in singularibus*. But the universal may also be considered as to the being it has in the mind, *secundum esse quod habet in intellectu*. In the latter event, since it is not taken as communicated to individuals in reality, but, on the contrary, as separated from them, it is taken neither universally nor particularly, but simply *as one*, *ut unum*, whether a predicate which refers to an operation of the mind be attributed to it—as, for example: "Man is attributable to several subjects"—or even whether a predicate which refers to the being which the nature seized by thought has in the thing be applied to it—as "Man is the noblest of creatures." "In fact this predicate belongs to human nature even as existing in individuals; for any individual man whatsoever is nobler than all irrational creatures. However, all individual men are not *one* man outside of thought, but only in the mind's conception: it is in this manner that the predicate is attributed to the subject here. That is—it is attributed to it as to *one* thing" (*ibid.*).

The following table shows the division of the (*collective* or *divisive*) concept as to extension, considering it from the point of view of its use in the proposition and reasoning.

			The Concept	
			Collective	*Divisive*
Subject-Concept	Singular		this army	this man
	Common	Particular	some army	some man
		Distributive (or universal)	every army	each man

DIVISION OF THE CONCEPT BY REASON OF EXTENSION

*(3) In thinking we arrange and assemble (abstract) intellectual objects which are applicable to an indefinite multitude of individuals though not necessarily constituting a part of their essential notes.

Because we act in this way it is absolutely imperative to consider the *extension* as well as the comprehension of our intellectual objects so as to define exactly the field within which their application is legitimate. For instance, we may reasonably apply the universal *liar* to individuals having human nature, and thus combine the object of thought, *man*, and the object of thought, *liar ;* but if we deduced from this that every philosopher being a man is a liar, our reasoning would be false. We should have considered the extension of the subject-concept, man (that is, we should have considered to what extent it is communicable to its inferiors), in relation to the concept liar ; this we do when we think : " SOME man is a liar." Since the subject-concept, man, is *restricted* or *particularized* in relation to liar, we cannot apply the term liar to a subject from the mere fact that this subject is human. In the same way we may reasonably combine the concepts triangle and isosceles, because the term isosceles is a term applicable to a category of triangle, but we would be reasoning falsely in deducing from this that in all triangles the median and the height are the same. The proper line of reasoning would be : " In an isosceles triangle, the median and the height are the same ; SOME triangle is isosceles ; therefore in SOME triangle the median and the height are the same."

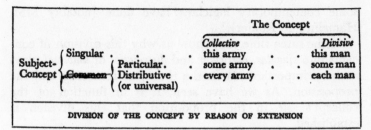

These elementary remarks suffice to show the futility of dreaming of a purely " comprehensive " logic, wherein all consideration of " extension " would be banned, as some contemporary logicians have done (notably MM. Hamelin and Rodier).[1]

At the same time they show us why this division of concepts into *singular*, *particular* and *distributive* or *universal* plays such an important *rôle* in the theory of reasoning and the proposition. As we have seen, it is in function of the concept's *rôle* in the proposition that this division is established.

Nevertheless, from the point of view of vocabulary (especially from the point of view of the use of the word *universal*) this division gives rise to a slight complication which it might be well to clarify. The object directly presented to the mind by every concept, being abstract, *is in itself universal*, that is, *it is one with an aptitude to be in many*. A "collective" concept, *e.g.*, family, is a universal concept, for it is applicable to all families, this one as well as that; a "particular" concept, *e.g.*, "some man" is a universal (viz., the concept "man"), whose extension we have restricted to an indeterminate individual subject. Finally an "individual" or "singular" concept, *e.g.*, "Peter" or "this man," is not singular in the sense that it would enable us to know an individual immediately *in his own individuality;* for we know that we have neither direct intellectual knowledge nor direct concepts of the singular as such.[2] This "singular" concept is in fact a *universal* (*e.g.*, man) that the mind has led back and pressed down, if I may use such a phrase, upon a singular thing, and whose extension it has restricted to one single determinate individual that may be pointed at—"this man" or that answers to some name—"Peter"—and to certain perceptions or sensible images (Peter presents himself to my sight or imagination under such and such an aspect).

[1] In spite of his personal prejudices against extension, M. Hamelin is altogether right in saying (*Système d'Aristote*, p. 164). "If experience plays a part in knowledge, especially if this part is not merely provisional but definitive, or, in other words, if there is contingency in the world, Logic, then, must take into account the quantity of propositions . . . and we must admit that Aristotle was right (in emphasizing the importance of logical quantity)." . . . We might add that since this is so, and since in a perfect syllogism the subject of the Major premise becomes the predicate of the Minor, it is impossible to construct the theory of reasoning without considering the extension of the predicate as well as that of the subject.

[2] See J. Maritain, *Introduction to Philosophy*, pp. 154–156, 170–172.

In short, it is only in an indirect manner, and by this bending back of the universal on the sensible, that such a concept may be "singular."

We may, however, have a *proper* and *distinct concept* of the singular. In fact the intelligence forms propositions about singular subjects, *e.g.*, "Peter is a man," "Socrates is not Plato," which presuppose that it knows these singular objects determinately, and distinguishes one individual from another. Furthermore, it compares the universal to the singular, which also indicates a proper knowledge of the latter.

But the proper concept of the singular is a *reflex* concept that brings the universal object of thought back upon the images from which it was abstracted, and upon the singular which they presented, and thus expresses this singular and has it as its term.[1]

But in the present division the word "universal" is taken in a special sense, and is to be understood in relation to the *rôle* of the concept *in the proposition* of which it is the subject. Thus in the proposition "*Every man is mortal*," the predicate "mortal" is attributed to the subject by reason of human nature considered in itself—abstracting from any individual modality. In such a proposition the concept man is *taken in all its universality*. Hence the name "universal" is given both to the subject "every man," and to the proposition itself.[2]

But, on the other hand, in the proposition "*some man* is a liar" the *predicate* liar is attributed to man only under certain individual modalities. The *subject* designates no longer the nature "man" as completely *de-individualized* and taken as communicable to all the individuals without

[1] Cf. John of St. Thomas, *Curs. phil. Phil. Nat.*, *De anima*, q. X, a. 4; Ferrariensis, *in I Contra Gentiles*, cap. LXV, §8, ad 3; Bannez, *in Sum. Theol.*, I, q. 86, a. 1, dub. 2.

[2] We must be careful to say "*every man*" and not "*all men*" (tout homme, et non pas "tous les hommes"). The first expression "denotes" the universal *nature* "man," which is derived by abstraction from individuals and is the first object of thought; the second designates only a *collection* of *individuals* possessing human nature. To make a systematic use of the latter manner of speech in formulating universal majors in the theory of the syllogism—as do so many modern logicians—is to betray great crudity in Logic.

exception to which it may be applied, but rather does it designate the nature " man," along with an individual although indeterminate manner of being, or, to be more precise, it designates an *indeterminate individual* (*individuum vagum*) possessing this nature.[1] In such a proposition the concept man is taken *as communicable only to one or to a few of the individuals contained under it.* Therefore, both the subject " some man " and the proposition itself are called " particular." [2]

Finally, in the proposition " *this man is wise*," the predicate is attributed only to a certain determinate subject possessing human nature and the concept man is restricted to a *determinate individual*. For this reason both the subject " this man " and the proposition itself are called *singular* or *individual*.

(*a*) As we have said above, the word *universal* should be differently understood according as it refers to the concept taken in itself, in which sense every direct concept is universal, let us say universal as abstract—or as it refers *to the concept as subject of a proposition*—in which sense only unrestricted common concepts are called universal, let us say universal as distributive.[3]

Likewise the word *particular* may be understood in two different senses :

(1) As related to the concept *considered as subject of a proposition* it is opposed to the *universal as distributive*, and designates a common restricted concept. This was the meaning explained in the text above : SOME man. We shall say that in this sense the concept is *particular-as-restricted*.

(2) But the word " particular " may also be related to the concept *considered in itself*, in which case it signifies a

[1] Cf. St. Thomas, *loc. cit.*, No. 13. In certain cases the particular subject does not designate an *indeterminate individual* but one of the inferior *universals* of the concept in question : " Some animal (viz., man) is rational."

[2] The same care should be exercised in illustrating this point as that mentioned above in note [4] that " some man " (quelque homme) should be understood in relation to the universal *nature* " man " and not in relation to a certain collection of individuals having human nature.

[3] Cf. St. Thomas, in *Anal. Post.*, 1, I, lect. 11, n. 2.

concept universal as abstract, but embraced within another more universal concept. Thus the concept "man" is less universal (universal as abstract) than the concept "animal." And because the concept "man" considered as an inferior of the concept "animal" has for its extension only *a part* of the latter concept, it may be opposed to the concept "animal" as the particular to the universal. For example, in going from the proposition "every animal is mortal" to the proposition "every man is mortal" we go from the universal to the particular. In this case the word "particular" no longer concerns the extension of the subject-concept as related to the predicate in a proposition, but simply the extension of the concept taken in itself as related to another concept. In this sense the concept may be called "particular as inferior."

Let us examine the proposition "every man is mortal." Obviously, if the *concept* "man" is *particular* in the *second* sense (particular as inferior), it cannot be *particular* in the *first* sense (particular-as-restricted), for its universality is not limited, it is a *universal-as-distributive* concept. The same is true of the proposition in question, which may be said to be *particular* in the second sense but is universal in the first.

Hence there arises a possibility of confusion whose source is in the profound law of analogy which rules the life and natural migrations of words and which entails almost inevitable linguistic imperfections. It is incumbent upon the logician to teach us to distinguish between the different meanings of the same word, and any evasion of this duty by imposing a mechanical rigidity upon linguistic signs would be foredoomed, for it would merely be an attempt to remedy a natural imperfection by an artificial and more injurious one.[1]

(*b*) This possibility of confusion is increased by the

[1] The vocabulary of the ancients (in which the words *extension* and *comprehension* themselves were not included) was less confusing than ours on this point. For whereas we say that a subject is *singular*, *universal* (as distributive) and *particular* (as restricted), the scholastics were wont to say that the subject was *singular*, *universal taken universally* and *universal taken particularly*.

use of the word " general " as synonymous (i) sometimes with universal as abstract, or (ii) sometimes with common, or, (iii) sometimes with universal as distributive, and thus as opposed respectively to (i) the particular as inferior or the *singular as such* (which is the direct object of sensation but never of a concept) (ii) the *singular concept*, (iii) the *particular as restricted.*

Once forewarned, however, it is not difficult to guard against such confusion, but it would be more easily avoided were we to agree once and for all

(1) to use " particular " only in the sense of *particular* as restricted, never " particular as inferior " ;

(2) to simply say " less universal " (*or less general*) instead of " particular-inferior " ;

(3) to use " general " only in the sense of *universal as abstract*, never in the sense of " universal as distributive."

In this way *particular* will always be opposed to *universal as distributive*, never to *universal as abstract*, and *general* will always be opposed to *less universal* or *less general*, but never to *particular.*[1]

The convention of never using the word *general* in the sense of universal-distributive seems acceptable and we will adhere to it. But it is doubtful whether what has been said here concerning the word " particular " should ever come into usage, for it would be a constraint upon the natural movement of language and would probably involve more confusion than clarity. Therefore we shall

[1] This is the general import of Goblot's interesting observations on the use of the words " general " and " particular " (*Traité de Logique*, Paris, 1918, §98, 108, 160). The author himself attaches excessive importance to these observations, because he has failed to understand that the words *universal* and *particular* may be used only according to a certain *analogy* between the *concept taken in itself* and the *concept as subject of the proposition.* Furthermore he does not see that the opposition of the *singular* (term or singular concept) to the *general* (understood as synonymous with common), like the opposition of the *particular* (as restricted) to the universal (as distributive), concerns the concept's *rôle* in the proposition in such a manner that propositions should be divided according to quantity into three groups : *singular*, *particular* and *universal* (although singular propositions are equivalent to universals both in the theory of the conversion of propositions and in the theory of the syllogism. See below No. 51).

not bind ourselves to it, but shall rely on the context to clarify our use of this word in each instance.

" Universal " and " Particular " in relation to the Concept itself.

Every direct Concept is UNIVERSAL (universal as abstract)	MORE UNIVERSAL (*more general*) or LESS PARTICULAR CONCEPTS .	" animal "
	LESS UNIVERSAL (*less general*) or MORE PARTICULAR CONCEPTS .	" man "
[Reflex concept of the singular	. . . . . .	" this man "]

" Universal " and " Particular " in relation to the Concept as Subject

Common Concept.	UNIVERSAL (distributive) .	" all man "
	PARTICULAR . . .	" some man "
Singular Concept.	. . . .	" this man "

USE OF THE WORDS " UNIVERSAL " AND " PARTICULAR "

SECTION 3. THE TERM

A. NOTION OF THE ORAL TERM

19. PRELIMINARY REMARKS. Man is naturally a " social " or " political " animal ; he is made to live in society (this is so, as we shall see in ETHICS, on account of his specific character, a *being capable of reasoning*, because he cannot make fitting progress in the work of reason except through help and instruction of others). Consequently, the aptitude for acquiring knowledge of things is not enough ; he must be able to express his knowledge verbally. From this necessity arose the system of conventional signs, called *language*, by which men communicate their thought : a wonderful instrument fashioned of articulate sound passing through the air, imparting through the most pliant and subtle of materials our innermost and most spiritual selves.

Furthermore, because man, unlike the animal, is not riveted to the present moment, it is fitting that he should make his thought known to those distant from him in time or space [1] ; hence the necessity for a second system of signs, more material and less perfect than the first which it represents, and this system is called *writing*.[2]

[1] Cf. St. Thomas, *in* I *Periherm*, lect. 2, n. 2.

[2] We speak here of *phonetic* and *alphabetic* writing which represents the oral signs of language. *Ideographic* writing (such as Egyptian hieroglyphics) does not represent the oral signs of language, but directly represents ideas.

Language and writing (oral and written signs) are essentially destined to the social manifestation of thought. However, because our sentient nature is ever in search of material support, these systems of signs offer to thought as their secondary effect the valuable assistance of precision, stability and economy of effort. But we must beware of thinking that these material signs are *absolutely necessary* to thought, that they could ever represent it as *perfectly* as a tracing, or that they could ever act as its substitute and *replace* it.

20. DEFINITION OF THE ORAL TERM. An *oral term* or simply a *term*, is the oral expression of a concept, or more precisely it is :

The term is an articulate sound conventionally signifying a concept.

every articulate sound that conventionally signifies a concept.

Let us note in what sense these terms are *conventional* signs : man's use of words to express his concepts is *natural* and derives from the faculties and propensities proper to his essence, but the fact that these particular words signify *these particular* concepts is not due to nature itself, but to an *arbitrary disposition* of man's own.

Since the "*mental term*" is the concept itself as the "*written term*" is the graphic sign of the oral term, it is evident that the written term signifies the oral term, which signifies the mental term or concept, which in turn signifies the thing. Hence the axiom : *words or terms are signs of ideas or concepts, and ideas or concepts are signs of things.*

*(*a*) Words are not pure signs ("formal signs") as concepts are. They strike the ear before speaking to the mind, and they signify ideas only by first calling up sense images. They have their own proper realm, their own resonances and associations, and it is only on condition that we master them by constant effort that we may come to use them well.

The psychological mechanism of oral expression is more complex than it would seem at first glance. Since the object of language is to lead the hearer actively to form within him the ideas which are in the mind of the speaker, the latter can succeed in his task only by re-forming in his own mind, beginning with the images which will supply him with words, the same ideas that he bids the hearer to form in his mind. Therefore the word is naturally ordained as to its end, not to an *image* which would be simply "plastered" on to the idea, but to form and manifest the *idea* itself, starting from images which merely serve as matter. The art of oral expression consists in disposing this sensible matter by means of words so as exactly to reveal the idea—which is an entirely spiritual thing. This is by no means easy to do. It has been said that perhaps the most striking and unusual poetic "images" originate in the difficulties that man experiences in telling himself and really making himself *see* even the most ordinary things by the help of the imagery of speech, difficulties which constantly constrain the poets to renew this imagery.

*(*b*) The term signifies simultaneously and in the same act both the *concept* and the *thing*, but it immediately signifies the *concept* (the mental concept or sign of the thing, and the objective concept, or the thing as object presented to the mind) and only signifies *mediately the thing itself* (as it exists outside the mind) by means of the concept: *voces significant intellectus conceptiones immediate, et eis mediantibus res* [1]; *nomina non significant res nisi mediante intellectu.*[2] For, (1) we intend to have our words impart "*what we are thinking about things*," that is—our concepts; (2) the word *man*, for example, signifies human nature, abstracting from individual human beings, but human nature thus abstracted exists only in our apprehension or in our concept, not in the real; (3) what we say signifies either the true or the false, but truth or falsity exists only in our concepts, not in things themselves; (4) if words themselves signified things directly there could be no equivocal terms.[3]

*(*c*) Which concept is more immediately signified by the term, the mental concept or the objective concept?

[1] St. Thomas, *in Perihermeneias*, lect. 2, n. 5; cf. q. IX *de Potentia*, a. 5.

[2] *Ibid.*, lect. 10, n. 4.—Thus the word "man" simultaneously signifies (*eadem significatione*) human nature and the individuals who have this nature (John of St. Thomas, *Log.*, p. 95).

[3] The division of terms into *univocal*, *analogous* and *equivocal* will be studied in Major Logic.

Thomists answer [1] that the term signifies the mental concept

MORE IMMEDIATELY (*immediatius*)

but signifies the objective concept

MORE PRINCIPALLY (*principalius*).

Indeed, that which is *first* made known by the term is the interior sign that we form in order to perceive the thing and to manifest it immaterially within us (the mental concept or *verbum mentis*). But the term signifies this concept simply as something known in the very exercise of the act of knowing (*in actu exercitu*), not as known in the act of signifying the known (*in actu signato*). For the mental concept, being essentially the sign of the thing, carries the mind directly to the objective concept (the thing that has been made an intellectual object by means of this mental concept) and it does not itself become an object of knowledge except by an act of reflection.

*(*d*) Strictly speaking, the definition of the term which we have just given is more applicable to the scholastic *dictio* (the word) than to the *term* properly so-called (the *terminus*) ; for the expressions "word" and "oral term," as a matter of fact or materially, designate the same thing but emphasize different formal aspects.

As its etymology would indicate, the proper meaning of the *term* (*terminus*) is the *ultimate element* into which a logical composite may be analysed or "resolved" (and consequently the first element of which such composites are made).[2] The oral term may therefore be considered from several different aspects ; when looked upon as the last element of the enunciation, it is defined as "an articulate sound, having a conventional meaning, with which a simple proposition is constructed"—that is, an

[1] Cf. John of St. Thomas, *Log.* Prima Pars, *Illustrationes*, q. 1, *de Termino* a. 5, Gredt, *Elementa*, n. 19.

[2] This is why the ancient logicians used "term" not only to signify the oral term, but also the concept or *mental term* itself.

enunciative term (see No. 23); when considered as the ultimate element of a syllogistic composition or argumentation, it is divided into subject and predicate and called the *syllogistic term.*

21. EXTENSION AND COMPREHENSION OF TERMS. The same may be said of the extension and comprehension of terms as was said of the extension and comprehension of the concepts which they signify (see Nos. 10–13).

B. THE DIFFERENT KINDS OF TERMS

1. *Generalities*

22. DIVISION OF THE TERM. A term may be considered simply as the expression of a concept, as part of an enunciation or proposition, or as a part of an argumentation.

Considered simply as the expression of a concept, the term is divided in the same manner as the concept and may be either incomplex or complex, concrete or abstract, collective or divisive.

(*a*) However, as we shall see in Major Logic, whereas concepts may be either *univocal* or *analogous*, terms may be either *univocal*, *analogous* or *equivocal.*

(*b*) Certain terms signify not concepts precisely, but rather aspects or modes which the mind is forced to isolate and consider apart because of the exigencies of oral expression. Such terms are called *syncategorematic.*

A term is

CATEGOREMATIC

Categorematic and syncategorematic terms.

(*significativus*) when it signifies an object that is something by itself (*aliquid per se*).

It is

SYNCATEGOREMATIC

(*consignificativus*) when it signifies a simple modification of something; *e.g.*, "all," "some," "fast"; "easily," etc.

The categorematic term is in turn divided into *absolute*

(man, humanity, whiteness) and *connotative* (white, learned) (see above, No. 16, *c*).—(Every adjective is a connotative term, but the converse is not true : " father," " creator " are connotative terms.)

(*c*) The division of the term into *complex* and *incomplex* corresponds to the division of the concept into *complex* and *incomplex* as to the manner in which it is conceived (see above, No. 15).

An incomplex term does not admit of parts that have a meaning of *their own*, *e.g.* : " man," " legislator." (Undoubtedly the syllables " legis " have meaning when considered apart but they do not *exercise* this meaning when in composition. Were we to forget the etymology of the word legislator for the moment and suppose its syllables to be devoid of meaning, the signification of the word would remain unchanged.) A complex term does admit of parts each of which has its own separate meaning, *e.g.*, " a learned man." [1]

The logician primarily considers the division of the term into *subject* and *predicate*.

The logician, considering the term and the proposition primarily as to their use in reasoning, is chiefly interested in the term's division into *subject* (S.) and *predicate* (Pr.), a division which is of essential importance in the syllogism wherein the term is considered as part of the argumentation (" syllogistic term "). The *subject*-term in a proposition is the term to which the verb *to be* applies a determination ; the *predicate*-term is the term which the verb *to be* applies to the subject in order to determine it. Inasmuch as it applies a determination to a subject the verb *to be* is called the *copula* (C.) because its function is to *unite* the Pr. and the S., or to affirm their real identity. " The snow is white," is equivalent to saying, " there is an identity between the thing which I designate by the word ' snow ' (the word which is subject or subjected to a determination in this proposition), and the thing which I designate by the word ' white ' " (the predicate-word which has the determining *rôle* in my proposition).

[1] See n. 39, note 2, on the difference between a complex term and imperfect discourse.

§2. *The Noun and the Verb*

23. DIVISION OF THE TERM CONSIDERED AS PART OF THE ENUNCIATION.[1] In considering the essential elements into which every enunciation or proposition is necessarily resolved we see that even the least significant enunciation requires two parts or terms—

THE NOUN

which has the *rôle* of stable extreme [2] in the proposition, and

The enunciative term is divided into noun and verb.

THE VERB

which plays the *rôle* of the uniting *medium*. For example :

(noun)	(verb)	(noun)	(verb)	(noun)
Peter	lives ;	Peter	is	living.

Every verb is equivalent to the verb *to be* followed by an attribute or predicate : "*I write*" is equivalent to "*I am writing*." Thus the verb *to be* is justly entitled the verb *par excellence*. In a proposition such as "I am" (we shall call such a proposition a "proposition with a verb-predicate"), which is equivalent to "I am existing," the verb to be exercises the function of both *copula* (inasmuch as it unites the subject to the predicate) and *predicate* (inasmuch as it signifies the existence attributed to a subject), but it directly *manifests* (*in actu signato*) the latter function only. In a proposition such as "Peter is a man" (which we shall call "a proposition with a verb-copula") in which the verb *to be* is followed by the predicate it applies to the subject, the verb directly *manifests* only its function as copula. This copulative function is always implied by the verb *to be* (and consequently by all verbs) because it corresponds to the

[1] The division in question—the essential division of the enunciative *term* into *noun* and *verb* is made from the point of view of language (oral sign, term). From the point of view of thought the *enunciative concept* is divided into subject and predicate ; but we must notice that this *enunciative predicate* is not the same as the predicate in the ordinary sense (the syllogistic predicate). The enunciative predicate is the undivided aggregate of the verbal copula and the predicate in the ordinary sense. The union of the S. and this Pr. results from the fundamental signification of the verb which expresses the act according to the very mode of the act, or inasmuch as it completes or terminates the subject.

[2] This includes "*nouns*" in general, *i.e.*, predicate adjectives used as nouns (Peter is *white*) and substantive adjectives used as subject (*white* is a colour), as well as substantive nouns.

very act of the mind itself applying a determination (a predicate) to a subject.

The verb *to be* signifies 1° actually exercised existence (Peter is); 2° as a copula the relation of Pr. to S. (Peter is a musician).

The first sense of the verb *to be* is that in which the copulative function is exercised without being directly manifested as it is in other verbs and in which existence is attributed as a predicate to a subject: "I am," "Hector is no more" (propositions with verb predicates).

From this first sense is derived the second wherein the verb *to be* directly manifests its copulative function: "I *am* sick," "Achilles *is* not invulnerable" (propositions with verb-copulas). It is important to note that, even when used simply as a *copula*, the verb *to be* continues to signify at least *ideal* or *possible* existence. In fact the copula does nothing but express the relation (*habitudo*) of the predicate to the subject; but what relation? The relation of identification of one with the other, the relation by which these two objects of thought, distinct as concepts (*ratione*), are identified in the thing (*re*) in *actual* or *possible real* or *ideal existence.* In other words, when used as a copula the verb *to be* affirms that the thing, with such and such determinations, exists either actually outside the mind or possibly outside the mind or, in the case of beings of reason, in the mind only. The proposition "a myriagon is a ten-thousand-sided polygon" is equivalent to: "the object of thought myriagon *exists* (*in possible existence outside the mind*) with this essential determination: "ten-thousand sided polygon." When I want to signify that the determination (the form), "unable to exist in reality" is found in a certain subject, *e.g.*, a "chimera" I have recourse to the notion of existence and the verb *to be* in order to combine these two objects of thought and I say "A chimera *is* unable to exist in reality" that is "the object of thought chimera *exists* (*in my mind*) with this property of being unable to exist in reality."

Nevertheless the verb *to be* always signifies this relation (of identification between S. and Pr.) as existing (in actual or possible real or ideal existence).

Thus the verb *to be* always signifies existence in a proposition with a verb-copula just as much as in a proposition with a verb-predicate [1]; and all propositions affirm or

[1] "Et ipsum verbum est, sive fiat propositio de secundo adjacente, ut quando dico: *Petrus est*, sive de tertio adjacente, ut cum dico: *Petrus est albus* semper significat idem, scilicet esse, quia ut dicit sanctus Thomas"

deny the *actual* or *possible*, *real* or *ideal existence* of a certain subject determined by a certain predicate. In other words, they either affirm or deny that this subject and this predicate are identified in actual or possible, real or ideal existence.

Therefore, as we shall see in Critique, truth, whether it be a truth in the "ideal" or in the "existential" order, always consists in the conformity of our mind with *being* or *existence*,[1] with possible existence in the first case, and actual existence in the second.

Hence the logical law: for an (affirmative) proposition to be true it is not enough that the predicate agree with the subject, *the subject must also exist in the manner of existence required by the copula*. For example, if I say "Bonaparte is first consul" the proposition is not true because the subject, Bonaparte, does not exist in the actual existence required by this copula (that is, in present time). Bonaparte was consul, but he is so no more (see below, No. 27).

*(*a*)[2] The propositions which we are designating as "*propositions with a verb-copula*" were called propositions *de tertio adjacente* by the ancients; these include all such propositions as "I am writing," "Peter is a man," in which the subject, predicate and copula are explicitly stated.[3] Likewise they called "*propositions with a verb-predicate*" "*de secundo adjacente*" (*e.g.*, "Peter lives," "I write"), in which the verb signifies the predicate itself at the same time as it unites it to the subject. In a proposition *de secundo adjacente*, "Peter is," the verb *to be* is attributed to the subject as a predicate, and signifies that Peter exists in reality. In a proposition *de tertio adjacente*, "Peter is a man," the verb *to be* is not attributed

(I, *Periherm.*, lect. 5, *in fine*): "ista actualitas . . . est communiter omnis formae, sive substantialis, sive accidentalis, et inde est quod, quando volumus significare quamcumque formam inesse alicui, significamus per verbum est, unde ex consequenti significat compositionem" (John of St. Thomas, *Log.*, *Sum.*, lib. I, cap. 6). Owing to a misunderstanding of this doctrinal point modern logicians—especially certain theorists in mathematical logic (cf. Rougier, *Structures des théories déductives*, pp. 5–13)—have involved themselves in many difficulties.

[1] *Verum sequitur esse rerum* (St. Thomas, *de Verit.*, q. 1, a. 1, 3rd sed contra).

[2] In this case the proposition is composed of only two words, the second of which (the verb-predicate) is united to the subject.

[3] In this case the proposition is composed of three words, the third of which (the predicate-noun) is united to the subject *by* and *with* the verb-copula.

to the subject as a predicate but merely as *joined* to the predicate "man," so as to form with it but a single member of the proposition attributed to the subject.

In all cases, whether it signifies the predicate itself, or is necessary in order to unite it to the subject, the verb "*stands with the predicate.*"

*(*b*) *The Noun.*[1] The noun is a term that signifies things "*sine tempore*" as intemporal. Time is excluded, not from the things that the nouns may signify (for there are nouns that denote time), but *from the manner in which the noun signifies.* For the noun signifies the thing *as stable*, as having a certain mode of permanence (even if the thing itself is not stable, *e.g.*, "movement," "change"; this stability *in the noun's mode of signifying* does not mean that the thing itself is stable, but means that the noun takes as its foundation in the thing the stability of the *essence* or *nature* of this thing. Time is always time; and as long as it exists "movement" qua movement, immutably keeps its nature, movement).

*(*c*) *The Verb.*[2] The verb is a term that signifies things

[1] Aristotle (*Periherm.*, I, c. II, 16a 19; lect. 4 in St. Thomas) defines the noun as (A) *vox significativa ad placitum*, (B) *sine tempore*, (C) *cujus nulla pars significat separata*, (D) *finita*, (E) *recta*. (A) is the general definition of the term. (B) distinguishes the noun from the verb. (C) excludes complex terms and imperfect discourse from the definition of the noun (see below No. 39). (D) excludes indeterminate terms (*infiniti*, non-man). (E) excludes oblique terms that cause the noun to "decline" from its proper nature [declension of nouns] (in such a case the noun is signified not as *tanquam quid, et ut extremum quoddam in se, sed ut alterius, respective ad alterum*) : liber *Petri*, *Peter's* book; video *Petrum* —I am *seeing Peter*.

[2] Aristotle (*ibid.*, c. III, 16b, 6; lect. 5 of St. Thomas) defines the verb as: (A) *vox significativa ad placitum*, (B) *cum tempore*, (C) *cujus nulla pars significat separata*, (D) *finita*, (E) *et recta*, (F) *et eorum quae de altero praedicantur, semper est nota*.

(A) is the general definition of the term.
(B) distinguishes the verb from the noun.
(C) excludes complex verbs.
(D) excludes indeterminate verbs (*e.g.*, non-loving).
(E) excludes oblique verbs: the past and future tenses "decline" from the proper nature of the verb, which is to signify things as acting and temporal, for they do not denote pure and simple action or movement, but denote it in the past or in the future. Therefore the present indicative alone corresponds to the proper notion of the verb: all the other forms participate in the verb's nature in an imperfect manner.—The verb always denotes the *attribution of a predicate* to a subject, and in this sense is said to always "stand with the predicate" (see above a).
(F) excludes the participle and the infinitive, which are both *reducible* to the noun as well as to the verb.

"*cum tempore,*" as temporal—in the manner of an *action* or movement or with a certain mode that consists in being effected in time: "Peter *speaks.*" Every verb (*e.g.*, "I see") signifies in a single concept and as a single object, both a certain thing (in this case, vision) and a certain mode that is characteristic of the verb. This mode consists in the *action* or *movement* according to which this thing flows from the subject and is joined to it. Thus the verb *to be* signifies *existence* as *exercised in time.* Whatever is independent of time or eternal is thereby excluded, not from the things the verb may signify (for the truths "every triangle *has* three interior angles together equal to two right angles," and "God *is* good" are independent of time), but from *the manner in which the verb signifies these things.* For of itself the verb signifies things as taking place in time; eternal things are grasped by our intellects by analogy with transitory things—they are signified with a temporal mode that relates not to themselves but to our mode of signification.[1]

*(*d*) Since language cannot simultaneously express both the stability of essences and the flux of movement it puts the burden once and for all upon two terms, the noun to express the former, and the verb to express the latter. Both of these terms accomplish their task *by the manner in which they signify* each, viz., stability of essences

[1] All the above notions are primarily true of the intellectual *rôle* played *de jure* by the elements of language considered in themselves. This analysis is in no way affected by the fact that *de facto* and in certain cases, language does not explicitly exercise all these functions, and that in some tongues the verb *to be* does not exist (its functions remaining unexpressed). That is the affair of descriptive Psychology but in no way concerns Logic. Undoubtedly there is no actually existing language, much less any artificial language constructed by some well-meaning philanthropist or logician, that absolutely satisfies the requirements of language considered as a purely logical type.

The Aristotelian definition of the verb needs to be well understood. *Cum tempore* does not mean that the verb must mark the difference between past, present and future time (on the contrary—the past and future *decline* (descend, or deviate) from the proper nature of the verb—see the preceding note). What this expression means is that it is essential that the verb signify something in the manner of an *action* or *movement*. Therefore the definition applies just as well to the verb of primitive languages that designates the metaphysical differences of action (the aorist for action *in fieri*, the perfect for *accomplished* action) as it does to the verb of modern language which designates the purely temporal differences in action. It would be well to note the importance of the linguistic category of *aspect* on this point (cf. Vendryes, *Le Langage*).

and flux of movement (and not by the *things* which they signify).

So, in accusing language of "parcelling out" reality into inert scraps and of depriving things of movement, the school of MM. Bergson and Le Roy not only mistakes a simple condition of the mode of signification for a condition of the signified thing, but entirely misunderstands the true notion of language in considering only the noun, and disregarding the verb.

*(*e*) The analysis of every enunciation reveals a subject united to a predicate by a copula ; in other words, the structure of an enunciation may always be reduced to two terms united by a copula, as S. to Pr., but the Pr. and C. may be united in the verb ("I run") and the S. and Pr. may be interchanged without affecting the truth of the statement ("some man is a liar," "some liar is a man"). Consequently the basic elements of every enunciation, considered simply in itself, are the *verb* (be it merely a copula, or copula and predicate united in one term) and the *noun* (subject or predicate). This is why we say that the division of the *enunciative* term into noun and verb is an *essential* one, whereas its division into S., Pr. and C. is an *accidental* division. However, the division of the *syllogistic* term into S. and Pr. is *essential*, for in this case the term and the proposition are considered *as parts of the reasoning*.

3. *The Subject and the Predicate*

The syllogistic term is divided into subject and predicate.

24. DIVISION OF THE TERM CONSIDERED AS PART OF ARGUMENTATION. Considered as part of argumentation (*the syllogistic term*), the term is the *last* element into which every argumentation is *necessarily resolved.* It is not the function of the argumentation, as such, to construct or state the truth "*Peter is a man,*" that is, to unite the term *man* to the term *Peter* by means of the copula *is.* (This is the function of the enunciation.) Argumentation as such *draws* or *infers*, from the fact that (I) "Man is mortal" and (II) "Peter is a man," the truth (III) "Peter is mortal": it unites *Peter* and *mortal* by means of *man.* Therefore the terms it admits of formally as an argumentation are the three terms

Peter, *mortal* and *man*. " Peter " is the *subject* of the conclusion, " mortal " is the *predicate* of the conclusion, " man," called the middle term, is the *predicate* of one of the premisses and the *subject* of the other.

The copula (and the verb inasmuch as it contains the copula) is not a syllogistic term ; it does not belong to the syllogism formally, but only by presupposition, as a part of the propositions of which the syllogism is composed. The proposition itself, *considered as part of argumentation* is resolved into two terms only : the subject and the predicate.

4. *Extension of the Subject-Term*

25. DIVISION OF THE SUBJECT-TERM ACCORDING TO EXTENSION.[1] As we have already seen (No. 18) the *concept considered as subject* of a proposition and in relation to the logical use we make of it as such, is divided into *singular*, *particular and universal* or *distributive*.

The subject-term is either *singular, particular, universal*, or *indefinite*.

The same is true of the term that signifies the concept thus considered. But it may happen that the extension of the subject-concept in relation to the predicate is not expressly manifested by any oral sign, *e.g.*, " *man* is mortal," " *man* is untrustworthy." In such a case the *concept* itself taken as it is realized in singular things is in reality either singular, or particular, or distributive, but the term does not indicate which. Therefore we say that this term is INDEFINITE. Accordingly, taken as the subject of a proposition, the term is divided according to extension into *singular*, *particular*, *distributive and indefinite*.

Subject-term	expressly manifesting the extension of the subject-concept in relation to the predicate	*Singular*		this man
		Common	*Particular*	some man
			Distributive of Universal	every man
	Indefinite (and occultly singular, particular or universal)			man

DIVISION OF THE SUBJECT-TERM ACCORDING TO EXTENSION

[1] This division, being related to the term considered as *subject*, concerns the *syllogistic term* treated in No. 24.

C. THE PROPERTIES OF TERMS IN THE PROPOSITION

Language serves thought but only in presupposing its activity, and without ever providing a substitute copy for it.

26. LANGUAGE AND THOUGHT. Everything directly conceived or thought of by our intellect, everything of which we have a concept or " mental word " may be expressed or translated into language.[1] But despite the flexibility, the docility, the delicacy of any system of language-signs, this expression is always more or less deficient in relation to thought. The loftiest intellectual knowledge, which reveals a world of consequences within a single principle, must, so to speak, be scattered and diluted in order to be orally expressed.

Indeed it would be absurd to expect material signs, uttered one after the other, to duplicate or furnish a facsimile of the vital and immanent act of thought. Nor is it the purpose of language to furnish such a facsimile of thought : its object is to permit the intellect of the hearer to think, by an active repetitive effort, what the intellect of the speaker is thinking. From this point of view human language performs its function perfectly. *Granted the interpretative effort* and the intellectual activity of the hearer, it is a perfect system of signs ; suppress this effort and this activity and there remains but a radically insufficient system of lifeless symbols.

In other words, language not only supposes an effort—often how bitter, authors know but too well—on the part of the one who expresses his thought, but also requires an effort on the part of the listener : a beneficent effort that keeps us from depending entirely on the sign and saves us from falling into what Leibnitz called "psittacism," a parrot-like use of language.

Nor would it be amiss to note in this connection that the more life and intellectual *quality* a philosophy possesses the more forcibly must that philosophy experience the distance between language and thought, without for all that cowardly forsaking all expression of the truth. Hence a twofold necessity accrues to philosophy : it must acquire a mastery

[1] *Omne individuum ineffabile.* Every individual taken in its individuality is inexpressible, because we have no direct concept of the singular ; we know it by our intellect, but only indirectly, by reflecting on images (*per conversionem ad phantasmata*).

over language by means of a whole technical apparatus of forms and verbal distinctions (terminology), and it must unceasingly exact from the mind an act of internal vitality such that words and formulæ can never replace, for they are there but to spur the mind to this act. All philosophy that relies upon words, all *over-facile* philosophy, is *a priori* a philosophy of lesser thought and consequently of lesser truth.

Language, then, expresses or signifies as much of our thought as is necessary in order that another intellect, hearing the pronounced words, may present the same thought to itself. The remainder is not necessarily, and even should not be, expressed, lest it overburden and infinitely complicate the winged signs of speech. This unexpressed margin of thought, to be supplemented by the intellect of the hearer, is remarkably evinced by the diverse properties that affect the term considered, not by itself, but *in the context of the proposition*, *as part of a proposition*. The ancient logicians made an exhaustive study of these properties, a study that may seem irksome to inattentive minds, but one that is most instructive from the point of view which we have just indicated and absolutely indispensable for anyone who would acquire the art of reasoning. As Aristotle says, since we cannot bring the things themselves into our discussions, we have to let words appear for them and testify in their stead.[1] But we shall inevitably fall into a host of errors unless we observe that not only may the same word have several different meanings but also that the same word, *even while having the same meaning* (for example, the one given in the dictionary) and consequently even while signifying the same intelligible nature, may, according to its use in the context, stand for very different *things*.

We give here a few points of information about the different properties of the term considered as part of the proposition, the principal of which is the *suppositio*. Since we are dealing with purely technical notions, it seems preferable to keep the Latin names by which these

[1] Aristotle, *I Elench.*, I, 164a, 5 : " In disputationibus nos utimur vocabulis loco rerum, quia ipsas res in medium afferre non possumus."

terms are signified, followed by an approximate translation.[1]

Hence the rules concerning the *suppositio* of terms, which we shall translate as their " substitutive value " (*suppléance*), that is to say the manner in which a term takes the place of, or becomes a substitute in discourse for, a thing. (*Terminus supponit pro re :* the term stands for the thing.)

The *suppositio* is the substitution of a term for a thing; this substitution must answer the needs of the copula.

27. THE SUPPOSITIO. (1) When I say " man is a species of the genus animal," " Man is a masculine noun," " Peter is a man," the term " man " has the same signification in all three cases—viz., " rational animal." But may I therefore say : " Peter is a man, therefore he is a species of the genus animal or a masculine noun "? Obviously not. For although the term " man " has the same signification in these three statements, yet *it stands for a different thing in each case*. We shall say then that the *suppositio* of a term, which we may translate as its " substitutive value," is *its function in discourse*—(the while its meaning remains the same)—*of taking the place of a thing. To be legitimate this substitution* (of term for thing) *must answer the needs of the copula.*[2]

Rule I. An affirmative is false if its subject does not stand for anything.

(2) What does the latter part of the definition mean in saying : " to be legitimate this substitution must answer the needs of the copula " ? It does not mean that, if it does, this substitution of the term for the thing will result in a *true* proposition. For example, if I say : " my friend Peter is vegetal," the term " my friend Peter " " stands for something " (*supponit*, has a substitutive value), since there really exists a thing to which this term applies considering the *present* time signified by the copula *is :* for I can at the present moment indicate by thought something of which I can truthfully say : this is my friend Peter. But, on the contrary,

[1] Although the logical properties considered here are easier to study in relation to the oral term, they belong just as much to the *concept* as they do to the *term* which is the material expression of the concept. A concept presents a nature or essence to the mind (*significatio*), but furthermore, when considered as part of the proposition that affirms or denies the existence of a certain thing with a certain predicate, it is a mental substitute for the subjects in which this nature is realized (*suppositio*).

[2] *Acceptio termini pro aliquo de quo verificatur juxta exigentiam copulae.* In his treatise *De Suppositionibus*, St. Vincent Ferrer treats the theory of the *suppositio* in a very remarkable and personal manner, but perhaps even too narrowly and systematically. We have preferred to draw upon the works of John of St. Thomas—with a little retouching of our own.

if I say : " Napoleon I. will be emperor," the term Napoleon I. does not " stand for anything " (*non supponit*) because, considering the copula *will be* (*future* time), there is nothing I can designate as Napoleon I. The same is true if I say " Adam is doing penance " or " Antichrist was a liar." So in saying that " the *suppositio* is the property of a term by which it stands for, or takes the place of, a thing in discourse, this substitution being legitimate considering the copula," we do not mean that this substitution is true in the nature of things, but only that : the sort of existence—actual (past, present or future), possible or " imaginary " —denoted by the copula permits this substitution. This is so because, as we saw above (No. 23), the verb *to be* always signifies existence (real or ideal) even when it is used simply as a copula. Accordingly, before verifying the conformity of predicate to subject, we must ascertain whether the subject itself exists in the manner required by the copula.

Hence the rule: *every proposition whose subject does not stand for anything is false* if it is affirmative. (This rule does not apply to negative propositions, for such a proposition may be true even if its subject does not stand for anything. The statement "Richelieu is not a member of the Chamber of Deputies " is true, by the very fact that Richelieu does not exist.)

(*a*) In propositions concerning pure essences (eternal truth, attributing an *essential* predicate to the subject), the subject-term always stands for something, for in this instance the copula denotes *possible* existence only, and is thus outside of time, *absoluta a tempore*. If I say, " the triangle has such and such a property," I can and always shall be able to show by thought a thing (an essence) in the order of possibles of which I may truthfully affirm " this is a triangle." Only when the predicate is *accidental* to the subject, as in " some man runs," "Napoleon was emperor," is there any reason for inquiring whether or not the subject of the (affirmative) proposition stands for something, for in this case the copula denotes existence *in act*—existence *in time*.

(*b*) Distinguish carefully between the "*signification*" and the "*suppositio*" of terms.[1] The *signification* relates to *that from which the giving of the name springs* (*id a quo imponitur nomen*), that is, to the form or nature which it represents to the mind (*qualitas nominis*). The "*suppositio*" of a word relates to that *to which the name is given* (*id cui imponitur nomen*), that is, to the things or subjects (*substantia nominis*) to which the intelligence *applies, in this way or that, the word itself in a proposition* in order that the word may act as a substitute for the thing to which the intelligence applies certain predicates. In other words, the "*signification*" (substitutio *repraesentiva* pro re) relates to the *natures* that are the proper object of the first operation of the mind, whereas the "*suppositio*" (substitutio *applicativa*) relates to the subjects in which these natures are realized and which the second operation of the mind signifies *as existing* with such and such predicates. When I say: "Man is social," the word "man" not only represents (renders present to my mind) human *nature* (considered in an abstract universal subject), but it also takes the place for me of the extra-mental thing, of the individuals to which sociability is attributed by the copula *is*.

(3) Before determining what the "*substitutive value*" (the *suppositio*) of a term may be, we must determine *whether there is any substitution.* We must also ascertain *to what kind of existence, real or ideal,*[2] *that substitution is related.* For instance, I should be guilty of very poor reasoning should I attempt to prove the existence of a chimera by the following argument:

(I) That which is an animal is,
(II) But the chimera is an animal,
(III) Therefore the chimera is.

[1] Cf. St. Thomas *in* III *Sent.*, dist. VI, q. 1, a. 3; John of St. Thomas, *Logica*, 1a Pars, Sum., p. 22.

[2] We may understand *ideal* existence as standing in contradictory opposition to *actual* existence; that is, we are defining it simply as existence *that is not actual* (whether it be possible or "imaginary"). Had it been thus understood in the table in No. 9a, the groups I, II, and III would have been bracketed together, and "real existence" would have referred exclusively to group IV, and would thus have designated actual existence as simultaneously opposed to both possible and "imaginary" existence.

For I play on the double meaning of *is* in proposition I: chimera being taken (substituting, *supponens*) in relation to to *ideal existence* in proposition II (for the chimera exists as an animal *in the mind* alone), and in relation to *real existence* in proposition III. It was in this way that the ancient sophists pretended to demonstrate that non-being is, because it is non-being.

It is evident that if the antecedent (the minor in a syllogism) [1] has a *suppositio* taken solely in relation to ideal existence (if it is a purely "essential" *suppositio* as we would say nowadays) then the conclusion cannot have a *suppositio* taken in relation to real existence, an "existential" *suppositio*. My reasoning would be defective indeed were I to infer from the propositions "Every centaur is half-man, half-horse," "but a centaur is a fabulous being" that "there *really exists* a fabulous being that is half-man, half-horse." The proper conclusion would be: "therefore some fabulous being is half-man, half-horse" (*in ideal existence*). Hence the rule:

Rule II. A sequence is invalid if the mode of existence in relation to which the *suppositio* is understood varies from the antecedent to the consequent.

For a sequence to be valid the mode of existence in relation to which the suppositio is understood must not vary from antecedent to consequent.

The "ontological" argument by which Descartes sought to prove the existence of God—starting with and proceeding from the *idea* of a perfect being (and not from some existing thing), violates this rule in passing from *ideal* to *real* existence.

(I) The perfect being exists necessarily,
(II) But God is the perfect being,
(III) Therefore God exists necessarily.

[1] In syllogisms of the third figure (see below No. 78) it may happen that although the Minor *considered by itself* has a purely "essential" *suppositio*, the *suppositio* of the Conclusion is "existential." Such is the case in the following example (in *Disamis*):

"Some angel is damned
But every angel is a pure spirit,
Therefore some pure spirit is damned."

But in this syllogism the existential *suppositio* of the Major is communicated to the Minor *taken as Minor*, that is, *thought of as subordinate to the Major*.

Proposition I results necessarily from the *idea* of a perfect being if the word " *exists* " relates to *ideal* existence, but not if it relates to real existence. This proposition simply means that among the constitutive notes of the object of thought I call " perfect being " is the object of thought I call " necessary existence " whether or not this being really exists (and without my knowing whether or not this represented existence is *exercised*). Likewise in proposition II, the substitutive value of the subject (God) relates to *ideal* existence. (Descartes did not prove that God *really exists* as perfect being, on the contrary, he began with the *notion* of God, with the principle that God *exists ideally* in our thought as perfect being). But in proposition III the substitutive value of this same subject relates to real existence, and Descartes concludes that God necessarily exists in real being. His premisses, however, justify such a conclusion in the *ideal* realm only ; in other words, his argument proves nothing beyond the fact that God exists necessarily, *if He exists.*

(4) Now let us examine the different " substitutive values " a term may have in a proposition.

A. In order to distinguish different substitutive values let us first consider the term as *subject of a proposition.* As we shall presently see, its substitutive value in this instance is determined by the signification of the predicate.

1 For example in the propositions :

Suppositio materialis.

" *man* is a noun of one syllable,"
" *lamb* is a four-letter word."

The term " man " or " lamb " stands for itself, for the oral or written *sign* itself : its substitutive value is *material, suppositio* MATERIALIS. More often, however, the term stands for the *thing* which it *signifies :* its substitutive value is *formal.*

2 In the latter case, if I say

Suppositio impropria.

" The *Lamb* was offered up for the sins of the world," the term " Lamb " stands for the thing it signifies only improperly or metaphorically : the substitutive value of the term is *improper, suppositio* IMPROPRIA. If, on the contrary, the term stands for the thing it signifies *in the proper sense*, its substitutive value is said to be *proper*.

3 For example in propositions such as :

" The vertebrate is a branch of zoology," or

" The lamb is a species of the genus animal," propositions in which the predicate is a logical being with the form of universality, the term " vertebrate " or " lamb " stands for a certain *nature* which it signifies without passing to the individuals who have this nature (for I cannot say : Fido is a vertebrate, therefore Fido is a branch of zoology). In other words, the term stands for the thing it signifies *primarily* and *immediately* (*primo et immediate*, *seu formaliter*) with a *precision* such that it does not pass on to the thing it signifies *secondarily* (*materialiter*) ; (for a common term signifies first and immediately a universal nature, and signifies secondly and mediately the individuals in which this nature is actualized).[1] In this case the substitutive value is *simple*, *suppositio* SIMPLEX.[2]

Suppositio simplex and *Suppositio personalis.*

However, the term may stand simultaneously for the thing it signifies *immediately* and for the thing it signifies *materially* and *mediately* ; that is, it may also stand for the individual subjects or " persons " in which is actualized the universal nature that it primarily signifies. In this case the term has, so to speak, a *double* substitutive value which is said to be *real* or *personal*, *suppositio* PERSONALIS.

4 In the latter case the substitutive value may be either *singular* (*suppositio* SINGULARIS) : " The *man* ran away at once," " The *lamb* will be sacrificed to-morrow," or

Suppositio singularis and *Suppositio communis.*

common (*suppositio* COMMUNIS).

5 The latter may in turn be either

particular determinate (*suppositio* DETERMINATE, *seu* DISJUNCTIVA) when the term stands for only a *certain determinate*

Suppositio disjunctiva, Suppositio disjuncta.

[1] See above No. 20 a.

[2] In the case of a *singular* term, which signifies the individual *immediately* and the nature *mediately*, the relation is inverse. There is *suppositio simplex* when the term stands for the individual subject without exercising its secondary signification, that is, without standing for the universal nature, as in all propositions wherein the predicate is a logical being with the form of singularity (incommunicable to many). For example, if I say : " Peter is an individual," that he is " something incommunicable to many contained in the species man," I cannot conclude by induction that man is an individual.

few of the things which it signifies : " Some *man* is a liar "[1]

or *particular indeterminate* (*suppositio* DISJUNCTA) when the term stands for *some* of the things which it signifies, but leaves them indistinct, *takes them as indeterminate or confused* " Some *instrument* is needed to make music."

Suppositio copulata.

or *collective* (*suppositio* COPULATA) when the term stands for the things it signifies taken collectively, or as a whole : " The *Apostles* were twelve," " The *Romans* were an imperialistic people."

or *universal* or *distributed* (*suppositio* DISTRIBUTA) when the term stands for each and every one of the things it signifies (*pro omnibus et singulis significatis*) : " *Man* is mortal," " Every *man* is mortal." In this case the extension of the term signifying a universal nature (*e.g.*, " man ") is in no way restricted.

THE SUBSTITUTIVE VALUE OF THE TERM

SUPPOSITIO — Propria — Personalis — Communis

Distributa:
- Completa : " Every *man* is mortal "
- Incompleta : " Every *animal* was in the Ark "
- Exceptiva : " Every *man* is born in sin "

Confusa (the things for which the term stands are considered *indeterminately*)

- Copulata : " The *Apostles* were twelve "
- Disjuncta : " Some *tool* is necessary in order to work "

Confusa Tantum

- Disjunctiva : " Some *man* is a liar." *Determinata.*

Singularis : " The *man* ran away," " *Peter* is seated."

Simplex : " *Man* is a species of the genus Animal."

Impropria : " The *Lamb* was offered up for the sins of the world."

Materialis : " *Man* is a noun of one syllable."

Suppositio completa, incompleta, exceptiva.

6 *Universal* or distributed substitution may be either *complete*, when the term stands for *all the individual subjects* to which its signification extends (*pro singulis generum*) : " man is mortal," " every animal is sentient."

[1] " *Some man* is a liar." The S. in this proposition *first* and *immediately* signifies an individual at large—an indeterminate individual (*individuum vagum*) with human nature, and *secondly* or *mediately* signifies certain determinate individuals with this nature—this man, or that man, is a liar.

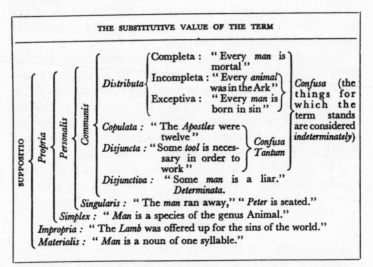

or *incomplete*, when the term stands only for *all the kinds of subjects* to which its signification extends (*pro generis singulorum*) : "*Every animal* was in Noah's ark" (that is, each species of animal). "God summoned *every animal* before Adam."

or *exceptive* : "*every man* that is merely man is born in sin" (exception being made for the Mother of God), "*every man* is fallible" (except the Pope speaking as Doctor of the Universal Church).

Descensus et Ascensus.

The ancient logicians called the legitimate progression from a common term to the inferior or singular concepts it contains, or from inferior terms to the common concept which contains them, the *descensus* and *ascensus* of terms. This progression constitutes a true inference in the case of the *particular-determinate* (*suppositio disjunctiva*) or *universal* (*suppositio distributa*) substitutive value of a term. In the first instance (*suppositio disjunctiva*) the *descensus* has the following form : "some man is a liar, therefore either this man is a liar, OR ELSE this one is a liar, OR ELSE this other one is a liar, etc.," "some body is sentient, therefore either this body is sentient, OR ELSE this one is sentient, OR ELSE this one (this animal for example) is sentient (*descensus disjunctivus*). . . ." In the second case (*suppositio distributa*) the *descensus* has this form : "Every man is mortal, therefore this man is mortal AND this man is mortal, AND this other man is mortal, etc.," "all corporeal substance is destructible, therefore non-living bodies are destructible, AND vegetables are destructible, AND animals are destructible (*descensus copulativus*)." In both cases we pass from a more universal proposition to a series of less universal propositions of which some (*descensus disjunctivus*) or all (*descensus copulativus*) should be true.

If the substitutive value in question is *collective* (*suppositio copulata*) or *particular-indeterminate* (*suppositio disjuncta*) the term is said to be "*immobile*" because it does not admit of a *descensus* or *ascensus* that resolves the truth that was stated about the term itself into other less universal or more universal truths. The *descensus copulatus* legitimately corresponding to the *suppositio copulata* has the following form: "The Apostles were twelve," therefore "Peter AND Paul AND John AND James, etc. (*taken together and as subject of a single proposition*) were twelve." The *descensus disjunctus* corresponding to the *suppositio disjuncta* has the following form: "some instrument is needed in order to make music, therefore a piano, OR a violin, OR a flute OR, etc. (*taken together and as subject of a single proposition*) is needed to make music." In neither of these cases is there any inference from a more universal to a less universal proposition.

We shall meet with the notion of "*the ascensus and descensus under a common term or concept*" again in dealing with *induction.*

Thus the substitutive value of a particular term may be *determinate* (*disjunctiva*), or *indeterminate* (*disjuncta*). In the former case it stands for determinate subjects, so that the truth stated about the term itself may be applied to each one of these subjects considered individually. In the latter case, it stands for a vague and indeterminate subject considered as a whole, so that the truth stated about the term cannot be applied to individual determinate subjects.

B. The *predicate* of an affirmative proposition belongs to the latter class: its substitutive value is *particular indeterminate* (*suppositio disjuncta*).

The substitutive value of the Pr. of a proposition: (*Suppositio disjuncta.*) particular indeterminate.

1 Its substitutive value is particular: for example in the proposition: "every man is an animal" the term *animal* is not taken as communicable to all the individuals contained under it, it stands only for an *individuum vagum* with animal nature; for there are animals that are not men.[1]

2 Its substitutive value is *particular indeterminate;* for example, if I say "Every sentient being is an *animal*" obviously I cannot conclude by descending to the particulars

[1] *Convertible* propositions (see below No. 52, #2, and No. 83) are also subject to this law. "Every man is rational." The concept rational *has the same extension* as the concept man; but as predicate, that is, as attributed to the universal subject *man* and to the individuals contained under it, *it is not taken universally.* It is not taken as communicable to the subject according to all the singulars contained therein, but only according to a certain individual and indeterminate restriction. For we cannot say: "each man is all rationality."

contained under the term *animal* that "therefore every sentient being is this animal (*man*)," or "therefore every sentient being is that animal (*beast*)"; I may only say: "therefore every sentient being is either *man* or *beast*." In the same way, if I say "Every musical performance *requires an instrument*" I cannot conclude "therefore every musical performance requires a *piano*, or every musical performance requires a *flute*, etc."—every one of these statements would be false. I may only say: "Every musical performance requires either a piano or a flute or, etc."

That is why the subject has a *particular indeterminate* substitutive value (*suppositio disjuncta*) in propositions such as "some instrument is *necessary* to produce music," "workmen *are needed* to build a house," "the animal *alone* has the power of spontaneous motion." [1] We cannot particularize immediately under the common term "workmen" and say "therefore the workman Peter is needed to build a house, or the workman Paul is needed to build a house, or the workman John . . . etc." (for no particular workman is needed), nor can we specify under the common term "*animal*" and say "therefore *man alone* has the power of spontaneous motion," or "the *beast alone* has the power of spontaneous motion," we must simply say, "therefore man and beast alone have the power of spontaneous motion."

Whence two rules to remember:

Rule III. In every affirmative proposition the Pr. is taken particularly.

In every AFFIRMATIVE *proposition*, the *substitutive* value of the PREDICATE IS PARTICULAR INDETERMINATE (*suppositio* DISJUNCTA).

Rule IV. In every negative proposition the Pr. is taken universally.

Counter to this, *in every* NEGATIVE *proposition the substitutive value* of the PREDICATE is UNIVERSAL (*suppositio* DISTRIBUTA).

For example in the proposition, "man is not a pure spirit" the term "*pure spirit*" is taken as communicable to all the singulars contained thereunder; no pure spirit is a man.

[1] Such propositions do imply or presuppose some universal affirmative proposition wherein their subject has the *rôle* of predicate. Cf. John of St. Thomas, *Log.*, I, P., *Sum.*, lib. II, cap. XII.

there are exceptions to these rules
The pred. might be singular

These two rules are used a great deal in the theory of the syllogism.

Rule V. The S. stands for the thing according to the needs of the Pr.

As for the SUBJECT, as we have already said, *its substitutive value is always determined by the signification of the predicate.*

(*Subjectum supponit juxta exigentiam Praedicati, talia sunt subjecta qualia permittuntur a suis praedicatis.*)
This is the fundamental rule in regard to the *suppositio* :

S. Pr.

"The Apostles were men"—*suppositio distributa* (universal).

"The Apostles were twelve"—*suppositio copulata* (collective).

"Apostles were necessary to preach the Gospel to the world"—*suppositio disjuncta* (particular indeterminate).

"Apostles were present at Mount Tabor"—*suppositio disjunctiva* (particular determinate).

Suppositio naturalis et *suppositio accidentalis.*

C. The "real" or "personal" substitutive value of a term (*suppositio personalis*) may be divided from another aspect besides the one noted above in 4—viz., in relation to the verb or copula. From this point of view it is either *essential* (*suppositio* NATURALIS), or *accidental* (*suppositio* ACCIDENTALIS). In the first case, *e.g.*, "*man* is rational" the subject-term stands for something to which the predicate belongs *intrinsically* and *essentially ;* consequently its substitutive value is *universal* (if it is a common term). In the second case, *e.g.*, "*man* is a liar," the term stands for something to which the predicate belongs *accidentally.* Therefore its substitutive value is *particular determinate* (*suppositio disjunctiva*), if the term is neither taken collectively nor rendered indeterminate (*suppositio disjuncta*) by any particular modifying sign. Hence the rule :

Rule VI. The substitutive value of an unmodified subject is universal in necessary matter,

When the *subject of a proposition* is not modified by any sign its *substitutive value* is UNIVERSAL in NECESSARY *matter*, PARTICULAR DETERMINATE *in* CONTINGENT *matter.*

Thus a proposition such as: "the *animals* are able to feel" (a proposition in the scientific order) is equivalent to a *universal* proposition ; a proposition such as "*the animals* listened to the preaching of Anthony of Padua" (a proposition in the historical order) is equivalent to a *particular* proposition. **particular in contingent matter.**

Furthermore, as we saw above, when the subject has a *suppositio naturalis*, the copula of itself signifies only the relation of predicate to subject in possible existence, so that the subject need not exist in order that the affirmative proposition be true. "Every animal is sentient" would be a true statement, even if no animal existed on earth.

On the contrary, when the subject has a *suppositio accidentalis*, the copula of itself denotes actual existence, for since the predicate is not of the subject's essence, it is received accidentally in a subject presupposed as existing. Consequently the subject must exist (in the time designated by the copula) in order that the proposition be true. "Peter runs" ; if Peter does not exist, this proposition is false. Similarly, "Racine is writing *Iphigenia*" and "Charlemagne will be crowned" are false propositions.[1]

D. Therefore—*every sequence is invalid in which the genus of the suppositio of a term changes from one proposition to another*.[2] For example : **Rule VII. In a valid sequence the genus of the *suppositio* must not vary.**

The logical categories were created by Aristotle,
But quantity is a logical category,
Therefore quantity was created by Aristotle.

Likewise it would be faulty reasoning in Theology to say : "The Father is God, the Son is God, therefore the Son is the Father." For the *suppositio* of the term "God" changed here from one premise to the other. In the Major it stood for *the divine essence subsisting in the person of the Father*—

[1] See below No. 84.

[2] We say the *genus* of the *suppositio*, because the species may vary : thus a particular may be inferred from a proposition whose subject has a universal substitutive value (every man is mortal, therefore some man is mortal). But were we to pass from one *genus* of suppositio to another (for example, from *suppositio simplex* to a *suppositio personalis*) the sequence would be invalid. The same is true when, as cited in the second example in the text, a single term with a *suppositio personalis* stands for two different subjects.

" The Father is God (the Father) " ; in the Minor it stood for *the divine essence subsisting in the person of the Son*—" The Son is God (the Son)."

DRILL.

(1) In the following examples indicate the *suppositio* of the italicized terms (as to mode of existence and as to their subjects) :

The *Romans* were an imperialistic people.
A *square circle* is impossible to conceive.
Every *creature* is finite.
Nebuchadnezzar is not in Paris.
Every *metal* is a heat-conductor.
The *Lion of Judah* has conquered.
Philosophers are arrogant.
Some *angel* is damned.

In this proposition *angel* is subject of the predicate damned.

Every *man* is fallible.
Man is rational.
I can find no rhyme for *epidermis*.
All the *nations* were at this congress.
The *serpent* betrayed the woman.
I need some *enemy* to teach me my faults.
Every created *essence* is distinct from existence.
This *man* is wicked.
No *circle* is square.
Napoleon I. will win the battle of Austerlitz.
Napoleon I. won the battle of Waterloo.
Some *triangle* is isosceles.
Romans were needed to build this empire.
Every *centaur* is half-man, half-horse.
The *Romans* destroyed Carthage.
Pious has two syllables.
All the soldiers are *French*.
The *Romans* were men.

(2) Find some examples of the *suppositio* in relation to possible existence, and in relation to ideal existence.

Find examples corresponding to each *suppositio* in the table in No. 27 (3), A. 5.

*28. OTHER LOGICAL PROPERTIES OF THE TERM.

I. The *ampliatio* (amplification, enlargement) extends or broadens a term's substitutive value. For instance, the term "*man*" is *broader* in this proposition: "every *man* (as a possible essence) is fallible" than it is in the proposition: "every *man* (actually existing) is fallible" (*ampliatio ad esse possibile*). Similarly this term is *broader* in the proposition "EVERY *man* is unhappy on this earth" than in "the POOR *man* is unhappy on this earth" (*ampliatio ad plura supposita*). *Ampliatio* or Amplification.

II. The *restrictio* (restriction), on the contrary, restricts the substitutive value of a term. In the proposition "every (actually existing) *man* is fallible" "the POOR *man* is unhappy," "the *men* OF THIS COUNTRY are liars" the term *man* has a more *restricted* substitutive value than it has in the propositions: "every *man* (as a possible essence) is fallible." "*Man* is unhappy on this earth," "*men* are liars." Likewise, in saying, for example, "*everyone* knows it, the expression "everyone," which stands for all the people of a certain country or a certain category, is employed with *restriction*. *Restrictio*

Rule. In order to proceed legitimately from the broad to the less broad in an *affirmative* proposition (*ab amplo ad non amplum, sive a non restricto ad restrictum*). 1. The broader term must be *universal* (distributive). 2. The less broad subject must be posited as existing: I cannot say: "every man is rational, therefore Napoleon I. is rational," for Napoleon I. does not actually exist. I should say: "every man is rational (Napoleon I. existed), therefore Napoleon I. *was* rational."

III. *Alienatio* transfers the substitutive value of a term from proper to improper or metaphorical: this transfer may occur either in the S. on account of the Pr. or in the Pr. on account of the S. *Alienatio* or transfer

The *Apostle* is carved in stone.
This philosopher is an *ass*.
This man is a *tiger*.
The *parrot* is a mast rigged on the main-top.

Diminutio or Diminution.

IV. By *diminutio* (diminution) the term is made to stand for a lesser (less extended) subject than it would stand for if taken by itself.

" *Every argument* is good in so far as it is true."

Appellatio or Reimposition.

V. The *appellatio* (reimposition) clothes the subject designated by the term with a determination other than the one which the term itself signifies. In other words, it imposes upon this term a formality that is properly signified by another, and thus causes it to stand for a thing taken from a determinate point of view which it does not signify when considered by itself.

Peter is a heavy eater.

The subject *Peter* is said to be heavy here, as or under the formality of an eater. Before being attributed to the subject *Peter* the term *heavy* (*terminus appellans*) " calls down " or " reimposes " upon him the determination or formality signified by the term *eater:* the term heavy is not *absolutely* applicable to Peter, but only *in relation* to the faculty of eating, *by means of the determination* signified by the term *eater*.

(*a*) Be careful not to confuse the *appellatio* with the *simple attribution* (*praedicatio*) of a predicate to a subject. In propositions such as: " *this poet is an aviator*," or " *the painter plays the violin*," the predicate is simply attributed to the subject. In order for there to be *appellatio*, the subject must be considered not only as subject, but as endowed with a certain determination by means of which it receives the predicate: " Peter is a *heavy* eater," " Alexander the Great was a *little* man " (small in stature), " this poet is *sublime* as an aviator," " the painter is *unrivalled* on the violin."

(*b*) Such terms as *to know*, *to love*, etc., that signify an interior act of the soul, cause " *appellatio* " in their *objects*, and clothe them with the exact determination or the proper formality supposed by the act in question. For these objects are said to be known, loved, etc., *under the exact aspect* from which they are attained." " I love my neighbour "—*as such*, and I love him thus even if he is my country's enemy (but not *as* the enemy of my country).

" The imprudent desire the pleasures that will destroy them," that is, they want them as pleasures not as evil (although they know them to be evil).

" This historian is well acquainted with Plato "—he knows him as a philosopher and as the author of the Dialogues—but he did not converse with him at the Academy.

It was by a fallacious use of the *appellatio* that the sophists fabricated the *sophism of the veiled man.* " Do you see that veiled man ? " the sophist would ask.—" Yes, I see him." " But one cannot see what is hidden under a veil ? "—" Naturally not." " Well then you are saying that you see this man and that you do not see him, therefore you are contradicting yourself. . . ." Obviously to say " I see this veiled man " means that one sees him as a visual object, that is, as an object covered by a veil, not as an object in itself.

This brief survey of the diverse properties of the term in the proposition is instructive in several respects. For if we have really understood that a single term may stand for different things in discourse, even while it keeps the same signification (corresponds to the same concept, and to the same word in the dictionary)—if we have really understood this—then we shall also understand why thc necessity of " distinguishing," *i.e.*, making distinctions, dominates all human discussions. We shall comprehend also why this necessity arises from the specific character of our intelligence : not only because the same word may signify different concepts, but also because words being the material tools, and concepts the immaterial tools, of rational activity the reason may *put the same concept* and *the same word* with its signification unchanged *to different uses.* We shall also understand how useless it would be to attempt to substitute for the *Logic of ideas* or of *concepts*, which always supposes the activity of the mind using concepts and words as tools, a logic of written or oral *signs*, so perfect as to dispense with thought and be sufficient unto itself (the *universal characteristic* of Leibnitz—modern *Logistics*). Of course, a system of signs more perfect and more rigid than ordinary language may be conceived ; but, with the exception of certain limited domains, such as that of algebra, we shall never succeed in completely suppressing the margin of indetermination that subsists around the oral or written sign, and attests to the transcendence of thought over its material symbols.

Finally, from another point of view, if we understand that the same word stands for such and such a thing, and has such and such a value for thought, depending upon the structure of the proposition of which it is a part, we have already laid hold of an important truth, namely that : the proposition is not a mere juxtaposition of words considered as *things*, but forms a true unity, and is a true *whole* composed of words taken as *parts*.

SECTION 4. THE DEFINITION

29. NOTION OF THE DEFINITION—(*Definition of the thing*). When we express a thought orally we say or utter it externally by means of a vocal sign (a word). When we *conceive* a thing, we utter it intellectually, we " say "[1] it within ourselves by means of an immaterial sign (an idea or mental concept), in other words we *form* a sign within us, an immaterial likeness in which our mind sees this thing.

But in order for the mind to work to advantage, is it enough to say a thing *in brief*, to express it in a *concept ?* Does it suffice to say " man " in thinking of what Peter is, or to say " triangle " in thinking of this geometric figure ? If I really want to *know* anything whatsoever about this geometric figure, or about Peter's nature, must I not first *determine their precise limits*, in order to avoid the risk of attributing the properties of a circle or of a square to the triangle, or of attributing to human nature what is proper to the nature of oxen or of angels. Is it not likewise neces-

[1] The term " say " is evidently used here only by analogy. It refers neither to the act of really uttering something aloud, nor to the act of uttering it *imaginatively* within us, as we do when we talk to ourselves without moving our lips—but relates to the purely immaterial act of thinking (cf. above No. 3). It is a law of the mind that we designate spiritual things analogically by means of words that primarily signify sensible things.

sary to *discern* in so far as it is possible, the elements of their intelligible structure so that I may account for their properties? Again, in order to *determine the limits* of a nature and to *discern* its intelligible elements, must we not explain or develop its concept into a complexus of *several* concepts or ideas, must we not tell *at length* what the concept said *in brief*, and not merely say " man " but " rational animal," not simply " triangle " but " three-sided polygon "? For every nature presents *several* intelligible aspects to the mind, to each of which there corresponds an idea within us. Furthermore, there is necessarily a certain group of intelligible aspects which it *alone* can present, otherwise it would not be this or that, but might be anything. Therefore we may " say " it to ourselves (*i.e.*, think it) as having an intelligible structure, and we may form an immaterial likeness of it within us, by a group of two or more concepts that manifest it or make it known by distinguishing it from all others.

First notion of a definition: a complex term that makes known what an objective concept or nature is (definition of a thing, *quid rei*).

Thus our knowledge is not constituted of concepts left *in the bud*, that is, in the undeveloped state in which they are as they issue from abstraction. It requires that these concepts unfold, *bloom*, and so develop that they may become capable of articulation and use by the mind. The *complex concept* formed by the intellect explicitly to manifest the nature presented by an incomplex concept, or the *complex term* [1] that expresses this complex concept externally and places it in language, is the

DEFINITION

of this nature. We must be careful not to confuse the definition itself with the judgment or proposition that attributes it to a subject. The *definition* of a man, for example, is the *complex term* :

rational animal

and not the *proposition* :

man is a rational animal.

[1] Strictly speaking, we should use *locution* or *discourse* (oratio) here, rather than *complex term*. But since the *complex term* coincides materially with the word *imperfect discourse*, and really means the same thing, its present use will not result in any confusion.

It is clear that the application of the definition to the thing defined (this application being accomplished by the proposition) does not constitute the definition, but presupposes it.

(*a*) Evidently then definition stands related to the first operation of the mind, which prepares the materials for the proposition. Undoubtedly it is a logical work, a composite of concepts ; but it does not form a whole or a finished structure, it is only a part, a member.[1] Its logical fabrication depends therefore not on the second operation of the mind but on the first, on the activity of simple apprehension. This does not mean that the act of forming a definition takes place *independently* of the act of forming a proposition, nor that it follows *immediately* in the order of time upon the act of abstracting. We only think " rational animal " or " featherless biped " in order to think and at the same time as we think : " Man is this or that." Furthermore, in order to define something, a whole preliminary effort at intellectual elaboration through comparisons, judgments and reasonings, is usually necessary. But just as the part of this effort that deals with the abstraction of the concept " man " depends upon simple apprehension, so does the part that relates to the assembling of concept groups, such as " rational animal " or " featherless biped " depend upon this act. We may add that the definition necessarily precedes *demonstration*, for every demonstrative syllogism is based precisely upon the real, or at least nominal, definition of the thing.

As we shall see (Nos. 35, 36) the second operation of the mind begins by bringing two terms together and comparing them, and ends in the act of judgment properly so-called. Likewise in the first operation of the mind which is made up of two different acts : the act of forming a concept, and the act of forming a definition, the formation of concepts is only, so to speak, the first halting place, or phase, of mental activity. Thus simple apprehension should be considered as ordained to the definition as to its most evolved and perfect product,

[1] See above, No. 7.

the first operation of the mind itself being ordained to the judgment, and the latter in turn to the reasoning. Such is the unvarying teaching of St. Thomas [1]; the acts of the mind are not isolated one from the other, we must beware of pigeon-holing them, of shutting them up in little compartments to work for themselves alone. They are vital and synergetic, they converge dynamically towards one end . . . *the knowledge of things* (which the Logician considers under its highest form, *science*).

(*b*) We may also see, from what has been said, that it is the definition that gives the concept the explicit expression required by science. That is why it takes its place with division and argumentation, as an "instrument of knowledge" (*modus sciendi*) by which "unknown [or at least imperfectly known] things are made known to us."

(*c*) Since the definition makes known by means of *several concepts* an object of thought that a *single concept* presented to the mind, and since these concepts are themselves defined by means of other concepts, must not the mind be finally forced to stop in the face of primitive concepts which cannot properly be defined? We shall prove this to be the case in Major Logic.

30. DEFINITION OF THE NAME. Before inquiring into *what a thing is*, for instance what man is, and expressing it in a definition, we must agree on the meaning of the *word* by which we designate this thing, and which takes its place in discussion. Let us say that the locution or the complex concept that makes known the signification of a name, is also a *definition*—and thus *extend* the meaning of this word. In this extended or derived sense the definition is said to be a nominal *definition*, a definition of the name. By contrast we may call the definition in the sense of the word of which we

This notion may be extended and applied to the *word* itself (definition of the name, *quid nominis*).

[1] See for example: *de Verit.*, q. 1, a. 3; q. 14, a. 1; *Sum. theol.*, I-II, q. 90, a. 1, ad 2; I, q. 17, a. 3; *in III de Anima*, lect. 11; *Quod lib.* v, a. 1; *Comment in Joann*, cap. I, lect. 1, No. 1. "Intellectus autem duo format, secundum duas ejus operationes; nam secundum operationem suam, quae dicitur indivisibilium intelligentia, format definitionem; secundum vero operationem suam, qua componit et dividit, format enunciationem, vel aliquid hujusmodi. Et ideo illud sic formatum et expressum per operationem intellectus vel definientis vel enunciantis, exteriori voce significatur. Unde dicit Philosophus quod ratio, quam significat nomen, est definitio." Cf. above, No. 3.

have hitherto been speaking, the *definition of the thing*, or "real" definition (*realis*, that is, *rei*).

The definition is defined as: *oratio naturam rei aut termini significationem exponens.*

31. DEFINITION OF THE DEFINITION. Now we may define the definition . . .

The definition is a complex concept or locution that sets forth what a thing is or what a name signifies.

In saying "complex concept" we consider the *mental* definition; in saying locution (or complex term) we consider the *spoken* definition.

SECTION 5. DIVISION

32. NOTION OF DIVISION. Is the definition the only means we have of explicitly manifesting what an incomplex concept presents to the mind? The definition "rational animal" shows us the constitutive aspects or essential parts of the objective concept "man." It distinctly reveals to us *what* man *is*. But has not this concept an *extent* (a sort of quantity) which is as yet but confusedly perceived, and which we should try to know distinctly? To advance in the knowledge of man or of triangle, should we not discern that there are *white*, *black*, and *yellow* men, . . . *right-angle*, *isosceles*, and *equilateral* triangles . . . ? or, from other aspects, that a triangle has *three sides* and *three angles*, that man has a *body and soul*, that man has *certain faculties*, and may be considered in the *natural state*, or *in the state of original justice*, or *in the state of integrity*, of *fallen nature*, or of *redeemed nature*?

Division of a nature, or of the object of a concept, into its parts.

The complexus of concepts thus formed by the intelligence to manifest the parts which an incomplex objective concept presents confusedly to the mind as entering into its compass under one aspect or another, or the complex term that outwardly expresses this complexus of concepts and puts it into language, is what logicians call

THE DIVISION

of this concept.[1] Do not confuse division itself with the

[1] The logician considers strictly and immediately the work produced, the *accomplished division*, and not the act of dividing.

proposition that relates it to a subject. The division of a triangle would be, for example, the complex term :

isosceles or *scalene*

and not the *proposition*

the triangle is isosceles or scalene.

(*a*) From this we may see that, like definition, division is related to the first operation of the mind ; the logical fabrication of the concept-group which is called " division," and relates to a subject in a proposition, depends upon simple apprehension.

(*b*) It is likewise evident that, like definition and argumentation, division is an instrument of knowledge (*modus sciendi*).

33. DEFINITION OF DIVISION. Just as the notion of definition may be extended from the definition of the *thing* to that of the *name*, so may the notion of division which is primarily concerned with the different parts of an objective concept or of a nature (*division of the thing*, or " real " division) be extended to the diverse significations of a word (*division of the name*, or *nominal division*). The general definition of division is, then : Division of a word into its meanings

division is a concept or a complex term that distributes a whole (thing or name) into its parts. Division is defined as, *oratio rem aliquam per sua membra, aut terminum per varias significationes distribuens*

In saying " complex concept " we are considering *mental* division ; in saying " complex term " (or " locution ") we are considering *spoken* division.

CHAPTER II

THE PROPOSITION AND THE SECOND OPERATION OF THE MIND

SECTION 1. THE JUDGMENT

34. IT is not enough to think " delicate people," " unfortunate," " formal dress," or " a nuisance " in order to have something complete in the mind. I have a complete thing in my mind only when I think, for example, " delicate people are unfortunate," or " formal dress is not a slight nuisance." I see immediately that a completed thing of this kind is a whole, composed of several parts united by an affirmative verb, or separated by a negative verb. The act by which I affirm or deny something in this way is the judgment.

The judgment, as we already know,[1] is the second operation of the mind. It may be defined as

The Judgment is that act by which the mind unites by affirming or separates by denying.

that act of the mind by which it unites by affirming or separates by denying.

or, in traditional terminology, it is the act of the mind by which it " composes " or " divides " by affirming or by denying : *actio intellectus, qua componit vel dividit affirmando vel negando*. (We affirm or deny when we declare that something is, or is not.)

(*a*) In *categorical* judgments (*e.g.*, " man is mortal ") the judgment unites or separates two objective *concepts* : *man* and *mortal* ; in *hypothetical* judgments (see below, No. 45, " if Peter is human, he is mortal "), the judgment unites or separates two *enunciations* or propositions : " *Peter is human* " and " *Peter is mortal*."

It is evident that hypothetical judgments unite several previously formed categorical propositions ; therefore

[1] See above, No. 2.

that which the second operation of the mind forms primarily (*per se primo*) is the *categorical* proposition. Categorical judgments and categorical propositions will also be given primary consideration in this section.

(*b*) Considering concepts *in relation to the thing itself* " secundum rationes rerum quarum sunt similitudines," there is *composition* " when the intellect compares one concept with another in such a manner as to grasp the conjunction or identity between the *things* which these concepts represent ; and *division* when the intellect compares one concept with another in such a manner as to apprehend that these *things* are different." In this sense an affirmative enunciation is called " composition " *in quantum conjunctionem ex parte rei significat*, a negative enunciation, " division," *in quantum significat rerum separationem* and the second operation of the mind is called *composition and division.*

But considering concepts *secundum se*, as they are themselves in the mind, the intellect always formulates its (affirmative or negative) enunciations by comparing and combining concepts. From this aspect, the second operation of the mind always involves *composition* (St. Thomas, *in Periherm.*, I, Chap. I, lect. 3, n. 4).

Likewise, in relation to the *things* that the enunciation presents to the mind, the affirmative judgment is an *assent* (" assensus ") and the negative judgment a *dissent—a refusal of assent* (" dissensus "). But in relation to the enunciation itself as formed in the mind, every (affirmative or negative) judgment is an *assent :* " It is true that Peter is a man," " It is true that Peter is not an angel."

Not every union (*compositio, σύνθεσις*), nor every separation (*divisio, διαίρεσις*), constitutes a judgment ; for example, we may unite or " compose between " *Caesar* and *victorious*, and think *victorious Caesar*, but in so doing we are not judging—we are making an act of simple apprehension.[1] We do not judge unless, in combining or dividing the two concepts by

[1] Furthermore (see No. 35, inset) we may compose or divide two concepts *by means of the verb*, without making a judgment, if we do not attach a signification of assent to this verb.

means of the verb, we think " *Caesar is victorious* " or " *Caesar is not victorious.*"

We should also note that, in composing or dividing two concepts by means of a verb, the most important thing, and that which properly constitutes the judgment, is our act of affirming or denying which is joined to our act of composing or dividing. When I think "*Caesar is victorious* " or " *Caesar is not victorious* " I make a judgment only because, in using the word " *is*," I have the explicit intention of affirming that this is so, or in using the words " *is not*," of denying that this is so. There is no judgment until the mind affirms or denies something, until it determines or decides what is. For does not the very word " judgment " evoke the idea of an authoritative decree ? The act by which the mind makes such an inward statement by *affirming* or *denying* something is called *assent* (*assensus*) ; and it is this *irreducible act of interior affirmation or negation*, known to everyone through personal experience, *that formally constitutes the judgment. To judge is essentially to* " *assent.*" True, the act of assent is *purely immanent* and taken in itself does not consist in producing a term ; but it occurs in human minds only on condition that we unite or separate, " compose " or " divide " —that we produce or construct something within us.[1]

The act of judging (assent) bears on a proposition whose *matter* is the S. and Pr. and whose *form* is the copula.

35. JUDGMENT AND THE ENUNCIATION. By " composing " and " dividing," the mind forms within itself a certain immaterial product or " mental word," [2] a certain group

[1] See below No. 36.—The essential distinction between the act of the mind (the judgment) and the logical product constructed by it (the proposition or enunciation) has been lost sight of by many modern logicians, especially those under the influence of Kant by whom properly so-called (universal, particular, singular, synthetic, analytic, etc.) *propositions* are called (universal, synthetic, singular, etc.) *judgments*. However, there are some modern authors, Meinong, for example, who see the necessity of returning to this distinction. It is chiefly because Goblot has not understood this sound distinction between the judgment and the *proposition* that he has substituted for it the much less happy distinction between " actual judgment " (accompanied by what he most inexactly terms " belief "—that is, *assent*), and *virtual judgment* (*Logique*, n. 49–51).

[2] The expression " mental word " which is said primarily of the concept produced by the first operation of the mind may also be said by extension of the proposition itself produced by the second operation of the mind (cf. Hugon, *Curs. Phil.*, *Metaph.*, t. IV, p. 137). Thus the Thomistic theologians say that in the infused act of faith the impressed species are natural, and the mental word supernatural, in the sense that it is expressed by the intellect as elevated by the *lumen infusum fidei*. Here the *verbum mentale* designates the mental proposition (cf. Garrigou-Lagrange, *De Revelatione*, t. I, p. 510).

of concepts that constitutes a (mental) enunciation or proposition and is expressed by an oral enunciation or proposition : *e.g.*, " man is mortal." We cannot judge or " assent " unless we form within us a mental enunciation or proposition.

This enunciation or proposition has for its *matter* the things (objective concepts) which are united or separated, " composed " or " divided " : that is, the subject (S.) and the predicate (Pr.).[1]

It has for its *form* the union or the separation, the " composition " or the " division " itself. This form is signified by the affirmative or negative verb, that is, by the copula " is " or " is not."

The copula " is " or " is not " has a double function. This function may be said to be merely *copulative* when the copula as yet expresses *composition or division* in a material fashion only, and simply connects the S. and Pr., without the mind's actually considering the act of being *as an act*. For instance, in reading a book I may come across the statement : " there is a treasure buried here," and consequently formulate the proposition in my mind as an object of simple apprehension, but for all that I need not make any judgment.[2]

The copula has a properly judicative function in so far as it expresses a *vital act of assent* (*affirmation or negation*) made by the mind thinking formally of the act of being *as an act*. For example, if we were actually hunting treasure we could, in face of some discovery, formulate this proposition : " a treasure *is* buried here." In this case we would really be making a judgment—an explicit affirmation.

*36. ANALYSIS OF THE JUDGMENT. The analysis of the

[1] See above, Nos. 22 and 24.

[2] We have said above (Nos. 23 and 27) that every proposition signifies the real or ideal, actual or possible, *existence* of a subject with a certain predicate, and that therefore the verb *to be* always signifies (actual or possible) existence, even when it is used as a copula. When the function of the verb *to be* remains simply copulative, it is because the actual or possible existence or non-existence of a subject with a certain predicate is not yet formally thought as act, therefore as effectively held by the subject (*ut exercita*) : as yet there is no judgment, no proposition properly so called.

operations of the mind—which properly belongs to Psychology not to Logic—is a delicate affair, especially when it deals with operations which may be decomposed into diverse moments so subtle that we cannot find in everyday language adequate expressions to distinguish them. Nevertheless, in order to clarify our ideas, it will be expedient to trespass upon the realm of Psychology, and to inquire whether in the case of the judgment, there are not several distinguishable actions of the mind, all of which terminate in a single oral expression (an oral proposition).

Two terms, conceived by simple apprehension, are combined in a *simply enunciative proposition*

At the moment of judging, (1) I have two terms in my mind, *e.g.*, " human soul " and " immortal," each of which is conceived by means of simple apprehension.

(2) I arrange, or combine these two terms together, by setting them up as subject and predicate of an enunciation. That is the work of ***composition and division***, considered as the simple material construction which PRECEDES the judgment properly so-called.

(*a*) When we make a *doubtful* enunciation, we see with particular clarity that the act of constructing an enunciation, in which we already combine and divide, is not the same as the act of judging. In formulating such a proposition we have materially combined two concepts; we have not *judged* (for on the contrary, we are withholding assent, and taking care not to say " this is so " or " this is not so ").

(*b*) When we apprehend as such the enunciation constructed before judging, the enunciation as yet unjudged, we compare two concepts as subject and predicate *linked* together by the copula in an (actual or possible) existence, which is not yet thought of as being existence in act, as existence effectively held (*ut exercita*).[1] We do not compare them to each other in relation to what is, to what REALLY EXISTS (actually or possibly). In other words, we do not compare them as subject and predicate *affirmed* of one another by the copula (properly *judicative* function of the verb *to be*).

(*c*) This enunciation, which we construct before judging

[1] See the preceding note

and which expresses not a completed judgment, but a possible judgment or a judgment to be made, may for that reason be called a *proposition to be judged*, or a simply *enunciative* proposition. It is as the *matter* of the proposition taken formally, or the *judicative* proposition, by which the mind "*posits*" before itself a connection of concepts as true.

Such an enunciation must *necessarily* precede the judgment. The assent of the mind can bear only on matter capable of receiving it, on a complex truth whose terms are linked together by a verb and are therefore constructed as S. and Pr. In other words, the assent of the mind can bear only on a proposition or enunciation. Thus, first, the proposition is constructed (with the verb *to be* in its purely *copulative* function) and then, only, it is judged.[1]

The presence in us of these materially considered propositions that precede the judgment is easily established by observation. A question must be asked before it can be answered. Generally, before making an affirmation in which the very truth of our mind is involved we must first have gone through some process of discovery or "invention." It is by having before our mind a proposition that is already constructed, but as something "to be judged" as "invented," not as demonstrated [*e.g.*, "plants breathe" (?)] that we can in a reasoning (inductive in this case) compare the S. and Pr. with that which is, and *judge* that it is true: "yes, plants breathe."

It not infrequently happens that whereas some have light

[1] Judicium est assensus intellectus circa aliquid quod est capax talis judicii; sed solum est capax talis judicii veritas complexa significata per enuntiationem; ergo actus judicii distinguitur a formatione enuntiationis. Maj. constat. Quia judicium est id quo determinatur intellectus assentiendo quod ita est vel non est, hoc enim est judicare; sed non potest assentiri, aut pronuntiare quod ita est vel non est, nisi circa aliquid complexum, quod connectitur cum verbo, ut experientia constat, et hoc est enuntiatio; *ergo prius formatur enuntiatio, et deinde judicatur*.

"Quod etiam patet quia multoties apprehendimus et formamus enuntiationes de rebus dubiis sine ullo judicio, ut cum dicimus: astra sunt paria, thesaurus est in isto loco, de quibus nescimus judicare et determinare assertive; ergo aliud est enuntiatio, aliud judicium" (John of St. Thomas, *Log.* I.P., *Illustr.*, q.v., a. 1).

especially to judge, others are gifted rather to materially arrange in orderly sequence, to construct, or to "compose" concepts.[1] Some minds of fertile invention lack judgment; others of taste and sure judgment lack inventiveness. We may add that the constructive elaboration which precedes judgment may take place unconsciously (and often progress quite far), whereas the judgment itself is always conscious.

(*d*) If philosophers often disregard this distinction it is because simply enunciative propositions are masked, so to speak, by *judicative* propositions, which are absolutely similar to them as to verbal expression and which manifest a completed judgment. Again, at the moment in which the mind pronounces itself, it composes (formally) and judges simultaneously in a single act. Nevertheless, the fact remains that before the perfect formal composition which is made in, and by, the assent itself, there is a material composition which precedes the act of judging or assenting.[2]

Thus the mind does not arrive immediately at the judgment properly so-called, which is a "perfect" or completed operation. First of all, it prepares the matter. It "composes" concepts, it constructs enunciations (which are as yet objects of simple apprehension and not objects of judgment) wherein the verb *to be* has a simply *copulative* function and not yet *judicative* or "assertive." It is after materially grouping the concepts together that the mind completes their composition, formally, in the act of existence itself. That is, it declares them to be identified with one another in extra-mental existence, and thereby declares what I think of things to be conformed with what is or can be independent of my mind.

composed of a S. and Pr. of which the mind perceives

(3) The next step is the comparison of the subject "the human soul," and the predicate "immortal," in relation to what is, to what exists.

Whether this comparison be made by the simple examination of the two terms (*e.g.*, "the whole is greater than any

[1] Cf. St. Thomas, *Sum. theol.*, II–II, 173, 2; *de Verit.*, q. 12, a. 7.
[2] Cf. John of St. Thomas, *Phil. Nat.*, III, p. 515 (Vivès).

one of its parts"), or by means of sense experience (*e.g.*, "snow is white") or in virtue of a reasoning that resolves the enunciation under consideration into its principles (*e.g.*, "the human soul is immortal," "the sum of the angles of a triangle is equal to two right angles"), in any event it shows that the compared concepts *really conform* or *do not conform* to each other (in actual or possible existence).

No doubt the judgment itself adds something to the perception of the conformity or non-conformity of Pr. to S., for it consists formally only in the act of *assent*. Furthermore, the judgment may be made, even though the perception in question be lacking, for instance, when we judge on the testimony of another that a certain S. has a certain Pr., without having seen for ourselves that this is so.[1] But when this perception takes place—as it does in all "evident" or "scientific" judgments—it is but one *in concreto* with the judgment, and precedes it only with a priority of nature and not with a priority of time. This is the reason why, when this perception takes place, the judgment necessarily and infallibly takes place likewise.

and declares (the act of assent) their conformity or nonconformity

(4) Then seeing that the Pr. "immortal" really conforms to the S. "human soul," simultaneously and in the same act, I *affirm* the one of the other, thus making a statement about what is, and declaring that what is in my mind conforms to what exists. This is the *assent*, and the act of judging properly so-called.

in a *properly judicative proposition*.

(5) This act of assent bears on the proposition taken materially, the *simply enunciative* proposition which I had constructed before judging and in order to judge. Now I express it in the same enunciation: "the human soul is immortal," but this time I utter it as the sign of a completed judgment, as a judgment which has become a *properly judicative* enunciation or proposition. Thus the *mental word* (the proposition) which is proper to the act of judging and which that act necessarily requires, just as the act of appre-

[1] In this case, we see not that *this S. has this Pr.*, but that *we should affirm that it has*. In such a case the judgment is made under the influence of the will, not through *necessity*.

hension necessarily requires the concept produced by the mind, appears here under the double aspect : 1— as an indispensable condition, and as the matter on which the act of judging must bear (the proposition taken materially or simply enunciative proposition) ; and 2—as the sign of this act, the completed product wherein it is expressed in being made (the proposition taken formally or judicative proposition).

The judgment is a simple or indivisible act bearing upon a logical organism (a proposition) that is one and undivided.

37. THE SIMPLICITY OF THE JUDGMENT. It is evident from the foregoing that the judgment properly so-called is *simple*, that is to say, *indivisible*, not decomposable into parts. It consists in the act of " composing " or " dividing " only so far as this act is completed in the act of assent which formally constitutes the judgment, and wherein knowledge has its term in an *ita est*, " this is so."

The proposition itself by which this judgment is expressed is something *one* and undivided ; true, it is composed of parts, the S. and Pr., but these parts are presented to the mind *together*, as constituting by their union *a living whole*. Indeed, if we were to divide this whole not only would the whole itself perish, but its parts would cease to be what they are : we should have two concepts—but we should no longer have a subject and a predicate. It is this whole which is presented in its unity to the mind, and which the judgment ratifies by uttering it in such fashion that the mind, in the moment of judging, does not grasp the S. before the Pr., or the Pr. before the S., but grasps both the one and the other instantaneously in the same act.[1] Be careful here not to confuse the spoken or written proposition in which the S. comes before the Pr., with the mental proposition in which they are presented together (and of which we are speaking here).

(*a*) As Bossuet says : " the understanding of terms naturally precedes the grouping of them, otherwise we

[1] St. Thomas, *C. Gent.*, I, LV : " Quod quando aliqua multa accipiuntur quocumque modo unita, simul intelliguntur, simul enim intelligitur totum continuum, non partem post partem, et similiter intelligitur simul propositio, non prius praedicatum, et postea subjectum, quia secundum unam totius speciem omnes partes comprehenduntur." Cf. *Sum. theol.*, I–II, 113, 7, ad 2 ; VI *Met.*, lect. ult.

would not know what we are assembling."[1] That is why simple apprehension precedes judgment. The mind produces concepts before assembling them, and in this sense it must be said that we know the parts of a proposition (taken separately and *in themselves*) before knowing the proposition itself. *Compositionem non est intelligere sine compositis.*[2]

But once *formed and constructed*, the proposition, matter and expression of the simple act of judgment—the whole, that is this proposition itself, is known before the subject and predicate are known separately as such. In this sense it must be said that we know the proposition itself before knowing its parts (taken *as parts* of this whole).[3]

*(*b*) We have said that the proposition is *one* and *undivided.* The question of knowing if, in addition to this, it is presented to the mind *by a single* mental word newly produced by the mind at the moment in which it composes the S. and Pr., a " mental word " or " concept " proper to the second operation of the mind which would be *one*, not only with a unity of *order*, but with a unity of being or *quality* and consequently really simple, is a more difficult question to answer and one which is controverted. It seems that (as far as categorical propositions are concerned) the answer should be in the affirmative. For the

[1] Bossuet, *Connaissance de Dieu et de soi-même*, ch. I, 13. The spirit of systematization is so strong in some logicians that they even misconceive so obvious a truth and declare that the judgment *precedes* the concept. Thus Goblot (Log., p. 87) considers the concept to be nothing but the attribute of a possible infinity of judgments. This formula has a meaning, if it signifies that the concept, existing in the mind as a concept, is destined to be the attribute of possible judgments, which will exist by means of it—but it becomes perplexing if it signifies that the concept exists only as the attribute of judgments that do not yet exist ; (at this rate we come very near to having nothing at all exist in the mind).

As we shall see in Criticism, even as far back as Kant, although in another sense, the concept (category) was, in a certain manner, the fruit or result of judgment.

[2] St. Thomas, in *Periherm.*, lib. I, c. v, lect. 8, n. 9 ; cf. lect. 5, No. 21.

[3] St. Thomas, *Sum. theol.*, I, q. 85, a. 3, ad 3. " Pars aliqua dupliciter potest cognosci : uno modo absolute ; secundum quod in se est ; et sic nihil prohibet prius cognoscere partes, quam totum, ut lapides, quam domum. Alio modo, *secundum quod sunt partes hujus totius : et sic necesse est quod prius cognoscamus totum quam partes :* prius enim cognoscimus domum quadam confusa cognitione quam distinguamus singulas partes ejus."—Cf. a. 4, ad 3 ; et I, q. 58, a. 2, resp. : " Et sic etiam intellectus noster simul intelligit subjectum et praedicatum prout sunt partes unius propositionis, et duo comparata, secundum quod conveniunt in una comparatione."

truth is the objective of judgment

categorical proposition is indeed the product immediately and primarily formed by the second operation of the mind (*illud quod per se primo format secunda operatio nostri intellectus*) and it presents something new to the mind, viz., the identity of the S. and Pr. which it groups together and offers to the mind *per modum unius*. There is, therefore, justification for thinking that this proposition constitutes a unique *representative quality*, newly produced by the mind.[1]

It is by the judgment that the mind is true or false.

38. WHAT IS PROPER TO THE JUDGMENT. If I think merely "centaur," "man," "horse," "two," "three," do I think what is true or what is false? No. I have as yet neither truth nor falsity in my mind. But if I think "centaurs exist," "the horse is human," "two and three make six," I am mistaken. If I think, on the contrary, "centaurs do not exist," "the horse is not human," "two and three make five," I think what is true. We may say, then, that to contain truth or falsity of knowledge is proper to the judgment. We are merely taking note of this point here in passing for we shall meet with it again in Criticism. Truth is indeed the conformity between the mind and what is. But only when the mind declares: "*this is so, the thing exists thus*" (in actual or possible existence) does it perform an act of knowing, conformed or non-conformed as such to *what is*, to *what exists* really or ideally, actually or possibly.

Since in man the apprehension of intelligible natures (simple apprehension) by means of abstraction does not provide material for judgment or assent, this apprehension must be completed by a second operation: the composition or division of concepts, the only means by which we have—in judging—true or false knowledge. Note that this condition is due to the imperfection of our intellect. An intellect superior to man's which would

[1] Cf. St. Thomas, *in* III *de Anima*, lect. 6; *Metaph.*, lect. ult.; and *Quodlib.*, v, a. 9. "Duplex est operatio intellectus secundum Phil. III, *de Anima*, una quidem, quae vocatur indivisibilium intelligentia (id est simplex apprehensio), per quam intellectus format definitionem, vel conceptum alicujus incomplexi. Alia autem operatio est intellectus componentis et dividentis (id est compositio vel divisio) secundum quam format verbum. Et utrumque istorum per intellectum constituorum vocatur verbum cordis, quorum primum significatur per terminum incomplexum, secundum per orationem." Cf. likewise John of St. Thomas, *Log.*, I.P., *Appendix*.

penetrate the entire object, essence and attributes, in a single act of intuition or synthetic apprehension, which would see it immediately as having or not having such and such attributes in reality, would at the same time *judge* instantaneously *in the same operation without having to compose or divide.*[1]

SECTION 2. THE PROPOSITION

A. GENERAL NOTIONS

1. *Discourse in General*

39. COMPLETE (PERFECT) DISCOURSE AND INCOMPLETE (IMPERFECT) DISCOURSE. We may define discourse in general (*oratio*) as every concatenation or construction of concepts or terms.

Logicians define discourse as : *a succession of articulate sounds whose separate parts have their own meaning as terms.* This definition relates to *spoken* or *oral* discourse,[2] which is the expression of *thought*-discourse (a series of linked or connected *concepts*).

Perfect or *complete discourse* (*oratio perfecta*) presents to the intellect a meaning in which it may rest, *e.g.*, " the prudent man speaks but little " ; *imperfect* or *incomplete discourse* (*oratio imperfecta*) leaves the intellect in suspense, *e.g.*, " a prudent man." [3]

Logic makes an especial study of two types of *imperfect discourse*, namely DEFINITION and DIVISION, because they are

[1] Cf. St. Thomas, *Sum. theol.*, I, q. 58, a. 4 ; q. 85, a. 5. Likewise within due proportion, the external sense " judges " things at the same time and by the same operation by which it perceives them (cf. St. Thomas, *de Verit.*, q. 1, a. 9).

[2] We are using the word " discourse " here in order to translate the Latin " *oratio* " by a single word. We might also use " verbal expression," " v.e.," or " verbal enunciation," " v.e.," as suggested by the Dictionary of the Soc. franc. de Philosophie.

[3] Notice the nuance that distinguishes *imperfect discourse* from the *complex term*. A group of terms such as " the prudent man " or " a rational animal " is an *imperfect discourse* when considered *in itself* and *as a whole ;* this same group is a *complex term* when considered *in the proposition as a part ;* for example, in the proposition : " *the prudent man* speaks but little," " man is a *rational animal*."

modes or means of knowledge (there are three modes or means of knowledge, *modi sciendi* : 1—Definition (see above, Section 4, 29) ; 2—Division (see above, Section 5) ; 3—Argumentation (see below, No. 60). The *modes of knowledge* will be studied in Major Logic.

40. THE DIFFERENT KINDS OF COMPLETE OR PERFECT DISCOURSE. There are three kinds of perfect discourse :

The *enunciation* (or proposition) (*oratio enunciativa*) which expresses the judgment or the conception of the mind composing or dividing.

The *argumentation* (*oratio argumentiva*) which expresses the reasoning, and

From among the different kinds of perfect discourse Logic considers only the enunciation or proposition and argumentation.

Discourse for a practical purpose (*oratio ordinativa*) which expresses something *to be done*. No doubt the latter type of discourse presupposes some judgment, but that which it communicates to another is not precisely this judgment, but rather a certain motive for action. For this reason Logic, considering human language in so far as it expresses the true or the false, treats only of the first two kinds of discourse : enunciation and argumentation (that is, a series of enunciations linked in such a manner as to produce a conclusion).

(*a*) There are four kinds of *practical discourse* (*oratio ordinativa*) : discourse *that summons* (*oratio vocativa*) by which we move another to attention : " Rabbi " ; discourse *that interrogates* (*oratio interrogativa*), by means of which we move him to answer : " Ubi habitas ? " ; discourse *that commands* (*oratio imperativa*) : " Venite et videte," by which we move an inferior to perform some act, and discourse *that implores* (*oratio deprecativa*) : " Domine aperi nobis," by which we move a superior to perform an act (for we are unable to move our superior as such except by the expression of our desire). Discourse that expresses a wish (*oratio optativa*) may be reduced to *oratio deprecativa*.

*(*b*) Logic omits from its consideration not only these four kinds of discourse, but also all the nuances of expression which in everyday language are mixed with enunciative discourse itself in order to make it signify not only what is, but also the speaker's opinion about what

is. In language *Logic considers purely and simply the expression of thought from the point of view of the true and the false.*

For this reason it reduces every (categorical) enunciation to the expression of an identity by means of the verbal copula.

This is a point worth remembering. We make use of a great many forms of speech that express something other than the simple identity (*in re*) of a Pr. and a S., but that is because, in these cases, these forms of speech are themselves something other than a simple enunciation. No doubt the phrase " Behold three men " implies an enunciation, but one which is comprised within the *oratio vocativa.* What it actually means is " Look ! There are three men before you." Suppress this nuance (or any other similar to it) relating to action, reduce this discourse to the simple enunciation considered by Logic, and there remains : " three men are coming." In discourse, whatever differs from the attribution of a predicate to a subject, to that extent, goes beyond enunciation properly so-called.

It may very well be that a certain confusion on this point has accidentally strengthened the theorists of the " logic of relation," particularly Bertrand Russell, in their opposition to the logic of inherence or predication. For against this logic they cite the irreducibility of an " affirmation of number," such as " Behold three men," to an affirmation of inherence.

As a matter of fact, the speech with which we are concerned is either something other than an enunciation and is to that extent outside the domain of Logic, or else it is nothing other than an enunciation and is thus always reducible to the affirmation or negation of the presence of a predicate in a subject—or, in other words, of the identity *in re* of this Pr. and S. As we shall see in Major Logic, those who hold to the contrary are victims of a confusion between the *logical subject* and the *real subject.*[1] (" Three

[1] This confusion between the real subject and the logical subject lies at the core of Leibnitz's philosophy. It has passed thence to a great number of modern logicians and becomes the more increasingly serious as it assumes more metaphysical character.

men are here" : three real subjects, but a single *logical subject*, which is the objective concept " three men " and which receives the predicate " are here.") " Peter and Louis are first-cousins " ; two real subjects, but only one *logical subject*, which is the objective concept " Peter and Louis " which receives the predicate " first cousins," without there being for all that an " accident in two subjects having one foot in one subject and the other foot in the other " as Leibnitz would have had it.[1] For in speaking thus, Leibnitz was considering real subjects. Now the accident " Louis' first-cousin," exists only in the real subject Peter, and the accident " Peter's first-cousin " exists only in the real subject Louis, but that in no way hinders the logical subject " Peter and Louis " from receiving in the mind the predicate " first cousins " which precisely signifies this double relation.

2. *The Enunciation or Proposition*

The enunciation or proposition is a discourse signifying the true or the false

41. GENERAL NOTION OF THE ENUNCIATION OR PROPOSITION. Take some enunciation, for example : " It is a nice day." This is a construction of concepts furnishing matter for a judgment and we have seen that it is only when it thus " composes or divides," and judges, that the mind is properly true or false ; therefore we shall say that

> *an enunciation or proposition is a complete discourse signifying the true or the false,*

that is, expressing a complex object on which a judgment may bear.

(*a*) We have seen that just as the *thought-term* or *concept* must be distinguished from the *oral term* or *word*, so must the *thought-proposition* or construction of concepts be distinguished from the *oral proposition*, or *spoken expression of this thought-proposition* (see above, No. 3). Actually in studying one we study the other ; and, since concepts are more difficult to study in themselves than in the material signs which express them, Logic studies and

[1] Cf. Bertrand Russell, *The Philosophy of Leibniz* (Camb. Univ. Press, 1900), p. 13.

constructs the theory of the proposition in considering the *oral proposition* especially, but only *in so far as it is the expression* of the *proposition* in the mind.

(*b*) To say that the enunciation or proposition signifies *the true or the false* is to say that it presents to the mind an object to which it belongs to be *true or false*, and to which the mind can give or refuse its assent. To be *actually* and *determinately* true, or *actually* and *determinately* false is accidental to the proposition (as it is to the judgment itself). Indeed, in certain cases (contingent matters) the *same proposition* and the *same judgment* (*e.g.*, Peter is seated) may be alternately true (when Peter is seated) and false (when Peter stands). What is *essential* to the proposition and to the judgment is not to be *true* or to be *false*, but to be *true or false* according to the case.

This simple remark has a very important application in the question of the contingent future. A proposition such as "Peter will be admitted to the Institute of Technology in two years," considering the secondary causes upon which this event depends, is neither actually and determinately true nor actually and determinately false. It is *true* or *false*, but it is impossible to say that it is true or that it is false ; in other words its truth remains *undetermined* until the realization of the event (see below, No. 55b).

*(*c*) As we have seen above (No. 36) a distinction must be made between the simply *enunciative* proposition which precedes the judgment, and the *judicative* proposition, which follows and expresses the judgment. In the first, there is truth or falsity simply presented to the mind, or simply apprehended (*veritas vel falsitas per modum repraesentationis*), since no judgment has yet been made ; in the second there is truth or falsity judged or accepted (*veritas vel falsitas per modum assensus*). Only in this second type of enunciation or proposition is the mind itself rendered true or false, since it alone implies a judgment made.

The spoken enunciation or proposition is often called the *oral expression of the judgment*. If we adopt this manner of speaking, we must note that the simply *enunciative* proposition as met with, for example, in a doubtful enunciation wherein there is no judgment: "Is there an even number of planets?" is nothing but the expression of a possible judgment, a judgment *to be made.* The judicative enunciation alone is the expression of a *completed judgment.*

*(*d*) There is a shade of meaning between the word "enunciation" and the word "proposition": the enunciation becomes a proposition properly so-called only when it is put forward or "proposed" as *part of a reasoning.*[1] But this distinction remains purely theoretical, and for all practical purposes the two words are accepted as being synonymous "apud sapientes."[2]

The proposition has for its *form* the copula and for its *matter* the S. and Pr.

42. THE MATTER AND FORM OF THE PROPOSITION. What constitutes the unity and the being of the proposition? The copula. Without it we have no undivided organism, but only disjointed materials. We may say that the proposition considered from the point of view of its use in reasoning, as is suitable in Logic, has for *form* (or soul) the copula, and for *matter* the ("syllogistic") terms, S. and Pr.,[3] which are also called the "extremes." Every proposition has these three elements, (*Lego*, for example, is equivalent to *ego sum legens*) and may be reduced to them. "The plague waged war on the beasts" is equivalent to *the plague* (S.) was (C.) *waging war on the beasts* (Pr.).

But considered in relation to one another the S. has the *rôle* of matter and the Pr. the *rôle* of form.

43. THE RÔLE OF THE EXTREMES. If we compare the S. and the Pr. of a proposition to one another we see that the mind, in constructing the proposition, first posits the S., *e.g., Peter*, and then applies to it a determination signified by the Pr., "is a musician." Because the Pr. is thus applied by the copula to the S. which in some way receives it in itself, as the form of the seal is impressed on the wax, we say that the subject stands in the proposition as *matter* and the Pr. as *form* (*subjectum se habet materialiter, praedicatum se habet formaliter*).[4] And this universal form is brought down

[1] Cf. St. Thomas, *in Perihermeneias*, lib. I, cap. IV, lect. 7; *in Anal. post.*, lib. I, cap. II, lect. 5.
[2] John of St. Thomas, *Logica*, Prima Pars, Illustrationes, q. 5, a. 1.
[3] See above, Nos. 22 and 24.
[4] Cf. St. Thomas, *in Perihermeneias*, lib. I, cap. V, lect. 8, n. 9, 11; cap. VII, lect. 10, n. 10, 23.

on the S. by the copula as on a thing contained in its extension and in which it is realized.

This determination of the subject as *matter* by the predicate as form, exists not only in our manner of conception, or in our mind (in the logical order), but also in the real (in the *real* order, physical or metaphysical) when the object of judgment is a substance determined by an accident, *e.g.*, " This man is learned " (that is, he has the accidental determination *learning*, which is real and really distinct from the substance of this man). But obviously this determination exists only in our manner of conception or in our mind, in a proposition such as : " this statue is of marble " (for marble is the very matter of the statue), or again " the human soul is spiritual " (for spirituality is not an accident distinct from the substance of the soul, but is one of its metaphysical properties), or " God is good " (for the divine goodness is God himself).

Remember that in the theory of the proposition and of reasoning, the words S. and Pr. do not designate the concept which serves as S. in the proposition taken separately and in itself, or the concept which serves as Pr. taken separately and in itself, but designate these concepts with the determinations which accrue to them from their having been referred to one another in the proposition constructed by the mind. These determinations are translated into oral expression by the complementary signs " every," " all," " some," etc. (syncategorematic terms). Thus in the propositions " some man is unjust," " this man is guilty," the S. is not precisely the concept " man " considered in itself, but precisely the term " some man " and the term " this man."

B. THE KINDS OF PROPOSITIONS

44. We may divide the different kinds of propositions according to an *essential* division or according to an *accidental* division. In the first case we divide the proposition by reason of that which constitutes it as such, that is by reason of the form or *copula*. Hence three divisions : 1

According to the different kinds of copula (simple or categorical propositions and compound or hypothetical propositions) ; 2 According as the copula "*is*" composes or divides (affirmative and negative propositions) ; 3 According as the copula "*is*" composes or divides purely and simply (simply attributive or *de inesse* propositions) or implies a certain *mode* in its very function as a copula composing or dividing (*modal* propositions).

In the second case (accidental divisions) the proposition may be divided in a great many different ways. We shall treat only one of them here : the division of the proposition by reason of the *quantity* or extension of the S. (universal propositions, particular propositions, etc.).

§ 1. *Simple Propositions and Compound Propositions*

The proposition is *simple* (*categorical*) or *compound* (*hypothetical*).

45. DIVISION OF THE PROPOSITION BY REASON OF THE DIVERSITY OF THE COPULAS THEMSELVES. (1) Take for example a proposition such as : "man is mortal" or "man is not an angel." It has for its parts a S. and a Pr. united or separated *by means of the verbal copula* "*is*." Propositions of this type are called *categorical*, that is, attributive (*praedicativa*) ; or again

SIMPLE

Now take, on the contrary, a proposition that has for parts not two concepts but two previously formed (simple) propositions, united and conjoined *by means of a copula other than the verb*, such as the particles *and*, *if*, *or*. A proposition of this kind constructs a new truth, distinct from the categorical truths and *dependent* upon them. It is therefore called *hypothetical* or

COMPOUND

The compound proposition is *openly* or *occultly* compound.

(2) There are two kinds of compound propositions : the first *openly* compound and, the second, *occultly* compound. If the very structure of the proposition shows that it has for parts two propositions, we say that this proposition is *formally hypothetical*, or

OPENLY COMPOUND

If the structure of the proposition is indicated only by a word which it contains (and which is equivalent to one or several propositions), we say that this proposition is ***virtually hypothetical*** or

OCCULTLY COMPOUND

(3) In the case of the *openly compound* proposition, we may say : " The brave gave their lives *and* the cowards made money " : this is a

The openly compound proposition is *copulative, disjunctive* or *conditional.*

COPULATIVE

proposition ; or again we may say : " There must be one leader, *or* our affairs will be mismanaged " : this is a

DISJUNCTIVE [1]

proposition ; or else finally : " If the earth turns it moves " : this is a

CONDITIONAL

proposition

(4) In the case of the *occultly compound* proposition, we may say, for example : " The human species *alone* is such that evil befalls it more often than good " : this is an

The occultly compound proposition is *exclusive, exceptive or reduplicative.*

EXCLUSIVE

proposition. Or again : " Every substance *except* ether can be weighed " : this is an

EXCEPTIVE

proposition. Or finally : " The wicked, *as* wicked, should be hated " : this is a

REDUPLICATIVE

proposition.

[1] The DISJUNCTIVE proposition affirms that two propositions cannot be a the same time *true*, nor at the same time *false*. The CONJUNCTIVE proposition denies that two propositions may be at the same time *true*, but it does not deny that they can be at the same time *false*. *E.g.*, " One cannot be both actor and spectator at the same time." (But one may be neither actor nor spectator—by never going to the theatre.)

In cases where there is no mean, *e.g.*, " Things cannot be at the same time leaderless and well managed," or " No man can serve both God and Mammon at the same time," the conjunctive proposition expresses, under another form, the same truth as the corresponding disjunctive proposition : " We must have a leader or things will be mismanaged," " One must serve either God or Mammon."

DIVISION OF THE PROPOSITION BY REASON OF THE DIVERSITY OF COPULAS

PROPOSITION	*Simple* : . . . . is . . . . (Categorical)		
	Compound (Hypothetical)	*Openly compound*	Copulative : . . . . and . . . . . .
			Disjunctive : . . . . or . . . .
			Conditional : . . . . if . . . .
		Occultly compound	Exclusive : (only) . . . .
			Exceptive : (except) . . . .
			Reduplicative : (in so far as) . . . . .

EXERCISE. (1) What is the nature of the following propositions: "Art as such is infallible," "Man alone is rational," "St. Augustine and St. Monica stayed here," "All that is beautiful is difficult," "If you are not gifted you would do better to give up the fine arts," "All the deputies except two voted for the government," "Every creature manifests the justice or the mercy of God," "We will win or die"?

(2) Find examples of each of the propositions mentioned in the above table.

For a copulative proposition to be true, both of its parts must be true; for a copulative proposition to be false, it is enough that one part be false.

46. RULES CONCERNING OPENLY COMPOUND PROPOSITIONS. (1) In order that a COPULATIVE proposition be *true each* of its parts must be true; in order that it be *false* it suffices that *one* of its parts be false. Thus:

"The moon moves and the earth does not" is a false proposition because its second part is false.

(*a*) Thus the affirmation bears on another object of assent in the copulative proposition than it does in the categorical proposition. The conception of the mind declared to be true in the copulative proposition is something other than the simple juxtaposition of two categorical enunciations: for we have *but one false* copulative proposition: "The moon moves and the earth does not" for *two* categorical propositions, one of which is *false*: "The earth does not move," and the other *true*: "The moon moves."

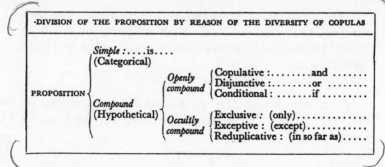

(*b*) *Rule of argumentation.* Granted a copulative as true, *e.g.*, "It is raining *and* it is cold," one thereby has the right to posit either one of its parts, taken separately, as true : " therefore it is raining," " therefore it is cold." But it is obvious that, inversely, it is not sufficient that one part, taken separately, be true in order that the other part, and consequently the copulative proposition in which the two are united, be equally true.

Given a copulative proposition as false, *e.g*, " It is false *that it is raining and that it is cold*," one does not thereby have the right to deny one of its parts taken separately (it might, for instance, be raining and yet not be cold).

(*c*) A proposition can be *occultly* copulative ; *e.g.* : " Peter *and* Paul died at Rome." Such a proposition (*de extremo copulato*) is resolvable into an *obviously* copulative proposition : " Peter died at Rome and Paul died at Rome."

(*d*) Do not confuse a proposition of the preceding type with a proposition such as " Peter and Paul are friends," in which " Peter and Paul " form but one subject, and which is consequently a simple or categorical proposition.

(2) In order that a DISJUNCTIVE proposition be *true*, it suffices that one of its parts be *true ;* in order that it be *false*, *both of its parts* must be *false*. Thus—" Good must be done and evil avoided or two and two do not make four " is a true proposition because its first part is true.

For a true disjunctive proposition one true part suffices. For a false disjunctive proposition both parts must be false.

(*a*) Thus the object of assent is not the same in a disjunctive proposition as it is in a categorical proposition.

(*b*) *Rule of argumentation.* " Given one part of a disjunctive as true, the whole may thereby be affirmed as true. Given a disjunctive proposition as true, and destroy one of its parts, the other part is thereby affirmed as true, *e.g.*, " There must be one leader or our affairs will be mismanaged " and " There shall be *no* leader, therefore our affairs will be mismanaged."

(*c*) This rule applies to every disjunctive proposition, be it *properly* or *improperly* disjunctive.

In a *properly* disjunctive proposition, the copula *or* signifies the necessity of a certain consequence. In an *improperly* disjunctive proposition, the word *or* merely denotes the fact of an equivalence or of a possible substitution ("or again," "or at least," "or even"); thus the proposition:

"To come thus far one may ride *or* (*i.e.*, *or one may*) go afoot," is an *improperly disjunctive* proposition.

In a properly disjunctive proposition, given the proposition as true and affirm one of its parts, you are thereby destroying the other part: "There must be one leader or our affairs will be mismanaged; there shall be one leader; therefore our affairs shall *not* be mismanaged."

In an improperly disjunctive proposition, given the proposition as true and affirm one of its parts, you do not by *that very act* (*in virtue of the form of the argument*) destroy the other part. For instance, if we say: "The violent man harms himself or harms no one," there is nothing to prevent both of these parts from being true at the same time.

(*d*) A proposition may be *occultly disjunctive*; *e.g.*, "A door must be open *or* shut"; "One may get there by wagon *or* on foot." Such propositions (*de extremo disjuncto*) may be resolved into the corresponding openly disjunctive propositions (properly disjunctive in the first case, improperly disjunctive in the second).

A conditional proposition is true if the *sequence* is valid, false if the sequence is invalid.

(3) For a CONDITIONAL proposition to be *true* it suffices that the *sequence* it signifies be valid, that is, that the second ("conditioned") proposition really follow from the first (the condition), even though the two propositions thus linked be false. For such a proposition to be *false* it suffices that the sequence be *invalid*, even though the two propositions be true. For in the conditional proposition the judgment bears only upon the conjunction of the two propositions—a necessary conjunction that we declare to be or not to be. Thus the conditional proposition:

"If 20 is an odd number, 20 cannot be divided by two," is true; and the conditional proposition:

"If England is an island, two and two make four," is false.

(*a*) Thus the object of assent, the conception of the mind on which the affirmation bears is altogether different in the conditional proposition from what it is in the categorical proposition. This is a point which we will have to recall in studying the conditional syllogism.

It is important to understand clearly that we may declare a conditional proposition to be true without for all that affirming in any way the truth or even the possibility of the categorical proposition stated as a condition. When St. Paul said : " *if* an Angel of God should come to proclaim another Gospel, do not believe him," he did not think that an Angel of God could really lie. When Joan of Arc said : " *if* the Church should command me to do an impossible thing (such as losing faith in her voices) I could not obey her," she did not think, as the judges of Rouen pretended, that the Church could really give her an order contrary to that of God. Likewise in saying : " *if* a number should measure the relation of two incommensurable magnitudes, I would call it an 'irrational number,' " I do not mean to say that such a number really exists.

(*b*) A distinction must be made between 1. conditional propositions *in the strict sense* (of which we are speaking here) wherein the word *if* signifies the necessity of a certain consequence, and 2. conditional propositions *in the broad sense* and *improperly conditional* propositions, in which the word *if* signifies a concomittance. Thus the proposition : " If Peter is silent (on the contrary), his brother is a chatterbox," is an *improperly conditional* proposition which may be reduced to a copulative proposition and obeys the same rules. The proposition " If the orator so much as opened his mouth, everyone yawned," is conditional in the *broad sense*. Such a proposition is subject to rules similar to those concerning strictly conditional propositions, but the conjunction of its two parts is given as a simple truth of fact, and not as a necessity. Furthermore, this proposition cannot be true unless both of its component propositions are verified by fact.

(*c*) *Rule of argumentation*. See below, the conditional syllogism.

(*d*) Do not confuse the term " *hypothetical* proposition " with the term " *conditional* proposition." The conditional proposition is only a kind of hypothetical proposition. True, it is the most important kind and plays the largest *rôle* in Logic, for it is closely akin to reasoning (since the affirmation in such a proposition bears on the necessity of a consequence, it really does nothing but declare the validity of an inference or a reasoning).

(*e*) *The disjunctive proposition may be reduced to a conditional proposition*,[1] for example, the disjunctive proposition : "We must have a leader or our affairs will be mismanaged," may be reduced to two conditional propositions : " If we do not have a leader our affairs will be mismanaged," " If we have a leader, our affairs will not be mismanaged."

The *causal proposition* [2] (" The human soul is immortal *because* it is spiritual ") and the *rational proposition* [3] (" The human soul is spiritual, *therefore* it is immortal ") may be resolved into a compound of categorical propositions. The same is true of the *relative proposition* when it has a *causal* signification [4] (" The human soul *which* is spiritual is immortal ") and of the *adversative proposition* when it signifies the negation of a causal relation [5] (" The human soul is spiritual *but* is not united to the body by violence ") —that is to say, the spirituality of the human soul does not cause it to be united to the body by violence. The causal proposition : " The human soul is united to the body by violence because it is spiritual " would be false.

[1] A *conjunctive* proposition " No one can serve both God and Mammon at the same time " may also be reduced to a conditional proposition : " If anyone serve God, he cannot serve Mammon."

[2] A causal proposition may be resolved into *three* categorical propositions : 1 The human soul is immortal, 2 The human soul is spiritual, 3 The spirituality of the human soul is the cause of its immortality. It is evident therefore that the truth of a causal proposition presupposes not only the truth of the sequence which links its two parts but also the truth of these two propositions themselves. (That is why a causal proposition cannot be reduced to a conditional proposition, nor conversely.)

[3] A rational proposition is equivalent to an argumentation properly so-called (enthymeme).

[4] In other cases the relative proposition may be reduced to a copulative proposition : " The man, whom I see, is running " = " I see a man and he is running." Again in other cases it may be only apparently compound "The leader who gives to every man his due, is obeyed" = " A just leader is obeyed," —a simple proposition.

[5] In other cases an adversative proposition may be reduced to a copulative proposition : " He may laugh about it, but I weep " = "He laughs about it and I weep about it."

It is plain that in regard to reasoning, only two propositions are important to consider: the *categorical* proposition and secondly, the *conditional* proposition (we say *secondly* because the *conditional proposition* itself 1—presupposes as logical material the categorical propositions of which it is constructed; and 2—signifies and affirms a conclusion, and therefore is not, like the categorical proposition, the first element of which the mind makes use in *discovering* or *establishing* a previously unseen conclusion).

47. RULES CONCERNING OCCULTLY COMPOUND PROPOSITIONS. These propositions are called "exponible" (*exponibiles*), that is, capable of being developed, because in virtue of a term which they contain they may be resolved into several propositions that "explain" or "develop" them.

(1) *Exclusive* propositions. Example: "The human species *alone* is such that evil befalls it more often than good," may be resolved into two propositions: "The human species is such that evil befalls it more often than good," "no other species is such that evil befalls it more often than good." It is not true unless both of these propositions are true.

Exclusive propositions are resolved into two simple propositions,

(2) *Exceptive* propositions. Example: "Every substance *except* ether can be weighed." May be resolved into three propositions: "All substances other than ether can be weighed," "ether is a substance," "ether cannot be weighed." It is not true unless all three of these propositions are true.

exceptive propositions into three

(3) *Reduplicative* propositions. Example: "The wicked, as wicked should be hated." This may be resolved into two propositions: "The wicked are specified as such by a certain determination (wickedness)," "that which accrues to them in virtue of this determination should be hated." It is not true unless both propositions are true.

and reduplicative propositions into two.

(*a*) In the example used above the "redoubling" particle, *as*, is taken in a purely "*specificative*" manner, that is, before the S. receives the Pr. the particle brings its own proper concept to it, viz., the formal reason that constitutes it in its species. Thus we say "that which is coloured is, *as such*, a visible object," "the prudent man, *inasmuch as* he is prudent, acts reasonably in all things."

(*b*) The "redoubling" particle is taken *reduplicatively* when, before the S. receives the Pr. the particle applies to the S. a particular determination other than its own proper concept, which determination is the reason, cause or condition in virtue of which this Pr. is attributed to the S. Example: "Man, as rational, possesses the power of risibility, as animal, possesses the power of nourishment, as having grace, may merit the vision of God." "Fire burns in so far as it is applied to combustible materials." [1] In such cases the reduplicative proposition is resolved into two or three propositions, the first of which expresses, either by a simple connotative term or by means of the copula *is*, the presence in the subject of the cause or condition in question:

(I) Man is rational; (he has rationality).
(II) Everything having rationality possesses the power of risibility.
(III) It is by reason of his rationality that man possesses the power of risibility.

(I) Man is an animal.
(II) Every animal has the power of nourishment.
(III) It is by reason of his animality that man has the power of nourishment.

(I) Every man having grace may merit the vision of God.
(II) Grace is the means by which men may merit the vision of God.

(I) Fire burns when applied to combustible material;
(II) Application to combustible material is the condition under which fire burns.

[1] We are following the terminology of John of St. Thomas here (*Log. Ia P. Sum.*, lib. I, cap. XXIV) in preference to Goudin's (*Log. Min.* II, P. a. 2, § 3).—Goudin considers as *specificative* reduplicatives, propositions such as: *homo ut homo sentit: homo ut homo videbit Deum; corpus ut corpus corrumpitur; justus ut justus peccare potest.* These propositions are but *improperly reduplicative*, and are *false* if considered as *properly reduplicative*. Properly speaking we must say, not (*specificative*): homo quatenus homo sentit, but (*reduplicative*): homo quatenus animal . . .; homo ut glorificatus . . .; corpus ut generabile . . .; justus ut homo . . .;

(*c*) It is evident from the last two examples that reduplication may, and in fact most frequently does, have a *restrictive* import. Such was the case in the proposition. "The wicked, as wicked, should be hated" (wherein the particle "as" was taken *specificative*). The same is true in the propositions, "Christ, as man, was created,"[1] "The Pope, as doctor of the Church, is infallible" (in which the particle "as" is taken as *reduplicative*). In reduplicative propositions with a restrictive meaning the subject-term has a *diminutive* substitutive value.

(*d*) Whereas an ordinary negative proposition, *e.g.*, "This man *is not* avaricious" is equivalent to an affirmative proposition wherein the negation falls on the predicate, *e.g.*, "This man is *non-avaricious*." Nevertheless, it must be noted that a reduplicative proposition, *e.g.*, "Man *as man* is not avaricious," signifying that such a Pr. is not essential to man, is in no way equivalent to the *reduplicative* : "Man *as man* is non-avaricious," signifying that the absence of this Pr. is essential to man. Man as man is neither avaricious nor non-avaricious.

A great many errors or misunderstandings arise from the mistaking of reduplicative propositions for simple or categorical propositions, especially when the reduplicative sense is understood but unexpressed, as it is in many formal philosophic propositions,[2] and inspired sayings, *e.g.*, in certain of the psalmist's behests : "Deleantur peccatores (*ut peccatores*) de Libro viventium, et cum justis non scribantur,"[3] etc.

Nevertheless, we must use reduplicative propositions at every turn be they speculative or practical ; for example, the enemies of our native land must be *hated* as such, and *loved* as men.

[1] This proposition may be resolved into three propositions : "Christ had a human nature," "Human nature is created," "It is because of His human nature that Christ is said to have been created."

[2] See J. Maritain, *Introd. to Philos.*, pp. 252–253.

[3] Ps. lxviii. 29.

the quality of propositions

The (categorical) proposition is either *affirmative* or *negative*.

§ 2. *Affirmative Propositions and Negative Propositions*

48. DIVISION OF THE PROPOSITION ACCORDING AS THE COPULA " IS " COMPOSES OR DIVIDES. From this point of view propositions are divided into *affirmative* or *negative* according as the copula *composes* or *divides* (unites or separates) the Pr. and the S. Like the division into simple and compound propositions, this division concerns the *form* of the proposition, that is the copula ; but instead of being made by reason of the different kinds of copulas it is made by reason of the unifying or divisive signification of the copula *is*. In order to settle our terminology let us say that such a division is made by reason of the *quality* (*i.e.*, the *essential* quality) of the proposition.[1]

(*a*) It is very important to note that a proposition is affirmative or negative by reason of the *copula* and the copula alone. Propositions such as " He who does not hope is unfortunate " or " This judgment is null and not to the point " are affirmative propositions.

(*b*) This division of the proposition into affirmative and negative is a subdivision of the simple or *categorical* proposition. *Compound* or hypothetical propositions cannot be divided in this way. The negation cannot fall on the copula " and," " or," " if " ; for in such a case it would destroy the union of the two parts of the proposition and consequently the proposition itself. Therefore every compound proposition as such composes but never divides. However, we may agree to consider as negative conditional propositions such as : " If Peter is a man, he is not a pure spirit," because the categorical proposition expressing the conditioned is itself negative.

*(*c*) Mr. Bergson thinks that a negative judgment, such as, " this table is not white," is nothing but a protest against a possible affirmative judgment, and that it consequently does not bear fundamentally upon the thing itself, " but rather on the (affirmative) judgment "

[1] Kant divides judgments from the point of view of quality into Affirmative, Negative and Indefinite (the soul is non-mortal). But, as he himself admitted, from the point of view of form, a proposition such as " the soul is non-mortal " is an *affirmative* proposition.

that someone might have made concerning it. As a consequence he maintains that, in contrast to affirmative judgments, negative judgments have an essentially "pedagogical and social" character.

Even if it were true that every negative judgment supposes that we have conceived a possible affirmative judgment, this would be a *purely psychological* consideration which would in no way prevent the mind from judging the thing itself in making a negative judgment. It is indeed evident that I cannot assent to an affirmative judgment without previously rejecting the contradictory negative, nor assent to a negative judgment without denying the contradictory affirmative and that, in both cases, it is to the thing that I declare my thought to be in conformity. In reality every judgment, whether it be affirmative or negative, presupposes that we have first asked ourselves a question, and have brought together the two objective concepts that we declare are united or divided in the real, in order that we may construct them in a proposition. And this bringing together may be made in the first place in a negative proposition. For in saying "essence and existence are not really distinct in God," I am not protesting against a possible adversary maintaining the contrary opinion any more than I am in saying: "essence and existence are really distinct in creatures." Consideration of an adversary is purely accidental in both cases, and may come into the second as well as the first.

Negative propositions are therefore in exactly the same class as affirmative propositions, and have no more nor less of a pedagogical and social character than the latter.

§ 3. *Propositions "De Inesse" and Modal Propositions*

49. **DIVISION OF THE PROPOSITION ACCORDING AS THE COPULA AS SUCH IS OR IS NOT MODIFIED.** If we say, for example, "Man is rational," "This man is overrun with debts," we purely and simply attribute a Pr. to a S. *These are the type* of proposition that have hitherto been chosen as

Simply attributive propositions (propositions *de inesse*)

examples. We may call them *simply attributive* propositions: in Logic they are called propositions *de inesse.*

This term *de inesse* signifies that the propositions in question simply affirm or deny that the Pr. *is in* the S.

Notice that we are concerned here with the presence of the Pr. in the comprehension of the S. *once the enunciation has been constructed by the mind.* The *logical* "inesse" has for its *raison d'être* a *real* "inesse," that is, the presence of the thing signified by the Pr. in the thing signified by the S, and this presence itself has for its *raison d'être* 1° EITHER the essence of the subject (in this case the Pr. is pre-contained in the notion of the S., *e.g.*, *rational* in *man*, or else the S. is pre-contained in the definition of the Pr., *e.g.*, number in *even*): 2° OR *an accidental or contingent determination* that it receives (in this case the Pr. *is not pre-contained* in the notion of the S.,—*e.g.*, *overrun with debts* is not pre-contained in the notion of this man.) Thus, contrary to Leibnitz's contention, the logical axiom, "*Praedicatum inest subjecto*" in no way signifies that every predicate is pre-contained in the notion of the subject, that is, that it is present in it by reason of the subject's essence (see below, No. 52 *a*).

must be distinguished from *modal* propositions.

But if, on the contrary, we say: "man is *necessarily* rational," or "*It is possible that* this man *be* overrun with debts," we not only attribute a Pr. to a S., but we also state the *mode or the manner* in which the copula links the S. to the Pr. in question. These propositions deserve especial study: they are called *modal* propositions.

A proposition is said to be modal when it states the *mode* or manner in which the copula links the Pr. to the S.

50. MODAL PROPOSITIONS. A modal proposition is a proposition in which we not only state that a Pr. is found in a S., but also state the mode according *to which* this Pr. belongs to the S. or is found in it. The word *mode* signifies in general *a determination that affects something* (*determinatio adjacens rei*). The determination with which we are concerned here *affects the verbal copula itself*, as to the manner in which it unites or separates the Pr. and the S.

Certain modes affect only the S. of the proposition, *e.g.*, "The *prudent* man is wise." Others affect only the

Pr. ; *e.g.*, " Peter runs *fast*," that is, he " is *running fast*." But it is not by reason of such modes that a proposition is said to be modal.

How many modes may affect the copula itself and thus make the proposition to be *modal?*

A predicate such as " ill " belongs to Peter *possibly*. Supposing that Peter is in good health, we would say : " Peter *can be* (EST POSSIBILITER) ill."

On the contrary, a predicate such as " angel " *cannot* belong to Peter. We say " Peter *cannot be* (EST IMPOSSIBILITER) an angel."

A predicate such as " in good health," belongs to Peter contingently. Supposing that Peter be in good health, we would say " Peter *might not be* (EST CONTINGENTER) in good health."

On the contrary, a predicate such as " man " belongs to Peter *necessarily* : " Peter *cannot not be* (EST NECESSARIO) a man."

There are four kinds of modes: possibility, impossibility, contingence necessity.

Thus there are only FOUR modes that can affect the copula itself :

POSSIBILITY.

IMPOSSIBILITY.

CONTINGENCE (possibility that it should not be).

NECESSITY (impossibility that it should not be).

It is evident that in every modal proposition two assertions are to be distinguished : the one (the *dictum*) concerns the thing itself, the attribution of the Pr. to the S., the other (the *modus*) concerns the manner in which this attribution is realized (be it in the thing itself or in the mind). To illustrate what we mean by *mode* we may say, for example, " *It is possible* that Peter be ill," " *it is impossible* that Peter be an angel," " *it is contingent* that Peter be in good health," " *it is necessary* that Peter be a man."

(*a*) We shall see in Major Logic that in those cases wherein the Pr. attributed to the S. is not of the latter's essence, we must distinguish again, within each of these four modes, between two types of modal propositions that differ in *meaning only*, and not in oral expression. This is the distinction between the *composite meaning* and the *divisive meaning* which plays a part of capital importance in philosophy.

*(*b*) The *impossible* may be reduced to the *necessary*, and the *possible* to the *contingent*. That is why Aristotle treats of but two modes, the necessary and the contingent. (*Anal. Pr.*, I, 9–22.)

*(*c*) Whereas Aristotle divided propositions in this way :

Propositions { *de inesse* or simply attributive
modal { *contingent* mode / *necessary* mode

Kant draws the following distinction :

Modality of the Judgment { *Reality* (assertory judgments)
Contingence (problematic judgments)
Necessity (apodeitic judgments)

By a singular abuse of language, Kant considers simple attribution itself as a special *mode* (" reality ") ; that is to say, he considers that case as modal in which *there is no mode* affecting the copula (propositions *de inesse*, which he calls *assertory*).

Furthermore, when he speaks of the *contingent* or *necessary* modality of the " judgment " (and not of the " proposition " as the ancient logicians would have done) he in no way interprets these words in the Aristotelian sense. " As Sigwart has said (*Logik*, I, 6, p. 189) . . . the matter in question for him [Kant] is the subjective possibility or necessity of the *act* of judging. When Aristotle draws the same distinction, [*Anal. Pr.*, I, 2, 246, 31], he speaks of the possibility or necessity of the *relation* expressed by the judgment " (Goblot, *Logique*, p. 158, note).

Stan. Dominczak's work on *Les Jugements modaux chez Aristote et les Scolastiques* may be profitably consulted on this subject. (Louvain, ed. de la Revue Neo-Scolastique.)

§ 4. *The Subject and Predicate from the Point of View of Quantity*

51. DIVISION OF THE PROPOSITION BY REASON OF QUANTITY. The proposition : " The triangle has the sum of its angles

equal to two right angles" applies to all triangles; for, in applying the Pr. to the S. "*triangle*," this proposition communicates it to all the individuals and to all the "inferior" objective concepts (isosceles triangles, scalene triangles, etc.) contained under the universal "triangle." But, in applying the Pr. to the S. "some triangle" the propositions "some triangle is right-angular" or "some triangle is equiangular," communicate it only to an indeterminate individual, or to a certain category of individuals, contained under the universal "triangle." Finally, in applying the Pr. to the S. *this triangle*, the proposition "*this triangle* is drawn with red chalk" communicates it only to a certain determinate individual subject. Thus, in applying the Pr. to the subject-concept, a proposition may communicate it either to the infinity of individual subjects contained under the universal subject, or to some of them taken indeterminately, or only to a certain determinate individual subject.

The quantity of a proposition is its breadth in relation to the individual subjects to which it communicates the Pr. in applying this Pr. to the S.

We shall call this property that the proposition has of communicating the Pr. to a greater or lesser multitude of individual subjects in applying it to the S., the QUANTITY of the proposition. The quantity or extension of the proposition is nothing else than the extension of the subject as determined by its relation to the Pr.[1] (see above, Nos. 10 and 25).

From this point of view there are FOUR kinds of propositions, according as the subject itself is a

From the point of view of quantity the proposition is either *universal*, *particular*, *singular*, or *indefinite*.

(1) *Universal*[2] or distributive term: "*Every* man is mortal." UNIVERSAL proposition; in relation to the Pr. mortal the concept man is taken as communicable to *all men*.

(2) *Particular* term: "*Some* man is unjust." PARTICULAR proposition; in relation to the Pr. unjust, the concept man is taken as communicable to an *indeterminate individual* (individuum vagum).

(3) *Singular* term: "*This* man is guilty." SINGULAR pro-

[1] "Sicut in naturalibus quantitas rei sequitur materiam, ita in propositionibus quantitas sequitur subjectum, quod est quasi materia respectu praedicati et copulae" (John of St. Thomas, *Log.*, p. 18).

[2] See the remarks in No. 18, above, on the meaning of the word *universal* in Logic.

position ; in relation to the Pr. guilty the concept man is taken as communicable to a *single determinate individual.*

(4) *Indefinite* term, that is, without any sign that explicitly manifests its quantity (which is in reality either universal, particular or singular) : " man is mortal," " man is unjust." INDEFINITE proposition.

(*a*) In every case the logician should obviously take an indefinite proposition for what it is in reality, albeit occultly—that is, as a *universal*, *particular* or *singular* proposition.

However, in some cases, for example : " Man is a species of the genus animal," " Man is the noblest of creatures," " The circumference is a line drawn through a series of points equidistant from the centre," an indefinite proposition whose subject is an *unrestricted universal nature* may be treated as a *singular*. In such cases the universal subject is *taken precisely as one ;* for it is taken not according to the being which it has in things, but according to the unity which it has *in the mind*—even though the predicate attributed to this universal nature (as in the two examples cited above) applies to the being which it has in singular things. For any individual man whatsoever is nobler than all irrational creatures, and any individual circumference is a line drawn through a series of points equidistant from the centre (see above, No. 18, 2, inset). Note in this connection that this is in general the case of the mathematical universal which some modern logicians by an odd blunder confuse with the singular.

*(*b*) In the *singular* propositions " Peter is guilty," " this man is guilty," the S. precludes all restriction in order to receive the Pr. just as it does in the *universal* proposition " Every man is mortal." But it does so for an altogether different reason ; in the former case the S. (this man, Peter) is not restricted because it is taken as *incommunicable ;* in the latter case the S. (every man) is not restricted because it is taken as *communicable to all the individuals* contained under it. Furthermore, the—indirect or reflex—singular concept " Peter " presupposes a

direct universal concept (man) whose extension is restricted to a single determinate individual subject, and thus restricted it stands to the Pr. in the proposition (see above, No. 18). Wherefore a special place must be given to singular propositions in the division of propositions according to quantity.

Singular propositions are, of course, assimilated to *universals* in the theory of the *conversion* of propositions (see below, No. 58, *c*) and in that of the *syllogism* (see below, No. 75). Nevertheless, they constitute a distinct category of propositions, and we would be entirely mistaken were we to say that they are *always* assimilable into universals. Thus, in the *opposition* of propositions, singulars do not behave like universals (between two singulars, one affirmative the other negative, there is the opposition of contradiction, not of contrariety (see below, No. 54, 3). In the *syllogism* itself the assimilation of singulars into universals which is valid for the Minor, would obviously be absurd for the Major (see below, Chap. III, footnote 2, p. 190). Finally the *expository syllogism* (see below, No. 85) admits of other modes than does the ordinary syllogism (for example, the second figure admits of the modes AA: this apostle is Judas, but this traitor is Judas, therefore this traitor is an apostle) which shows that the singular premisses are other than a simple equivalent of universal propositions.

*(*c*) Mr. Lachelier [1] distinguishes propositions such as "every man is mortal," from propositions such as "all the members of this family are learned," or "all the apostles were present at the Last Supper." He calls the former *universals*, because they bear immediately upon a nature concerning which they state a law, and bear only mediately upon the individuals having this nature; he calls the latter *collective*, because they bear immediately upon a *collection of individuals*, and express a simple fact.

He distinguishes similarly between propositions such as "some men are sincere" and propositions such as "some members of this family are learned." He calls

[1] J. Lachelier, *Études sur le Syllogisme*, Paris, 1907, p. 46 sqq.

the first propositions *particular*, because they bear upon a nature, restricted this time, indeed, in extension, and because they imply a sense of right as well as a *fact* (human nature is not exclusive of sincerity). He calls the second *partially collective* because they treat of a mere *collection of individuals* taken partially, and express nothing more than a fact.

In truth, propositions such as " all the apostles were present at the Last Supper " and " some members of this family are learned " *are not collective propositions;* only a proposition whose subject is taken collectively (in other words, has a *suppositio copulata*) [1] in relation to the Pr. is a collective proposition. *E.g.*, " the apostles were twelve, some of the members of this family are ambitious." Therefore Mr. Lachelier's terminology must be rejected. Furthermore, since the division he proposes is taken not from the form but from the *matter* of the proposition, it belongs to Major Logic, not to Minor Logic, and there is no reason for retaining it here. However, for clarity's sake we will say a few words about it.

A universal proposition such as " Every man is mortal " has a double signification: it bears first and immediately upon the *universal nature man* taken in all its universality, and mediately upon the separate *individuals* taken one by one who possess this nature. Thus a proposition such as " some man is sincere " bears primarily and immediately upon the *universal nature* man taken in a certain indeterminate individual (*individuum vagum*) [2] and mediately and secondarily upon *such* and *such* an *individual* having this nature. Now let us consider propositions such as " all men are mortal," " some men are sincere " ; they *also have a double signification*, but *in the inverse order;* they start with the individuals and proceed thence to the nature. Although these propositions (*universal*, in the first case, *particular* in the second) are used in everyday language, for the logician, from the strict point of view of the art of reasoning, they are *incorrectly formulated*. For reasoning is essentially con-

[1] See above, No. 27, 5.
[2] See above, No. 29, Section 3, Chap. I.

cerned with the universal *nature* communicable to individuals, and it is this nature that must be emphasized in a correct formulation. In the language of Logic, as we have remarked above,[1] universal propositions should be expressed by: "Every . . . is . . ." and not by "all . . . are . . . ," and particulars, by: "some . . . is . . ." not "some . . . are . . ." Finally, propositions such as those which Mr. Lachelier considers (all the apostles were at the Last Supper, some members of this family are learned), belong to the same type as those preceding (the first universal, the second particular), but by reason of their matter bear only upon a collection or series of individuals (taken divisively as Mr. Lachelier does not see), and are in the same act limited to the simple expression of a fact. However, Mr. Lachelier is quite right in saying that if a universal does nothing but signify a fact, without telling anything about a nature, then it cannot be used as a true Major in a syllogism of the first figure (see below, No. 81, 4).

(*d*) DRILL. What is the quantity of the following propositions: "Every bird has wings, some theologians are doctors of the Church, no man should despair of divine mercy, the child concentrates with difficulty, all these soldiers are French, some angels are damned, the women and children were massacred by the enemy, Judas was a traitor."

(*e*) *Other accidental* DIVISIONS *of the* PROPOSITION. The proposition may be divided accidentally, not only by reason of quantity, but also by reason of *matter* (*necessary*, *contingent*, *impossible*, propositions) by reason of *quality* (*accidental* quality; *true* or *false* propositions) and by reason of *origin* (*immediate* and *mediate* propositions). These divisions are studied in Major Logic and Criticism.

52. EXTENSION AND COMPREHENSION OF THE EXTREMES. (1) To say "This man is white," for example, is to identify the S. "this man" with the Pr. "white" or "having whiteness." But *how* is this identification made? Either the mind judges that: "That which I am calling *this*

In every affirmative judgment the mind makes the Pr. enter into the comprehension of the S., or

[1] No. 18, note 37, and note 39, Section 2, Chap. I

theory of predication

the S. into the extension of the Pr.)

man, and that *which has whiteness* is ONE and the SAME SUBJECT." Or else it judges (which amounts to exactly the same thing) that "There is an identity between THE SUBJECT which I call *this man*, and A SUBJECT *which has whiteness*."

In the first case the mind says that a same subject has the note humanity and the note whiteness and thereby makes whiteness enter into *the comprehension* of the S. "this man."

(In every negative judgment the mind excludes the Pr. from the comprehension of the S. or the S. from the extension of the Pr.)

In the second case the mind says that the subject which has the note humanity is one (of the) subject(s) that possess(es) the note whiteness, and thereby makes "this man" enter into *the extension of* the Pr. "white."

Thus the same act of judging may be made either from the point of view of comprehension (Peter is a saint, he possesses sanctity) or from the point of view of extension (Peter is a saint, he is one of those who possess sanctity). In both cases the mind accomplishes the same act of identifying the S. and the Pr., and does nothing else than that expressly (*in actu signato*). But by that very act and simultaneously with it, although without thinking about it (*in actu exercito*), the mind makes the Pr. enter into the comprehension of the S. or else it makes the S. enter into the extension of the Pr.

Which is the more *natural*, judgment in *extension* or judgment in *comprehension?* Judgment in comprehension. . . . For just as the comprehension of a concept is a more fundamental property than its extension, so, in affirmation, the logical function of making a Pr. enter into the comprehension of a S. is more fundamental than the function of making a S. enter into the extension of a Pr. Wherefore in the theory of the proposition, logicians say that the Pr. *is in* the S. (*Praedicatum inest Subjecto*) or that the Pr. *belongs* (ὑπάρχει) to the S.

*(*a*) In this instance the word *comprehension* does not designate the *comprehension of the concept* which serves as the subject of the proposition *taken in itself*[1]; for example, it does not designate the comprehension of the concept "man." It refers to this concept, *e.g.*, "this man," *in so far as it is used as subject of the proposition*,[2] and it

[1] See above, No. 10.
[2] See above, Nos. 18, 43 and 49.

designates the sum of the notes that belong to this S. *de jure* or *de facto*, necessarily or contingently, *in virtue of the concept itself* or *by accident*. Thus in saying " This man is rational," " This man is sanguine," I make the Pr. : " rational " (which is a part of the *comprehension* of the concept " man ") and the Pr. " sanguine " (which is not a part of the *comprehension* of the concept man) enter into the *comprehension of the S.* man. Likewise in saying " Cæsar was the victor at Pharsalia " I make the Pr. " victor at Pharsalia " enter *into the comprehension of the S.* " Cæsar," although it is not a part of the comprehension of the concept man, neither does it necessarily belong to the subject Cæsar, nor is it precontained in his individual concept.

The broader sense assumed by the word comprehension in the expression " the comprehension of the S. " must be very precisely defined. It is because he failed to understand this, that Leibnitz believed that he could deduce a whole system of metaphysics from the logical axiom " *Praedicatum inest subjecto* "—a chimerical metaphysics according to which all events and all accidents affecting an individual substance, *e.g.*, Cæsar in the course of his existence (and supposing the relations of this substance with a multitude of others and finally with the whole universe), are inscribed beforehand in the *notion* or in the essence of this individual substance or " monad," each " monad " being thus a " mirror " or view of the entire universe.[1] As an immediate consequence whatever Leibnitz may do, there is really no contingence or liberty in the world.

*(*b*) We must remember that in every affirmative proposition the Pr. is as a *form* that determines the S. (see above, No. 43), and the S. is as a matter that receives the Pr. Therefore the S. *as such* is *subjected* to the Pr. (*subjectum subjicitur praedicato*) ; this is the logical relation which characterizes essentially the one and the other. It is of the essence of the S.[2] to be under the Pr. as matter under a form ; it is of the essence of the Pr. to be applied

[1] Cf. Leibnitz, *Discours de Métaphysique* ; *Lettres à Arnauld*.
[2] We are speaking here of the *logical subject*. See above, No. 43, inset.

to the S. as a form to a matter. Thence we see that the act of the mind in forming a proposition, or in judging, consists necessarily either in bringing the Pr. as form over upon the S. as matter or, which amounts to the same thing, bringing the S., as matter, under the Pr. as form. In the first case the mind makes the Pr. enter into the comprehension of the S., saying that whiteness is one (of the) note(s) of "this man," in the second case it makes the S. enter into the extension of the Pr., saying "this man" is one (of the) thing(s) having whiteness.

It is therefore plain that an (affirmative) judgment is not the pure and simple identification of two concepts, but is rather the identification of a concept *functioning as S.* and a concept *functioning as Pr.*, so that, in establishing this identification, the mind must necessarily look upon things either from the point of view of extension or the point of view of comprehension.

*(*c*) Since these two ways of making a same judgment are absolutely equivalent, the logician, in *reflecting* upon the judgment from the point of view of his *art* (which is not the same thing as judging naturally) is free to consider every proposition either from the point of view of extension, or from the point of view of comprehension. However, if he wishes to simplify things, by considering the point of view of extension *exclusively*, as did Leibnitz and his school, he would risk misunderstanding the *natural* processes of the reason which actually employs the point of view of comprehension as well as that of extension, according to the case (and even makes more frequent use of the point of view of comprehension). Above all, he would run the extremely serious risk of falsifying the whole theory of judgment.

(2) Whether the mind judges from the point of view of extension, or from the point of view of comprehension, the logical properties concerning the extension and the comprehension of S. and Pr. in the proposition evidently remain the same. We shall first consider the logical properties that concern the EXTENSION of the PREDICATE.

A. First let us take the case of an *affirmative* proposition(s).

Given the affirmative proposition: "This man is white." In forming this proposition, we make the Pr. "white" enter into the comprehension of the S. "this man" or, which amounts to the same thing, we make the S. "this man" enter into the extension of the Pr. "white."

But from the fact that the Pr. "white" enters into the comprehension of "this man" it is evident that the comprehension of "this man" is taken in this proposition as being *greater* than that of "white." From the Pr. "white" the S. "this man" receives one of the determinations which characterize it, a determination which is added to those which it already has; therefore its comprehension is greater than the Pr.'s, for, besides the notes it has as "this man," it also has those given it by the Pr. "white."

As a matter of fact it happens that in certain cases the comprehension of the S. is *equal* to that of the Pr.[1] Such is the case in the universal affirmative propositions that are called *convertible*, that is, such that the S. and Pr. may be interchanged without changing the quantity of the proposition and without the newly formed proposition's ceasing to be true[2]: "Every man is a rational animal." Rational animal has the same comprehension as man, and I may say with truth: "Every rational animal is a man." But it is by reason of the *matter* of the proposition that this is so, not by reason of its form or of the logical relations it implies. In any case, the comprehension of the S. is *never smaller* than that of the Pr. so that we may write:

$$\text{Compr. S.} \geq \text{Compr. Pr.}$$

Since the comprehension and the extension of a term are in inverse ratio to each other, to say that the S. has a greater *comprehension* than the Pr. is also to say that the

[1] In the propositions which are called *unnatural*, because the natural order of the S. and Pr. is reversed (*propositiones innaturales, indirectae, violentae*) *e.g.*: "some man is Peter," the comprehension of the S. seems to be smaller than that of the Pr. But in reality the S. *some man* stands for a single individual and therefore has a comprehension *equal* to the Pr.'s.

[2] This new proposition is just as true as the first, but it affirms another truth. It is one thing to say "Every man is a rational animal" and another to say "Every rational animal is a man," just as it is one thing to say "A belongs to all B" and another to say "B belongs to all A." Cf. No. 58e.

S. has a smaller *extension* than the Pr. This may be directly verified by considering a proposition which has been thought from the point of view of extension. From the very fact that the S. " this man " enters into the extension of the Pr. " white," the extension of the Pr. " white " is taken in this proposition as *greater* than that of the S. " this man " ; the S. " this man " is brought under the Pr. " white " as one of the things to which this Pr. is applied in order to determine them, therefore its extension is smaller than the Pr.'s.

It does happen in certain cases (*convertible* propositions : " man is a rational animal "), that the extension of the Pr. is equal to that of the S.[1] But this occurs by reason of the *matter* of the proposition, not by reason of its logical constitution or *form*, *vi propositionis*. Considering only the logical function of the Pr. with respect to the S., or the logical structure of the proposition, this latter places the Pr. before the S. as a term of greater extension comes before a term of lesser extension.[2] In any case the extension of the Pr. *is never smaller* than that of the S., so that we may write :

$$\text{EXT. Pr.} \geq \text{EXT. S.}$$

In every *affirmative* proposition the Pr. is taken *particularly.*

Since, in every affirmative proposition, the logical function of the Pr. is to be applied to the S. as a *universal form* to a matter,[3] while the S. stands, in the proposition, for the singular subjects in which the Pr. is realized as a universal concept, it is evident that, when the Pr. is said of the S. or identified with it by the mind, it is not taken *according* to all its extension or universality, that is, as realized in all the singulars contained under it. In the proposition " Every man is mortal," I identify all the matter contained under the universal man (all the singular subjects in which this universal is realized) with something determined by

[1] Likewise true in an *unnatural* proposition, *e.g.*, " some man is Peter." Since the S. *some man* stands for a single individual in such a proposition, its extension is not greater than, but equal to, the Pr.'s.

[2] That is the reason why this proposition " man is a rational animal " does not in itself tell us that the extension of " rational animal " is equal to that of " man." In order to say that, we would have to have recourse to another proposition, *e.g.*, the *exclusive* proposition : " man alone is a rational animal."

[3] See above, No. 43.

the form or quality Mortal, but certainly not with all the matter contained under this universal form itself, nor with all the singular subjects in which " Mortal "(ity) is realized.

In every *Affirmative*
the Pr. is taken
PARTICULARLY.

*(*a*) To speak more precisely we should say that in every affirmative proposition, the Pr. as such has a *particular* " substitutive value " (*supponit particulariter, confuse tantum seu disjuncte*).[1] In the example given, mortal " stands for " " some mortal." To forget this and say, *e.g.*, Man = Mortal, therefore Mortal = Man, would be a tremendous blunder.

*(*b*) In fact, it sometimes happens—in convertible propositions [2] for instance : " Every man is a rational animal "—that the Pr. has the same extension as the S. (there are no rational animals other than man). Nevertheless, in this case, the *Pr. is not taken according to all its extension* (which is in fact equal to the S.'s) in being said of the S. The *Pr. is never taken in all its universality in being affirmed of the S.*, for then it would have to be said *according to all the singulars for which it stands as a universal*, and to all the singulars for which the S. stands in the proposition. I may very well say : " Every man is rational," but I cannot say " every man is every rational being," which would imply that " every man is all rational beings." [3] It is important to understand that, although the extension of the Pr. in a convertible proposition is no greater than that of the subject (*non est in plus*) (and thus its extension is not restricted when made to coincide with that of the S.), nevertheless, in its function of Pr. in an affirmative proposition it continues to be taken particularly in order to be attributed to the subject.

B. Now let us consider negative propositions. Here the Pr. and S. are separated from each other ; this separation implies that the Pr. does not constitute any of the notes of

And in every negative proposition, the Pr. is taken UNIVERSALLY.

[1] See above, No. 27.
[2] Every proposition in which the subject is attributed its own definition is a convertible proposition.
[3] Cf. St. Thomas, *in Perihermeneias*, lib. I, cap. VII, lect. 10, n. 23.

comprehension of the S., and, at the same time, that the S. is not one of the things to which the Pr. may be applied. Therefore the S. is excluded from the whole extension of the Pr. In the proposition " Man is not a pure spirit," I separate from all the matter contained under the universal man the universal form, pure spirit, and thus all the matter contained under universal form.

In every *negative* proposition
the predicate is taken
UNIVERSALLY.

Precisely speaking, in every negative proposition the Pr. has a universal " substitutive value " (*suppositio*); *pure spirit* " stands for " *any pure spirit*, in this case.

The above survey suffices to show the futility of the *quantification* of the Pr. proposed by the English logician Hamilton. It is nonsense to want to " quantify " the Pr., that is to say, to manifest explicitly its quantity (see below No. 83) since it is of the *very essence* of the Pr. in virtue of its logical relation to the S., to be taken particularly in every affirmative, and universally in every negative.[1]

EXTENSION AND COMPREHENSION OF THE PREDICATE

	in every AFFIRMATIVE PROPOSITION	in every NEGATIVE PROPOSITION	
The predicate is taken	Particularly	Universally	as to EXTENSION
	Totally	Partially (Considered divisively)	as to COMPREHENSION

(3) Now let us consider the COMPREHENSION of the PREDICATE.

[1] For the same reason it is nonsense to accuse traditional Logic of having paved the way for the theory of Hamilton by emphasizing the properties that concern the extension of the Pr., as if the logical function of the Pr. in the proposition, and what it implies as to the extension, or the latter were the result of a more or less arbitrary theory, and did not depend upon the very structure and essence of the proposition.

" Man is mortal " : all the notes constituting mortality are found in man. That is to say that

in every *affirmative* proposition
the predicate is taken
in *all* its COMPREHENSION.

In every *affirmative* the Pr. is taken in all its *comprehension*,

On the other hand, if I say : " Man is not a pure spirit," not *all* the constitutive notes of a pure spirit are thereby excluded from man (man like a pure spirit is a substance). Therefore

in every *negative* proposition
the *predicate* is taken
only in *a part* of its COMPREHENSION
—if its notes be considered *divisively*.

but in every *negative* only a *part* of its *comprehension* (considered divisively) is taken.

(For the Pr. is taken *in all its comprehension* when its *notes* are considered collectively).

(*a*) *Extension of the subject.* As we have seen above (No. 51) the SUBJECT is, by definition, taken universally in every UNIVERSAL PROPOSITION and *particularly* in every PARTICULAR PROPOSITION.

In every SINGULAR PROPOSITION, *e.g.*, " This man is mortal," the subject-term signifies a (reflex) singular concept, which in turn presupposes a (direct) universal concept. The (universal) direct concept is taken only in a *part of its extension*, being restricted to a single determinate individual, but the reflex or indirect (singular) concept itself is obviously *taken in all its extension ;* therefore in the theory of the syllogism and the theory of conversion of propositions, singular propositions are practically equivalent to universal propositions.

On the other hand, every INDEFINITE PROPOSITION is equivalent either to a universal (in necessary matter, when the Pr. must *necessarily* or must *necessarily not* belong to the S.) or to a *particular* (in contingent matter when the Pr. *may or may not* belong to the S.), or even to a singular (when the subject stands for a single determinate individual : " the man is come ").

(*b*) *Comprehension of the subject.* The S. is taken *in all its* COMPREHENSION, that is, with all its constitutive notes, in every proposition (except *reduplicative* propositions implying restriction).

(*c*) *The use of these notions.* We will encounter these notions concerning the comprehension and, especially, the extension of terms (in the proposition) in several important theories. As we have already remarked [1] because of the fact that we handle abstract (and therefore universal) concepts, we cannot think correctly without taking their extension into account. That is why the study of the extension of terms plays so important a *rôle* in Logic (the extension of the subject in the theory of the *opposition* of propositions, the extension of the two extremes in the theory of *conversion* and, above all, in the theory of *reasoning*). Not that the logician demands that this study reveal the very essence of discursive thought, that would be absurd ; but he does ask that it fix certain conditions indispensable for the legitimate use of this thought.

(*d*) DRILL. How are the subject and predicate taken from the point of view of comprehension and extension in the following propositions : " All power is weak, unless it be united, Peace is good of itself, I am not a great prophet, Wolves eat gluttonously, No miser is at peace with God, Some fruits are poisonous, A triangle is a three-sided figure, My friend is gone, Some boisterous people are not brave, This diplomat is renowned as a dancer."

C. THE OPPOSITION OF PROPOSITIONS

53. GENERAL NOTION OF OPPOSITION. The two propositions, " Man is fallible " and " Man is not fallible," are constructed of the same terms, but they cannot subsist together in the mind : they are repugnant to each other. We say that propositions exclude or are repugnant to each other, when one affirms and the other denies the same Pr. of the same S. This is

Logical opposition or the opposition of propositions is the affirmation and negation of the same Pr. in regard to the same S.

LOGICAL OPPOSITION

or the *opposition of proposition*, which we define as the affirma-

[1] See above, No. 18.

tion and negation of the same Pr. in regard to the same S. (*affirmatio et negatio, ejusdem de eodem*). Evidently it will be greatly to the logician's interest to make an inquiry into the laws that govern this opposition. For they will enable him to know, in the face of two propositions constructed of the same terms, when to proceed from the affirmation of one to the negation of the other and inversely ; and when to say that if the one is true the other is false, or if the one is false the other is true.

As we have seen, propositions are AFFIRMATIVE OR NEGATIVE as to their *form* (or " essential quality ") ; UNIVERSAL OR PARTICULAR as to their *quantity* (see above, Nos. 48 and 51). For purposes of abridgement and in order to construct mnemonic formulas, logicians have agreed to designate propositions by means of the following abbreviations :

AFFIRMATIVE UNIVERSAL propositions

Capital A means yes, E means no universally. Capital I means yes, O means no, particularly.

by the letter A (first vowel of the word *affirmo*) ;

AFFIRMATIVE PARTICULAR propositions

by the letter I (second vowel of the same word) ;

NEGATIVE UNIVERSAL propositions

by the letter E (first vowel of *nego*) ;

NEGATIVE PARTICULAR propositions

by the letter O (second vowel of the same word). We shall use these letters with this conventional signification from now on. The following mnemonic formulas provide a convenient way of remembering what these letters A, E, I, O mean.

Asserit A, negat E, verum generaliter ambo,
Asserit I, negat O, sed particulariter ambo.

54. THE THREE KINDS OF OPPOSITION. (1) Given the (A) proposition : " Every man is blond." This proposition *affirms* the Pr. blond of the (*objective*) *concept man taken in its universality*. How can this Pr. be denied of this S. so as to *purely* and *simply* destroy the proposition in question ? By purely and simply saying : it is not true that every man

is blond, that is by *denying* that the Pr. blond belongs to the concept man taken in its universality, by constructing the (O) proposition, " Some men are not blond," or, as is preferable in Logic : " SOME MAN IS NOT BLOND." This is the opposition of

CONTRADICTION

in which one proposition *purely and simply* denies what another proposition affirms, and in which there is *absolutely nothing* wherein the two propositions can agree.

(2) The Pr. of this same proposition, " EVERY MAN IS BLOND," may be denied of the S. in another way : by denying not only that the Pr. blond belongs to the concept man *taken in its universality*, but also that it belongs to the concept man *taken in any way whatsoever*, by saying : " It is not only false that every man is blond, but it is also false that some men are blond "—in other words, by constructing the (E) proposition : " NO MAN IS BLOND." This is the opposition of

CONTRARIETY,

in which a proposition denies not only what the other affirms, but also what a *less extended* proposition would affirm. It follows that in this type of opposition there is something in which the two opposed propositions may agree, namely, *falsity ;* for the two propositions " every man is blond," " no man is blond," are equally false—the truth being that some men are blond and others are not.

(3) Now let us take the (I) proposition : " SOME MAN IS BLOND." We may oppose it by CONTRADICTION, by purely and simply destroying it, that is by constructing the (E) proposition : " NO MAN IS BLOND." But we may also oppose it in another way, by constructing the (O) proposition : " SOME MAN IS NOT BLOND " (which no longer denies the proposition " Some man is blond," but denies the more extended proposition : " Every man is blond "). This is the opposition of

SUB-CONTRARIETY,

in which a proposition denies not exactly what the other affirms, but rather what a third *more extended* proposition would affirm. Consequently, in this kind of opposition, there is something in which the two opposed propositions may agree—namely *truth*: for these two propositions "some man is blond," "some man is not blond" are equally true.

*(*a*) There is the opposition of *contradiction* between the two *singular* propositions: "Peter is wise," "Peter is not wise," for the second proposition purely and simply destroys the first.

*(*b*) The same is true of two propositions such as: "Man is the noblest of creatures," and "Man is not the noblest of creatures." Although that which is attributed to the universal subject in these propositions relates to the being which it has in things, the universal subject itself is taken according to the being which it has in the mind—that is, *precisely inasmuch as it is one* (under the condition of *unity* which belongs to it in the mind alone).[1] That is why propositions such as these, whose universal subject is considered *as one*, behave like singular propositions from the point of view of opposition (they admit of but one kind of opposition, the opposition of contradiction, which does not suppose a difference in the *quantity* of the propositions).

But apart from these two cases it is clear from the foregoing that two propositions are

There are three kinds of logical opposition: contradiction, contrariety, sub-contrariety, to which may be added subalternation.

CONTRADICTORY

when they have the same S. and Pr.[2] and are opposed not only in *quality* (the one affirmative, the other negative), but also in *quantity* (the one universal, the other particular);

CONTRARY

[1] See above, No. 18 (2), inset, and No. 51a.—"Quandoque attribuitur aliquid universali sic considerato, quod scilicet apprehensitur ab intellectu ut *unum*, tamen id quod attribuitur ei non pertinet ad actum intellectus, sed ad esse, quod habet natura apprehensa in rebus quae sunt extra animam, puta si dicatur quod homo sit dignissima creaturarum. Hoc enim convenit naturae humanae etiam secundum quod est in singularibus. Nam quilibet homo singularis dignior est omnibus creaturis irrationalibus; sed tamen omnes homines singulares non sunt *unus* homo extra animam, sed solum in acceptione intellectus; et per hunc modum attribuitur ei praedicatum, scilicet ut *uni* rei" (St. Thomas, *in Perihermeneias*, lib. I, c. VII, lect. 10, n. 9).

[2] In two opposed propositions not only must the S. and Pr. be the same, but the S. must have the same *kind* of "substitutive value" or *suppositio* (material, logical, or real). However, the S. may sometimes pass from a real particular *suppositio* to a real universal *suppositio* (substitutive value) or inversely.

when they have the same S. and Pr., and are opposed in *quality*, but not in quantity—both being *universals*.

SUB-CONTRARY

A is the contradictory of O, I the contradictory of E.

A is the contrary of E, I the sub-contrary of O.

when they have the same S. and Pr. and are opposed in *quality* only, not in quantity, both being *particulars*.

There is therefore opposition of *contradiction* between A and O, and between E and I; opposition of *contrariety* between A and E, opposition of *sub-contrariety* between I and O. These facts are presented in the following scheme which is called the " square of opposition."

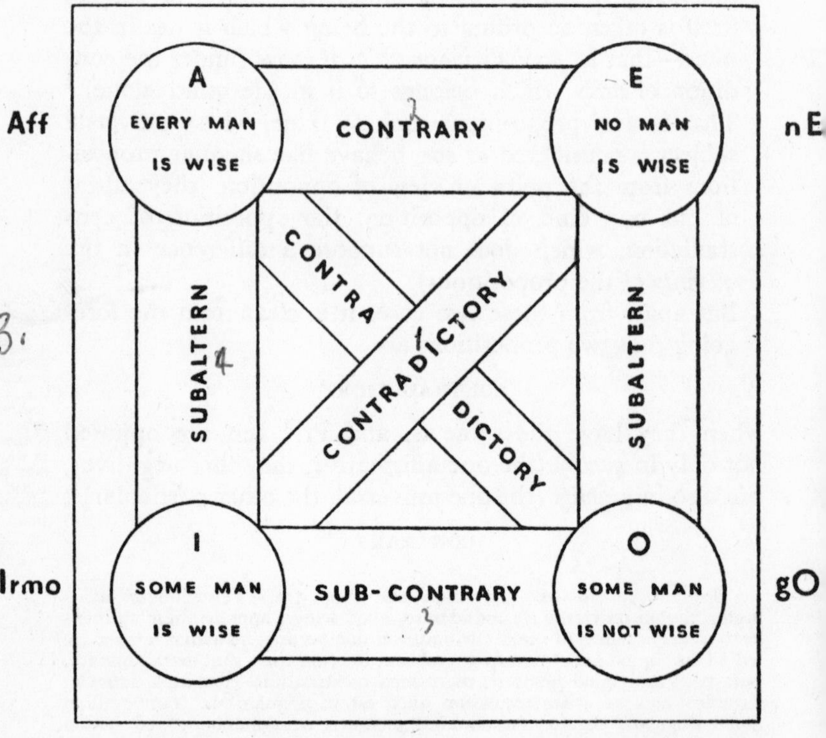

I is the subaltern of A, O the subaltern of E.

I is said to be the SUBALTERN of A, O the SUBALTERN of E. Subalternation does not really constitute logical opposition, but only a relation between superior (a more universal proposition) and inferior (a less universal proposition).

A universal proposition and its subaltern are not *opposed* in the proper sense of the word. On the contrary, for the subalternate (I or O) does but express in a partial or diminished fashion the same thing as the subalternant (A or E). Therefore we must say that there are the THREE kinds of logical opposition : contradiction, contrariety and sub-contrariety, although, in order to unite in one same classification all the kinds of relation that may exist between two propositions having the same S. and Pr. we often say that there are FOUR kinds of logical opposition : contradiction, contrariety, sub-contrariety and subalternation. But in this case the word opposition in so far as it concerns subalternation is understood in an improper sense.

Contradiction is the perfect type of opposition.

Which is the *greatest or strongest* of these different kinds of opposition—that in which the negation is the most destructive ? It is not, as one might think at first sight, the opposition of contrariety but the opposition of

CONTRADICTION

in which the negative proposition is the *pure negation* of the affirmative proposition. The opposition of *contrariety*, in which a proposition denies not only what the other affirms, but also what a *less extended* proposition would affirm, is really *less negative* than the opposition of contradiction, for in passing from a proposition to its contrary the subject continues to be taken *universally* ; wherefore these two propositions have something in common, namely falsehood.

*(*a*) Note that the definition of opposition : " the affirmation and negation of the same Pr. in regard to the same S." applies perfectly to the first three kinds of logical opposition recognized by the logician, if by S. we understand precisely the *word* which is the subject of the proposition. In the opposition of sub-contrariety " some man is wise," " some man is not wise," the Pr. " wise " is affirmed and denied of the same *word* subject, " some man." If, on the contrary, we understand by S. the *things* for which a word stands, then this is a definition by the most typical or eminent case : it is completely verified only by the most perfect type of opposition, namely contradiction. In order to apply this definition

to the opposition of contrariety, we must extend it and give it a certain leeway (for in this type of opposition the S. of the negative proposition stands not only for the subjects of which the affirmative is false, but may also stand for other subjects of which the affirmative would be true—and inversely). And we must understand this definition in an even broader sense in order to apply it to the opposition of sub-contrariety (for in this case the S. of the negative proposition may possibly not stand for the same subject for which the S. of the affirmative proposition stands). As for subalternation, it is only for reasons of symmetry that logicians have admitted it into the Square of Opposition. This blind window does not figure in the theory of opposition formulated by Aristotle.

*(*b*) In regard to conditional propositions, we may say *by analogy* that there is 1 *Contradiction* between "if I were rich I would be happy" and "it is not true that if I were rich I would be happy" (that is: "if I were rich I might not be happy") and *contradiction* between "if I were rich I would not be happy" and "it is not true that if I were rich I would not be happy" (that is "if I were rich I might be happy"); 2 *Contrariety* between "if I were rich I would be happy" and "if I were rich I would not be happy"; 3 *Subcontrariety* between "if I were rich I might not be happy" and "if I were rich I might be happy"; 4 *Subalternation* between "if I were rich I would be happy" and "if I were rich I might be happy" and also between "if I were rich I would not be happy" and "if I were rich I might not be happy."

Law of Contradictories: if one is true the other is false, if one is false, the other is true.

55. THE LAWS OF OPPOSITION. (1) CONTRADICTION. *Two contradictory* propositions *cannot* be at the same time *true*, nor at the same time *false*. If one is true, the other is necessarily false; if one is false, the other is necessarily true. "Some man is blond" is *true*: therefore "no man is blond" is *false*. "Every man is just" is false: therefore "some man is not just" is *true*.

Law of Contraries: if one is true the other is false; but if

(2) CONTRARIETY. Two *contraries cannot* be at the same time *true*, but they *may* be at the same time *false*. If one is true, the other is necessarily false; but if one is false, the

other may also be false.[1] " Every man is just " is false, but that does not prove that " no man is just " is true. one is false the other may equally be false.

(3) SUB-CONTRARIETY. Two *sub-contraries cannot* be at the same time *false*, but *may* be at the same time true.[2] If one is false, the other is necessarily true ; but if one is true, the other may also be true. " Some man is just " is *true*, but that does not prove that " some man is not just " is false.

Law of Sub-contraries: if one is false the other is true; but if one is true the other may be equally true.

(4) SUBALTERNATION. Subalterns obey the following law : If A is true, I is true ; if A is false, I may be true. If I is true, A may be false, if I is false, A is false. Likewise for E and O.

These laws are evidently of very great practical value. We must be especially careful not to confuse the opposition of contradiction with the opposition of contrariety. *It does not necessarily follow* from the falsity of a proposition that the *contrary* proposition is true. For instance, because the proposition " *Every* religion is good," is false, it does not follow that the proposition " *No* religion is good " is true ; for, on the contrary, it is false. Nor is the truth of the proposition : " *No* sin may be avoided without the help of grace " consequent upon the falsity of the proposition : " *Every* sin may be avoided without the help of grace " (see No. 56, the opposition of modal propositions).

*(*a*) Note that the *contradictory* of a COPULATIVE proposition is a DISJUNCTIVE. Example : " Every rich man is sad *and* honoured." Contradictory " Some rich man is not sad *or* not honoured." Actually if this disjunctive is false, the copulative is true, and if either one of its members is true, the copulative is false.

*(*b*) *The opposition of contradiction and future contingencies. If* a proposition is true, its contradictory is false ; *if* a proposition is false, its contradictory is true. But a proposition concerning the contingent future is neither *determinately true* nor *determinately false* (see above, No. 41 *b*),

[1] *In necessary matter*, that is when the Pr. is of the essence of the S. two *contrary* propositions cannot be at the same time false. Ex. : " Every man is mortal," " No man is mortal." *In such a case* (but only in such a case) we may conclude to the falsity of one contrary from the truth of the other—as in the opposition of contradiction.

[2] *In necessary matter*, that is, when the Pr. is of the essence of the S., two *sub-contrary* propositions cannot be at the same time true. Example : " Some man is mortal," " some man is not mortal." *In such a case* (but only in such a case) we may conclude from the truth of one sub-contrary to the falsity of the other—as in the opposition of contradiction.

so that its contradictory is neither *determinately true* nor *determinately false*. For instance, in speaking of some future event, such as a naval battle, if we said : " there will be—there will not be—a naval battle to-morrow," we could not say that since these two propositions are contradictory, one of them is actually false and the other is actually true. All that we can affirm is that they exclude each other *indeterminately*. On the supposition that either one of them is true, the other is false, and inversely. But at the moment neither one of the two (this one rather than that one) can be said to be determinately true, nor the other rejected as false. For at present neither one nor the other is true or false. *Discourses are true*, says Aristotle, recalling his definition of truth, *in so far as they are conformed to things*. It is evident then that when an event does not yet exist and does not even exist as pre-formed in its cause since it is contingent, no discourse about this event can be either true or false, nor can we say that since one of the opposed discourses is true, the other is false, or inversely.[1]

*(*c*) Does the opposition of propositions give rise to *immediate inferences ?* (see below, No. 68).

*(*d*) *Modern criticism of the theory of subalternation* (see below, No. 84).

(*e*) DRILL. (1) Indicate the type of opposition existing between the following propositions :

Every rich man is selfish, no rich man is selfish.

Every mammal has hairy tegument ; some mammal does not have hairy tegument.

No philosopher has erred, some philosopher did not err.

Some soldiers fled, no soldier fled.

Some mammal has wings, some mammal does not have wings.

Some man is a liar, every man is a liar, etc., etc.

(2) Given the following propositions : Every truth should not be told. Some severity is necessary. No bird is viviparous. Some philosophers were not virtuous. Indicate

[1] Hamelin, *Le Système d'Aristote* (Alcan, Paris, 1931), p. 167. " The question of knowing whether or not there are contingent futures is quite another thing"; adds Mr. Hamelin, "if there are any, the doctrine of Aristotle upon the application of the principle of contradiction to these futures, is the only correct and rational one." Cf. Aristotle, *Perihermeneias*, chap. IX, and St. Thomas's masterly commentary, lect. 13 and 14.

their contradictions, contraries, sub-contraries and subalterns.

*56. THE OPPOSITION OF MODAL PROPOSITIONS. In a modal proposition there are *two qualities* to be considered: that of the *mode*, and that of the "*dictum*," that is, of the enunciation itself that unites or separates the Pr. and S. Thus in the proposition: "It is possible that Peter will not come," the mode is affirmative, the *dictum* is negative.

Similarly there are *two quantities* to be considered in modal propositions: that of the *dictum* and that of the *mode*. *Necessary* and *impossible* modes denote *universality* (the thing in question must *always* happen or can *never* happen); *possible* and *contingent* modes denote *particularity* (the thing in question may sometimes happen, or may *sometimes* not happen).

(1) *Let us first abstract from the quantity of the dictum* and suppose the singular S.: "that Peter be cured," for instance. Then we shall have only the quantity of the mode, the quality of the mode, and the quality of the *dictum* to consider.

Granted that "impossible" is equivalent to "not possible," and consequently to a *negative* mode we may say that if both the mode and the dictum are affirmative the proposition is purely and simply affirmative, and that the same is true if both are negative; if the mode is affirmative and the dictum negative, or inversely, the proposition is purely and simply negative.

(Aff.) Necessary	(Aff.) that it be	= Aff.
(Aff.) Necessary	(Neg.) that it not be	= Neg.
(Aff.) Possible	(Aff.) that it be	= Aff.
(Aff.) Possible	(Neg.) that it not be	= Neg.
(Neg.) Impossible	(Aff.) that it be	= Neg.
(Neg.) Impossible	(Neg.) that it not be	= Aff.

It is clear, on the other hand, that the following combinations [1]

Impossible that it not be
Not possible that it not be } are equal to *Necessary that it be* (Affirm. univ.)

Likewise the combinations

Necessary that it not be
Not possible that it be } are equal to *Impossible that it be* (Neg. univ.)

The combinations

Not impossible that it be
Not necessary that it not be } are equal to *Possible that it be* (Affirm. partic.)

And the combinations

Not necessary that it be
Not impossible that it not be } are equal to *Possible that it not be* (Neg. Partic.)

consequently we may represent the opposition of modal propositions whose S. is singular in the following schema :

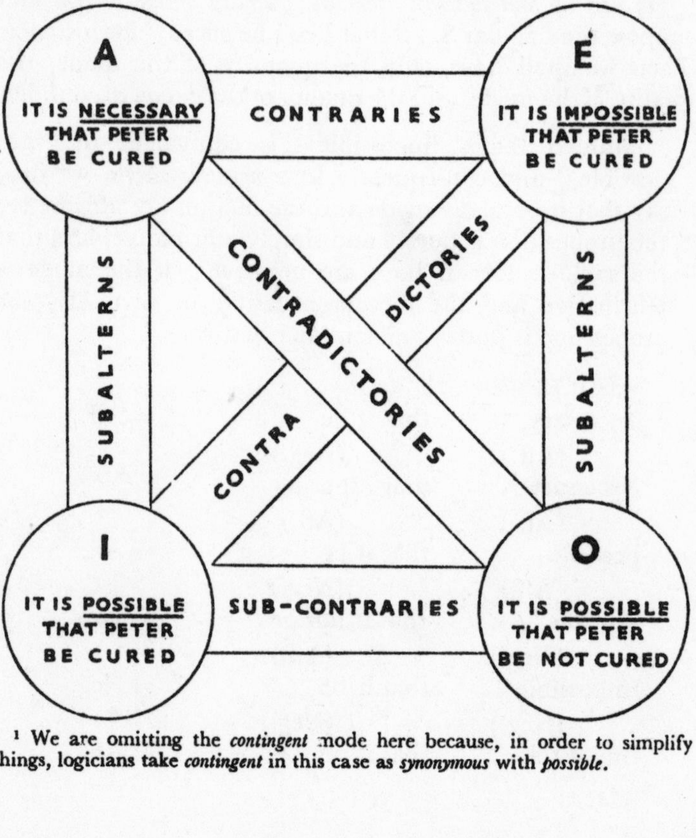

[1] We are omitting the *contingent* mode here because, in order to simplify things, logicians take *contingent* in this case as *synonymous* with *possible*.

(2) Now, *taking the quantity of the " dictum " into account* we have the following outline.

In the example we are using, (1) and (2) are false ; their contradictories (3) and (4) are true, (5) is true, *e.g.*, a man who studies the first principles of mathematics must necessarily be a metaphysician ; their contradictories (7) and (8) are false.

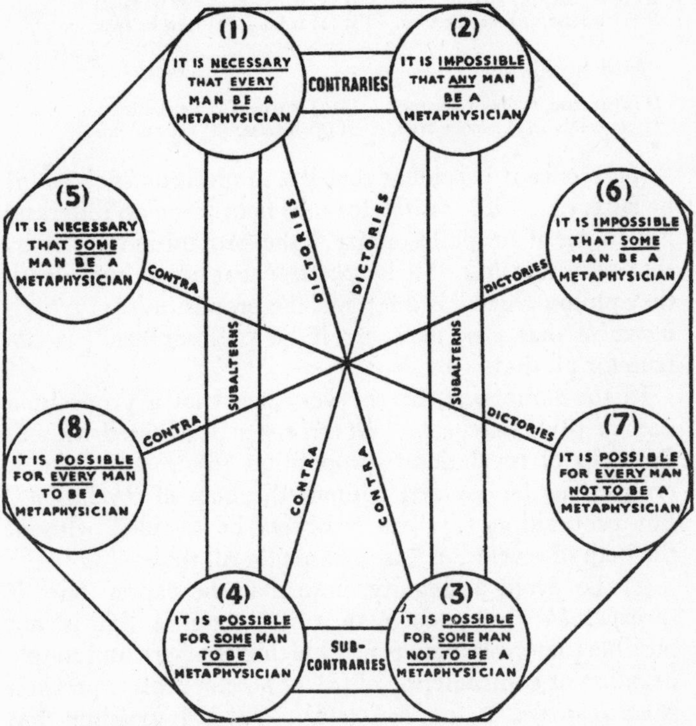

(*a*) The proposition (5) being subalternated to (1), it follows that :

If (1) is true, (5) *must* be *true*. If (5) is true, (1) *may* be false.
If (1) is false, (5) *may* be true. If (5) is false, (1) *must* be false.

Likewise :

If (2) is true, (6) *must* be true. If (6) is true, (2) *may* be false.
If (2) is false, (6) *may* be true. If (6) is false, (2) *must* be false.

Likewise:

If (7) is true, (3) *must* be true. If (3) is true, (7) *may* be false.
If (7) is false, (3) *may* be true. If (3) is false, (7) *must* be false.

Similarly:

If (8) is true, (4) *must* be true. If (4) is true, (8) *may* be false.
If (8) is false, (4) *may* be true. If (4) is false, (8) *must* be false.

Or again:

If (1) is true, (4) *must* be true. If (4) is true, (1) *may* be false.
If (1) is false, (4) *may* be true. If (4) is false, (1) *must* be false.

And finally:

If (2) is true, (3) *must* be true. If (3) is true, (2) *may* be false.
If (2) is false, (3) *may* be true. If (3) is false, (2) *must* be false.

(*b*) Hence it is evident that if a proposition such as (7) be false, *e.g.*, " it is *possible* for *every* man (even an illiterate) not to err if he philosophize," the proposition (5) is by that very fact *true*, " it is *inevitable* that *certain* men err if they philosophize," is *true*; but the proposition (1): " it is *inevitable* that *every* man err if he philosophize," is not true for all that.

In the same way, by the very fact that a proposition such as (8) is false, *e.g.*, " *all* error *may* be avoided without the help of revelation," proposition (6) is *true*: " *some* error *cannot* be avoided without the help of revelation." But proposition (2) " *no* error *can* be avoided without the help of revelation " is not true for all that.

(*c*) To avoid ambiguity, note that the expression " it is *impossible* that *every* man run " signifies " it is not possible that every man run," which is the pure and simple negation or contradiction of (8). Therefore this expression is *not equivalent to* (2), *but to* (6): " it is impossible that certain men run "; in order to express (2) we would have to say: " it is impossible that *any* man run," or simply " no man can run."

(*d*) Logicians have chosen four vowels, A, E, I, U, as mnemonic symbols to be used in the opposition of modal propositions. Their significance is as follows:

A signifies a proposition that is affirmative as to *dictum* and as to *mode*.

E signifies a proposition that is negative as to *dictum* and affirmative as to *mode*.
I „ „ that is affirmative as to *dictum*, negative as to *mode*.
U „ „ negative as to *dictum* and as to *mode*.

These may be remembered by means of this line :

E dictum negat, Ique modum, nihil A sed U totum.

Logicians have made up the mnemonic words *Purpurea*, *Illiace*, *Amabimus*, *Edentuli*, in each of which

the *first* vowel designates the mode of Possibility,
the *second* the mode of Contingency,
the *third* the mode of Impossibility,
the *fourth* the mode of Necessity.

There is *equivalence* ("*equipollence*") between the four propositions signified by each mnemonic word, *contradiction* between Purpurea and Edentuli, Amabimus and Illiace (as there is between A and O, I and E, in propositions *de inesse*), *contrariety* between Purpurea and Illiace, *sub-contrariety* between Amabimus and Edentuli. Hence the following schema :

PUR	It is not possible that Peter be not cured		it is not possible that Peter be cured	IL
PU	it is not contingent that Peter be not cured	(A) CONTRARIES (E)	it is not contingent that Peter be cured	LI
RE	it is impossible that Peter be not cured	CONTRA DICTORIES	it is impossible that Peter be cured	A
A	it is necessary that Peter be cured		it is necessary that Peter be not cured	CE
A	it is possible that Peter be cured	CONTRA DICTORIES	it is possible that Peter be not cured	E
MA	it is contingent that Peter be cured		it is contingen tthat Peter be not cured	DEN
BI	it is not impossible that Peter be cured	(I) SUB-CONTRARIES (O)	it is not impossible that Peter be not cured	TU
MUS	it is not necessary that Peter be not cured		it is not necessary that Peter be cured	LI

D. THE CONVERSION OF PROPOSITIONS

To convert a proposition is to invert its extremes in such a manner as to express the same truth.

57. NOTION OF THE CONVERSION OF PROPOSITIONS. Given a proposition expressing a certain truth, *e.g.*, "*No man is a pure spirit*"; we may express *the same truth* by inverting the order of the extremes, that is, by making the S. the Pr., and the Pr. the S., and saying: "*No pure spirit is a man.*" The first proposition has been *converted*. The conversion of a proposition is therefore,

> *the inversion of the extremes, in such a way as to express* THE SAME TRUTH.

There are three kinds of conversion: simple, accidental, by contraposition.

There are three kinds of conversion.

SIMPLE (*simplex*) conversion, when the *quantity* of the proposition *remains unchanged.*

ACCIDENTAL conversion (*per accidens*), when the *quantity* of the proposition *is changed.*

Conversion BY CONTRAPOSITION (*per contrapositionem*) when a *negative particle* is added *to the interchanged extremes* (without changing the quantity of the proposition).

58. RULES OF CONVERSION. Since the Pr. of the original proposition becomes the S. of the new one, it must evidently *keep, as S., the same extension which it had as Pr.*, otherwise the truth of the proposition would be impaired. Hence all the rules of conversion.

These rules rest, then, on the substitutive value (*suppositio*) of the Pr. in the original proposition, and of the S. in the new one.

(1) Given a negative universal proposition (E), *e.g.*, "No man is a pure spirit." How is the Pr. taken in negative propositions?—*Universally* (see above, No. 52). Therefore we convert this proposition by saying: "*No* pure spirit is a man" (SIMPLE conversion).

The truth of the latter proposition implies that of its subaltern: "*some* pure spirit is not a man." Which means that E is also converted ACCIDENTALLY (in this case the converted proposition expresses *the same truth* as the original proposition, but in *a partial or diminished fashion*).

(2) Given a particular affirmative proposition (I), *e.g.*, "Some man is wise." How is the Pr. taken in affirmative

propositions ?—*Particularly*. Therefore the converse of " I " will be : " Some wise (being) is a man " (SIMPLE conversion).

(3) Given an affirmative universal proposition (A), *e.g.*, " Every man is mortal." For the same reason, it will be converted into " some mortal is a man " (ACCIDENTAL conversion).

But it may also be converted by CONTRAPOSITION : " Every non-mortal is a not-man."

(4) Finally, given a particular negative proposition (O), *e.g.*, " Some man is not just." May we convert it by saying : " Some just (being) is not (a) man " ? No, for in the original proposition the negated Pr. " just " signified just *man* (it " stood for " just *man* : some man is not (a) just (man)).

E may be converted in two ways ; simply or accidentally, A, accidentally or by contraposition. I admits but one : simple conversion, and O, conversion by contraposition.

But in the new proposition, on the contrary, " some just (being) is not (a) man," the S. " some just (being) " does not " stand for " just *man*, but for some other being, *e.g.*, God or some angel. (It does not " stand for " just man.) This new proposition does not express *the same truth* as the first—nor is it its converse. Hence it follows that O may be converted only BY CONTRAPOSITION, " Some *non*-just (being) is not *not*-man," *i.e.*, " some non-just (being) is a man."

Logicians have summed up these rules in two mnemonic lines :

Simpliciter fEcI convertitur, EvA per accid,
AstO per contrap ; sic fit conversio tota.

(the words fEcI, EvA, AstO are meaningless syllables and have no other purpose than that of grouping the figurative vowels A, E, I and O).

(*a*) *Practical utility* of studying the conversion of propositions. As the English philosopher Bain has remarked, a great number of sophisms spring from the fact that careless thinkers have the tendency to convert universal affirmatives *simply* ; for instance, to pass from this proposition : " Every artist of genius astonishes common people," to this one : " Every artist who astonishes common people is a genius" ; or from this proposition (supposed as true) : "Every man of superior intelligence has a large head," to this other : "Every man with a large head has superior intelligence" (see No. 59).

(*b*) Note that, in order to be suitably converted, a proposition must first be reduced to its logical structure (which admits of no verb except the copula *is*) so as to entirely convert the whole Pr. into the whole S. The converse of "Peter sees a bear" is not "a bear sees Peter," but "some (man) seeing a bear is Peter."

*(*c*) A *singular* proposition is converted into an I, if it is *affirmative*, into an E if it is *negative*. "Peter is a saint," "some saint is Peter," "Peter is not impious," "No impious (man) is Peter." Thus, in the theory of conversion, an affirmative singular is assimilable into an A proposition and a singular negative into an E proposition.

*(*d*) In the conversion of *modals*, the mode does not change. "Every man is necessarily animal" (A) ; some animal (viz., rational animal) is necessarily man."—"No man can think without images" (E) ; "no being that thinks without images is a man."

*(*e*) An affirmative proposition may be converted simply when it happens, as it does in affirmatives whose Pr. is a definition (convertible propositions) that the extension of the Pr. is equal to that of the subject.

But this is not *conversion* properly so-called, for the second proposition expresses another truth than does the first, for even when its extension is equal to that of the S. the Pr. has a *particular* substitutive value in every affirmative proposition, consequently the first proposition of itself says but one thing : "Each man is a rational animal (regardless of the question of knowing whether there be rational animals other than man) ; and the second proposition, in saying : "Each rational animal is a man," *adds* to, and expresses something *other* than, the first.

To say that a convertible proposition may be converted simply is to say that, supposing the proposition in question to be true, its converse is equally *true :* it is not to say that its simple converse expresses *the same truth*.

*(*f*) Is the conversion of proposition an *immediate inference?*—(See below, No. 68.)

*(*g*) *Modern criticisms of the theory of conversion.*—(See No. 84.)

*(*h*) THE EQUIPOLLENCE OF PROPOSITIONS. Besides *opposition* and *conversion* there is another property of propositions to be considered; this property is called *equipollence*. When two propositions are opposed and are made equivalent to one another by the addition of a negative particle, we say that these propositions have become *equipollent*. Example: given the original proposition *Nullo homo est justus*. Its contradictory is: *aliquis homo est justus*, and its contrary: *omnis homo est justus*. By adding the particle *no* to both of the latter propositions we have: NON *aliquis homo est justus*, and: *Omnis homo* NON *est justus*, which are equivalent to the original proposition. The rules of equipollence concern language more than thought, and since the English language does not readily lend itself to them, we shall not study them here.

OMIT

*59. RECIPROCAL PROPOSITIONS. Given an affirmative universal (A): "Every square is a right-angled rhombus." The

RECIPROCAL

The reciprocal of an affirmative universal is this same proposition converted simply.

of this proposition is an equally affirmative universal (A) in which the two extremes are transposed: "Every right-angled rhombus is a square." [1]

Thus the reciprocal of an A is this same proposition converted simply. And, if we keep in mind the fact that the Pr. was taken particularly in the original proposition, as it is in every affirmative, it is clear that, whereas the *partial converse* "some right-angled rhombus is a square" expresses *the same truth* as does the original proposition—the *reciprocal* expresses *another truth* than does the latter and *is independent* of it. Even though the original proposition be true, the

[1] Likewise in the conditional propositions, often used for convenience' sake in geometry: "If two circumferences are inwardly tangent, the distance between their centres is equal to the difference between their radii.—Reciprocal: If two circumferences are such that the distance between their centres is equal to the difference between their radii, they are inwardly tangent.

reciprocal may yet be false. The truth of the propositions " every man is an animal," " every square is a parallelogram " does not give us the right to conclude: " every animal is a man," " every parallelogram is a square."

When the reciprocal is true (as it is in " *convertible* " propositions) it must be proven on its own account; and its truth may sometime demand the addition of some condition. For example, the theorem: " A line drawn through two sides of a triangle, parallel to the third side, divides those sides proportionally." Its reciprocal is true, but by means of the addition of a condition: " A straight line cutting off proportional segments on two sides of a triangle is parallel to the third side, if both the points of intersection fall on the unextended sides of the triangle, or both fall on their extensions."

To conclude from the truth of an affirmative universal to the truth of its reciprocal is a crude sophism which is all too frequently committed.

(*a*) THE INVERSE OF A PROPOSITION. The inverse of an (A) proposition is a proposition having the same terms and the same quantity as the original, but whose *subject* and *copula* are affected by negation. It is *independent* of the original proposition, it may be false while the latter is true: " Every man is an animal," " Every ~~not~~ NON-man (*e.g.*, a dog) is not an animal.

But this inverse proposition expresses in the negative form the same thing as does the *reciprocal* of the original proposition: " Every not-man is not an animal " = " every animal is a man."

And the *inverse of the reciprocal*, in this case: " Every non-animal is not a man " expresses the same thing as does the original proposition (" Every man is an animal ").

Consequently if both a proposition and the inverse of its reciprocal are true, it does not follow that its inverse and reciprocal are true. But if both a proposition and its reciprocal are true then its inverse and the inverse of its reciprocal are true; and if a proposition and its inverse are both true, its reciprocal and the inverse of its reciprocal are true.

Obverse E inverts to I
A inverts to O

{Every square is a right-angled rhombus

↗ *Reciprocal :* Every right-angled rhombus is a square ↖

(Equivalent Propositions) — (Equivalent Propositions)

↘ *Inverse :* Every non-square (every rhombus that is not square) is not a right-angled rhombus. ↙

{*Inverse of the reciprocal :* Every non-right-angled rhombus is not a square.

{If in a trihedral two dihedral angles are equal, the opposite surfaces are equal.

↗ *Reciprocal :* If in a trihedral two surfaces are equal the dihedrals opposite these surfaces are equal. ↖

(Equivalent Propositions) — (Equivalent Propositions)

↘ *Inverse :* If in a trihedral two dihedrals are not equal, the opposite surfaces are not equal. ↙

{*Inverse of the reciprocal :* If in a trihedral two surfaces are not equal, the dihedrals opposite these surfaces are not equal.

(*b*) In this paragraph we have been speaking of the *reciprocal* in the strict sense. Certain authors, Renouvier for example, give this word a broader meaning, and use it as synonymous with *converse*.

(*c*) DRILL. (1) Convert the following propositions : Every man is a liar, No created intellect is able to understand God, Every created intellect is capable of knowing God, Some rich man is merciful, Some painters are not talented.

(2) Find the reciprocal, the inverse and the inverse of the reciprocal of the following propositions, and say in each case whether they are true or false : Every man is a creature, Every animal is sentient, Every bat is mammal, Every rectangle is a parallelogram, Every circle is a conical section, Every rhombus has its diagonals perpendicular to each other.

CHAPTER III

REASONING

SECTION 1. REASONING IN GENERAL

A. GENERAL NOTIONS

Reasoning is the act by which the mind progresses in knowledge through the help of what it already knows.

60. NOTION OF REASONING. Reasoning, as we already know,[1] is the third operation of the mind. It may be defined as:

the act by which the mind acquires new knowledge by means of what it already knows.

To reason is to proceed from one thing that has been intellectually grasped to another thing intellectually grasped by means of the first, and to advance thus from proposition to proposition in order to know intelligible truth: *procedere de uno intellecto ad aliud, ad veritatem intelligibilem cognoscendam.*[2] Such an act implies a progressive *movement* of thought, or a *discursus* (discourse), and consequently implies a succession of moments, a succession of " before " and " after."

By reasoning the mind goes from the known to the unknown, it acquires something new, *either* by *discovering* a hitherto unsuspected truth (order of discovery or *invention*), or by *proving or establishing as certain* a truth which it had previously discovered but which it possessed in an imperfect manner (order of *judgment* or *demonstration*).

61. REASONING AND ARGUMENTATION. Take, for example, the following reasoning:

(I) Every perfection possessed by creatures has God for its first cause; but the operation of free will is a perfection possessed by creatures.

(II) *Therefore* the operation of free will has God for its first cause.

By a first act we perceive as true the proposition " Every

[1] See above, No. 2.
[2] St. Thomas, *Sum. theol.*, I, q. 79, a. 8, resp.; cf. q. 58, a. 3.

perfection possessed by creatures has God for its first cause" ; then by a second act we perceive as true the proposition : "the operation of free will is a perfection possessed by creatures" ; and not only do we perceive this proposition as being true in itself, but we also perceive it as bearing instructive and fruitful *relationship* with the first, as putting something (viz., the objective concept "the operation of free will") under the dependence of the first proposition ; that is why we say : "but."

These two connected acts come first or *precede* in the reasoning, hence those propositions upon which they bear are called the *antecedent*. But the second of these acts is pregnant with a third ; to know under the dependence of this truth—that every perfection possessed by creatures has God for its first cause this other truth—that the operation of free will is a perfection possessed by creatures—is *already* to know in act [1] this third truth—that the operation of free will has God for its first cause, . . . without indeed having formulated it for itself, but in seeing it instantaneously in the second proposition illumined by the first. So *at the same time*, "αμα" [2] in which the mind knows the truth of the

In reasoning the mind is moved by two propositions, perceived as true (the antecedent), to posit the truth of a third proposition (the consequent).

[1] On the contrary, when I know only the Major : "Every perfection possessed by creatures has God for its first cause" without relating it to the Minor by an act of reason, I may say that I already know the conclusion "Free will has God for its first cause," but with only a *potential* knowledge (my intelligence is *in potency* to this truth) or *virtual* knowledge (this truth is contained *virtually* in that of the Major). This potential or virtual knowledge can be actualized only by the movement of the reason.

[2] Aristote, *Anal. Post.*, lib. I, cap. I, 71a, 20, St. Thomas, lect. 2 ; n. 9 ; "Ut si sic demonstraret aliquis, *omnis triangulus habet tres angulos aequales duobus rectis*, ista cognita, nondum habetur conclusionis cognitio : sed cum postea assumitur, *haec figura descripta in semicirculo, est triangulus*, statim scitur, quod habet tres angulos aequales duobus rectis. . . . Inducens hanc assumptionem, scilicet, quod hoc, quod est in semicirculo, sit triangulus, *simul*, scilicet tempore, cognovit conclusionem." Cf. John of St. Thomas, *Phil. Nat.*, III, q. XI, a. 4, p. 520.

Unless the mind reasons about a previously formulated argumentation suggested to it by someone else, in which case all the propositions it considers are constructed beforehand (for instance, in teaching, when a professor gives an example of reasoning to a pupil), the construction of the conclusion as a proposition is posterior in time to the construction of the Minor ; *anima in componendo et dividendo necesse habet adjungere tempus, ut dicitur in III de Anima*, cap. VI (St. Thomas, *in Periherm.*, I, c. IX, lect. 14, n. 19). But the truth of the conclusion is seen in the Minor taken as such before the conclusion itself is constructed. Thus the perception of the truth of the Minor causes the perception of the truth of the conclusion, but precedes it only with a priority of nature not of time, and thereby causes and precedes with a priority of time the construction of the conclusion.

Minor taken as such (that is, perceived under the dependence of the Major), it also knows *in actu signato* the truth of the conclusion, in a vision which contains all that is formally signified by the word *to know*, and has only to realize this knowledge *in actu exercito* in formulating the proposition which expresses it.

By a third act we immediately construct the third proposition as being linked to those preceding it (*therefore* the operation of free will, etc.) for we simultaneously perceive its truth as necessarily consequent upon the truth of the other two. Once the mind has performed the two preceding acts it cannot avoid the third, just as a diver who has jumped from a spring-board cannot avoid diving.

The mind stops in this third act ; by it it has come to the term of its discourse ; this is the act of *concluding*. And the proposition on which it bears is called the *consequent*. It springs from the other two propositions in virtue of a movement of the mind actuated by the antecedent whose truth it has perceived. Our mind does not see the consequent *in* the propositions which constitute the antecedent considered separately (in such a case it would not reason, but would know intuitively after the manner of pure spirits) ; it sees the consequent *by means of* these propositions. Neither the light sufficing for the perception of the truth of the first proposition in the antecedent, nor the light sufficing for the perception of the truth of the second proposition in the antecedent, suffices for the perception of the truth of the consequent. But the bringing together of these two lights, one under the other, necessarily gives birth in the mind to another light (lights another light, if we may so speak) by which the mind perceives the truth of the consequent. This third light is the perception of the truth of the antecedent as antecedent, the perception of the truth of the Minor under the Major.[1]

[1] Cf. John of St. Thomas, *Logica*, IIa, Pars, q. 24, a. 3, pp. 672–673 : " In eodem instanti quo minor cognoscitur, ut minor, deducitur assensus conclusionis, ut asseritur a D. Thoma (I, *Post.*, lect. 2, n. 9) quia posita cognitione minoris formaliter ut coordinata et subordinata majori, atque adeo supponendo cognitam bonitatem consequentiae, hoc ipso ponitur lumen sufficiens et necessitans ad manifestandum conclusionem ; nec enim alio lumine manifestatur conclusio, quam lumen illativo quod in praemissis continetur ; sed illuminatio fit in instanti, multo magis in spirituali lumine

To sum up then, the act of reasoning supposes that certain propositions have already been constructed by the mind. Considering these propositions in a certain order and perceiving them as true, the mind also perceives—in simple act (act of "inference") which is the essential thing in reasoning—that by this very fact, another proposition which it has constructed is true and must necessarily be affirmed in view of the assent given to the preceding propositions.

Thus, in reasoning, the antecedent is as an absolutely indispensable means or *instrument* by which the mind *is moved* to posit the consequent. The consequent thus *caused* is the term, which was at first unknown and is now known, in which the mind rests.[1] That which constitutes the reasoning is the fact that the consequent does not merely come *after* the antecedent (unum *post* aliud, *discursus secundum successionem*), as it does when we pass from one idea to another by means of the association of ideas, but it comes *from* it (unum *ex* alio, *discursus secundum causalitatem*).

The logical organism formed by the *antecedent* (the moving

quam in corporali, quia illud est efficacius et perfectius ; ergo in eodem instanti quo ponitur lumen praemissarum quo determinatur major ultimate per minorem, ponitur assensus conclusionis, tanquam a causa non impedita et operante instantanee."—*Curs. theol.*, t. IV, q. 58, disp. 22, a. 14 : "Discursus secundum causalitatem addit supra successionem cognoscendi, quod una cognitio causetur ex alia, ita quod ex uno noto seu cognito moveamur ad aliud ignotum ex vi prioris cogniti seu manifestati ; et sic manifestatio unius debet esse causa manifestationis alterius, non solum quia unum objectum illuminat aliud (hoc enim etiam in simplici intuitu plura objecta attingente obtinere potest), sed quia ipse cognoscens prius illuminatur circa unum, et in illo nondum illuminatur circa aliud, sed movetur ad educendum ex illo aliud lumen, seu manifestationem alterius. . . . Requiritur ergo ad discursum quod sit diversitas et ordo etiam in ipso lumine ut tenet se ex parte cognoscentis et unum lumen oriatur ex alio, sicut ex lumine principiorum oritur lumen scientiae, ita quod primum lumen non sufficit ostendere per se ea quae inferuntur, sed habet se ut lumen probativum, id est, quod manifestat alterum per deductionem et illationem unius luminis ex alio, quia primum non est sufficienter in se comprehensivum totius."

[1] Cf. John of St. Thomas, *Log.*, I. P. Illustr., q. 8, a. 3 : "Syllogismus est quasi organicum instrumentum, quod constat ex parte movente, et ex parte mota, sicut in viventibus una pars movet aliam. Constat enim quod ipsae praemissae sunt motivum et ratio cognoscendi conclusionem, unde ad rationem syllogismi, quo tamquam instrumento fit ista cognitio conclusionis, necessario et essentialiter requiruntur praemissae. Similiter ipsa conclusio est objectum cognitum ; ad hoc enim tendit syllogismus, ut conclusionem cognoscat per illationem. Syllogismus est instrumentum logicum, quo intellectus movetur de uno ad aliud cognoscendum, unde debet includere partem moventem, quae sunt praemissae, et partem motam, quae est objectum illatum, seu conclusio."

part) and the *consequent* (the " moved " or caused part) is called ARGUMENTATION.

(*a*) If the propositions constituting the argumentation are *mental propositions* the argumentation is mental. If the propositions are oral, the argumentation is *oral*—*material expression* of mental argumentation and consequently of the act of reasoning. In studying argumentation Logic considers it in its oral form, but we must not forget that its principal object is mental argumentation.

As we have already remarked, the word reasoning (which in the strict sense signifies only the operation of the mind and not the result produced), is used in English to mean argumentation.

*(*b*) From the preceding analysis we see that the reasoning taken as a whole (the preliminary acts bearing upon the antecedent, the definitive act bearing upon the conclusion) is a *complex* operation. But this complex operation is really *one* and *undivided*, for reasoning is a single continuous (that is, unarrested) movement by which the mind goes from a starting-point to a goal.

The argumentation formed by the propositions with which reasoning is concerned is itself *one*, but its unity is one of *order* and co-ordination, not of being or *quality*, as is that of the categorical proposition presented to the mind by a single mental word (see above, No. 37 B).

Furthermore, the act of inference which constitutes the essential thing in reasoning, the act by which the mind necessarily sees the truth of the consequent, and posits the latter, is itself a *simple* act.

*(*c*) We have already indicated that there are *two distinct* functions in mental activity[1]: 1 the mind *produces* or *constructs* something; 2 the mind *acts* in a purely *immanent* manner according to a mode of activity which, when taken formally or in that which properly constitutes it, is not a production. This latter function consists either in seeing or *apprehending*, or in *assenting*.

[1] These two distinct functions are two aspects of the same formally immanent and virtually productive act (which is itself preceded, in the second operation of the mind, by a preliminary constructive phase which is more dependent on simple apprehension than on judgment). Cf. Nos. 8 (note 1) and 36.

In a general way, the mind *produces or constructs in order to see and assent.* First, by means of abstraction, it forms a *mental concept* in which it sees or apprehends an essence (an objective concept, or the object of a concept). Then it *constructs* an enunciation (composition and division), to which in *apprehending* the real conformity or non-conformity of the S. and Pr., it may give its assent expressed in a judicative proposition.

In the same way, reasoning supposes that two previously constructed enunciations have been grouped and co-ordinated in such a manner as to form an *antecedent.* By reason of the two successive acts of *apprehension* or intellectual perception (and assent) that bear upon this antecedent, the mind is moved to *apprehend* or to perceive the necessary truth of a third proposition (the consequent) which it immediately *constructs* and to which it assents in a judgment wherein it rests.

It is therefore evident that, although the second operation of the mind, inasmuch as it *composes* or *divides,* that is, inasmuch as it constructs enunciations, is ordained to reasoning as to the most complex operation, nevertheless, the reasoning itself is ordained to the second operation of the mind—inasmuch as it is consummated or perfected in *judgment* or assent—as to the end of knowledge [1]: we reason (in making use of other judgments) *in order to judge* (in the conclusion).

The necessity of reasoning bespeaks the natural *imperfection* of the human mind. An intuitive intellect of the type possessed by pure spirits, apprehending at first glance all that can be known in an object, has no need for discourse: in knowing the principle it knows distinctly all the conclusions; it does not have to draw them bit by bit from the principle. Such an intellect sees *that* one truth follows from another, it knows the influence exercised by the antecedent upon the consequent (inference), but it does not do so *by moving* from something *known before* to something *known after.* The

[1] Cf. John of St. Thomas, *Phil. Nat.*, III, q. XI, a. 3, p. 516: "Secunda operatio, quantum ad enuntiationem, praebet materiam discursui, et ordinatur ad illum, sed secunda operatio quantum ad assensum et judicium est finis, et terminus ad quem ordinatur discursus, ut ad perfectionem, quam intendit."

human mind, however, when it reasons knows the inference only by living it, by submitting itself to the movement which it implies.

62. ARGUMENTATION, INFERENCE, SEQUENCE. As we have said, the argumentation is the logical organism formed by the antecedent and the consequent. Now we must define this notion more precisely.

We say that the antecedent INFERS (*infert*) the consequent, or that there is a real INFERENCE (*illatio*) from one to the other when the antecedent (supposed as true) necessarily implies the consequent, or, in other words, when it has the property of *being unable to be true unless the consequent is true.* It is for this reason that when our mind has laid hold of the antecedent as such, as involving the truth of the consequent, it cannot *not* perceive the truth of the consequent.

But our mind cannot grasp the antecedent as such unless the propositions [1] about which it is reasoning be disposed in a certain *order which manifests* the property in question.

Therefore we may define argumentation as :

The argumentation is a group of propositions one of which is signified as inferred by the others.

a group of propositions in orderly sequence one of which (the consequent) is posited as inferred by the others (the antecedent).

or, again, if we consider the argumentation in its oral expression : *oratio in qua uno dato aliud sequitur*—a discourse in which one thing being given, another is said to follow.

The sequence is the connection existing between two propositions th: signifies an infe.ence.

The SEQUENCE (*consequentia*) is none other than the argumentation taken in what we may call its most vital point, that is, in the relation which unites the antecedent and the consequent to one another. We may define it as : *a connection existing between two propositions necessarily linked together because the one infers the other, connexio illativa duarum propositionum.* [2]

In short a sequence may be called *the statement of an*

[1] We are speaking here not only of oral propositions but also, and *principally*, of the *mental* propositions that co-ordinate *concepts*. As Aristotle says (*Anal. Post.*, I, 10, 76 b, 25) the syllogism is not in the words but in the soul.

[2] By the connection of *two* propositions is meant the connection of the minor *as such* (*thought under the dependence of the major*) with the conclusion : " . . . but Peter is a man, therefore Peter is mortal." In a conditional proposition " if Peter is a man he is mortal" the sequence does not move the mind to pass from one affirmation to another, for the inference is itself the object of affirmation.

inference. We often say " inference " in the same sense as " sequence " or " argumentation." For clarity's sake, however, it is expedient to reserve the word " inference " (*illatio*) to indicate the antecedent's property of inferring the consequent, and to use the words " sequence " (*consequentia*) and " argumentation " to signify the connection between the propositions which presupposes this property. In such a case the sequence is *valid* if the property in question *exists*, that is, if there actually is an inference ; when, on the contrary, this property does not exist, the sequence is *invalid*.

63. VALID AND INVALID, MATERIAL AND FORMAL SEQUENCE. When there is an inference, when the antecedent really infers the consequent, we say that the argumentation or sequence is *valid*. (In this case the antecedent cannot be true without the consequent's being true.)

A sequence is *valid* when there is an inference

When there is no inference, when the antecedent does not really infer the consequent, the argumentation or sequence is *invalid*. (In this case the antecedent may be true without the consequent's being true. Example : " Man is mortal, but an angel is not a man, therefore an angel is mortal," " all living beings have the power of self-movement, but man is a living being, therefore man is a pure spirit." As a matter of fact, an invalid sequence is but a *pseudo-sequence* (it unites two propositions *as if* they were necessarily connected because one infers the other, whereas in reality this inference does not exist.) It deserves the name of sequence only by analogy, just as a corpse with a life-like appearance deserves the name of man only by analogy.

***invalid* when there is not.**

In every argumentation we must distinguish between the *matter* (the objective concepts assembled in the propositions) and the *form*, that is to say, the disposition of these same objective concepts, thanks to which their grouping signifies an inference, or more precisely *that disposition in which propositions and concepts are so arranged, according to quantity, quality and the other logical properties that they make known an inference.*[1]

The matter and form of the argumentation.

[1] " Forma est dispositio propositionum et terminorum secundum quantitatem et qualitatem, et alias proprietates logicales, in ordine ad inferendum unum ex alio." The " other logical properties " in question are the *suppositio*, the *ampliatio*, etc., of which we have spoken above.

*A sequence may be invalid as to form, and nevertheless valid as to matter, for example: " Every man is *rational*, but Peter is a man, therefore Peter has the *power of laughter*." There is inference here, but only by chance or " by accident " because it happens that everything that is rational has the power of laughter. But were we to say in using the same logical disposition (in having, in the conclusion, a predicate other than the predicate in the major) : " Every man is rational, but Peter is a man, therefore Peter is a musician," the sequence would be invalid. The same is true in induction ; for example, supposing that we had verified by a particular instance, the fact that man is mortal, but that we did not know that to be mortal or immortal is a predicate which of its nature depends *necessarily* upon the essential constitution of a thing, and that we said : " *One* man is mortal, *therefore every* man is mortal." The sequence is invalid as to form, but nevertheless valid as to matter, since mortality cannot be in one man without being in all men. There is an inference, but it exists only by chance, or " by accident," because it so happens that the attribute " mortal " is an essential attribute. (Were we to say in the same way that " *one* man is a knave, *therefore every* man is a knave," the sequence would be invalid.) Sequences like " every man is rational, therefore Peter has the power of laughter," or " one man is mortal, therefore every man is mortal " are said to be *materially valid*, or *material*.

A sequence is valid as to form, or FORMALLY VALID, when it is valid *by reason of the very disposition* or of the very order of the concepts which signify the inference. In this case the antecedent infers the consequent with a *universal* necessity *de jure*, whatever the matter may be (that is, once this disposition has been made, whatever the matter may be, the antecedent cannot be true without the consequent's also being true), and the sequence is valid because it denotes an inference. Needless to say Logic treats only of formally valid sequences.

When the sequence is valid on the side of form (" formally valid "), that is, when the manner in which the concepts

VALID OR INVALID, MATERIAL OR FORMAL SEQUENCE				
Sequence	valid (in which there is an inference)	*formal* (the only one studied in Logic)	Every man is rational therefore Peter is rational Every man is an angel therefore Peter is an angel	The conclusion is secure as to the manner in which it follows from the antecedent
		material	Every man is rational therefore Peter has the power of laughter Every man is an angel therefore Peter is immortal	The conclusion is not secure as to the manner in which it follows from the antecedent
	invalid—(in which there is no inference)		Every man is rational therefore Peter is a musician Peter is a miser therefore every man is a miser	

and propositions are co-ordinated according to their logical properties is such that the antecedent infers the consequent in virtue of the logical relations which obtain between the concepts so arranged, we say that the conclusion is posited *vi formae*, in virtue of the form. To study such sequences (which are the proper object of Logic) from the point of view of the form of the reasoning, the logician reduces them to types wherein the properties and logical relations alone are made clear, and the matter remains entirely indeterminate ; for example : Every B is C, but every A is B, therefore every A is C.

The expression *vi formae* (a conclusion posited *vi formae*) refers to the form of mental propositions, of which the form of the oral or written proposition is but the material sign. It means that the conclusion is posited in virtue of a *disposition of concepts* (*e.g.*, the concept " man " serving as a middle term between the concepts " mortal " and " Peter ") and that this disposition is such that, whether these concepts or any other concepts *having the same logical properties and the same disposition* be used, the evidence of the truth of the consequent necessarily imposes itself in an absolutely necessary manner on the thinking mind (if the antecedent is true). But it does not mean that the conclusion is posited in virtue of a disposition of oral or written *signs* which impose a mechanical necessity on a mind in which no intellectual perception is going on. If this point were always well understood we would be spared a great many mistakes and misunderstandings concerning Logic. Descartes, for instance, completely misapprehended the meaning of the expression *vi formae*. It is extremely curious to note that his criticism of the logic of the ancients [cf. *Regulae ad directionem ingenii*, reg. X (Vol. X, p. 705, *Œuvres de Descartes*, Cerf, Paris): " quasdam formas disserendi praescribunt, quae tam necessario concludunt ut illis confisa ratio, *etsi quodam modo ferietur ab ipsius illationis evidenti et attenta consideratione*, possit tamen aliquid certum ex vi formae concludere, etc."] exactly applies not to the Logic he was criticizing, but to the logical system which Leibnitz tried to build up, inspiring himself from Cartesian ideas (the theory of " simple natures," the idea of a universal philosophical language) and which has become the Logistics of our day.

*64. "SEQUENCE" AND "ARGUMENT" The distinction between these two notions is very important.

The *sequence* is concerned solely with the manner in which the consequent *follows* from the antecedent, prescinding from the value of the propositions in relation to what is and from the truth or contents of the propositions. It is concerned with the act of inferring (*illatio*).

The *argument*, on the contrary, refers to the action of proving (*probatio*). It is the means used to *establish a conclusion* in a *pure and simple* manner (absolutely speaking), taking into account not only the matter but also the form of the argumentation.

An argument may be either *demonstrative* or *probable*, but a sequence does not admit of such division ; it may only be either valid or invalid. And if a sequence is valid it is always and in every case *necessary* precisely because it is a sequence or inference.[1]

[1] Cf. John of St. Thomas, *Log.* I, P., Illustr., q. VIII, a. 1.

For example the following syllogism:

(I) Every son loves his mother,
(II) but Paul is a son
(III) therefore Paul loves his mother,

A *valid sequence* is always *necessary* as such, even if the *argument* is only *probable*.

is only a *probable* ARGUMENT. Why is this so?—Because the principle (I) stated of the antecedent is not a *necessary* truth—it is true only in the majority of cases and admits of exceptions. But the SEQUENCE is *necessary* as such, for inasmuch as the mind posits (I) and (II) it cannot not posit (III).

Thus every valid sequence is, as such, *necessary*, even when the argument is merely probable and deficient on the material side; in other words, a valid sequence is necessary even when the sequence is not necessary *in the sense* that it does not render the conclusion necessarily and infallibly true.

65. THE ESSENTIAL LAW OF ARGUMENTATION. I As we have already seen (No. 62) the essential law of (inductive or deductive) argumentation is—

From the true follows the true, never the false;

> *in a valid sequence it is impossible for the antecedent to be true and the consequent false*

or, in other words,

> *by the very fact that the antecedent is true the consequent is likewise true.*

This law is directly allied to the primary principle of reason (the principle of *identity: a thing is what it is*) which is expressed in Logic under the negative form of the principle of *non-contradiction: to be is not to not be; it is impossible for a thing to be and not be at the same time and under the same aspect.*

Indeed, to suppose that a true antecedent infer a false consequent would be to suppose that this *true* antecedent is *false* in *some respect* (in so far as it makes a false consequent appear to be true); and since, to be untrue it suffices to be false in some respect, this antecedent would be supposed as both true and not true at the same time.

Hence it follows that *if the sequence is valid and the consequent is false, the antecedent is necessarily false.*

2 Although a false consequent cannot follow from a true antecedent, yet

in a valid sequence a true consequent may follow from a false antecedent.

but sometimes from the false follows the true.

This would be the case, for example, in the following reasonings : " My purse is in the moon, but the moon is in my pocket, therefore my purse is in my pocket " ; " every square has three sides, but every triangle is a square, therefore every triangle has three sides." [1] Obviously such reasonings beget true conclusions only by chance.[2]

It follows that *even though the sequence be valid and the consequent true, the antecedent need not necessarily be true.*

(*a*) As a matter of fact, in order to be true in some respect it does not suffice to be *not* false ; a false antecedent may be *true in some respect* without for that reason being *not false* (that is, it may be true in so far as it makes a true consequent appear to be true). Thus the principle of contradiction does not prevent a true consequent from following from a false antecedent.

In such cases the false (a false antecedent) does not *prove*, *cause*, or *manifest* the true (the truth of the consequent). But the true may *follow* from the false by accident, in the sense that, supposing as true that which is not true and is alleged by the antecedent, something may follow therefrom which happens to be *true*, *but for other reasons.*[3]

(*b*) With the exception of these fortuitous cases, the antecedent normally *causes* the truth of the consequent, and therefore the antecedent, containing within it the

[1] Similarly in an argumentation with but one false premise, *e.g.*, " Every angel has free will, but every man is an angel, therefore every man has free will.

[2] Thus chance acting on the material side of the argumentation, may either make the true follow from an argumentation that is invalid on the formal side (see above n. 63, *material sequence*) or else it may make the true follow from a valid argumentation whose antecedent is false.

[3] " Ex falso dicitur sequi verum, non quia possit causari, vel manifestari per falsum, sed *quia stat bene* cum assensu falsae praemissae assensus verae conclusionis " (John of St. Thomas, *Log.*, I. P. Illustr., q. VIII, a. 1). Cf. Aristotle, *Anal. Pr.*, 1, II, c. 2 (53, b 7) ; St. Thomas, *in Metaph.*, I, II, lect. 2.

truth of the consequent, must be "truer," as Aristotle says, that is more certain, than the consequent.

B. DIVISION OF REASONING

66. THE DIFFERENT KINDS OF ARGUMENTATION. Argumentation is divided *essentially* into *two* kinds, according to the manner in which it manifests the truth. For there are but two ways in which we may manifest the truth. Either our mind takes as its starting-point the *first universal principles known immediately by the intelligence*, and links these principles to a conclusion, or " resolves " a conclusion into these principles ; in this instance the mind moves purely

There are two kinds of reasoning or argumentation: the *syllogism* and *induction*.

ON THE INTELLIGIBLE PLANE

and makes known the truth of the proposition in so far as it is contained in the *universal truth* from which it is derived.

Example : Everything that subsists immaterially is indestructible,
but the human soul subsists immaterially,
therefore the human soul is indestructible.

This is a *deductive argumentation*, or a

SYLLOGISM

in which the S. (the human soul) and the Pr. (indestructible) of the conclusion are united to each other *by their mutual union to a third term* called the *middle term* (" that subsists immaterially ").

Or our mind takes as its starting-point *sense data and the facts of experience*, which are the primary source of all our knowledge and belong to the order of the *individual* or *singular*. In this instance the mind moves

FROM THE SENSIBLE TO THE INTELLIGIBLE PLANE and

makes known the truth of a proposition in so far as it is the *universal* enunciation of which these singular data are the parts.

Example : this lot of water boils at 100°, this other does

the same, this other, and this other also . . . therefore water boils at 100°. This is *inductive argumentation* or

INDUCTION

in which the S. and Pr. of the conclusion are not united in virtue of their union to a third term, but in virtue of the enumeration of the " subjective " parts [1] of the subject.

The syllogism itself is either *categorical* or *conditional*.

There are, therefore, but two kinds of argumentation : the SYLLOGISM and INDUCTION (to which may be reduced the *example* and *reasoning by analogy* (see below, No. 100). [2]

The syllogism itself is divided into the *categorical* syllogism (the syllogism pure and simple) and the *conditional syllogism*, accordingly as it is founded on the identity of two terms with a same third term, or on the positing (or destruction) of one of the members of a conditional proposition (see below, Nos. 69 and 87).

Conditional propositions are already related to argumentation in the sense that they are precisely the affirmation of a sequence or inference. Nevertheless, they remain *propositions* and do not properly speaking constitute *argumentations* because they do no more than affirm that a proposition (be it true or false) infers another, without positing *a conclusion as true* in reason of this inference.

C. " IMMEDIATE INFERENCE "

read from here to 169

67. ARE THERE ANY IMMEDIATE INFERENCES ? It is often said that we make an immediate inference when we pass from the affirmation of a proposition, *e.g.*, " No man is an angel " to its *converse :* " therefore no angel is a man " or to the *negation* of its *contradictory :* " therefore *it is not true* that some man is an angel " ; that is, we say that in this case an inference or conclusion follows from the positing of *a single* proposition.

[1] See above, No. 13. The parts of a potential or logical whole (*e.g.*—*animal* in respect to its species, *man* in respect to Peter, John, etc.) are called *subjective* parts.

[2] Cf. Aristotle, *Anal. Pr.*, lib. II, c. 23, 68 b 13 : ἅπαντα πιστεύομεν ἢ διὰ συλλογισμοῦ ἢ ἐξ ἐπαγωγῆς.—*Anal. Post.*, lib. I, c. 18, 81 a. 40 : μανθάνομεν ἢ ἐπαγωγῇ ἢ ἀποδείξει. ἔστι δ' ἡ μὲν ἀπόδειξις ἐκ τῶν καθόλου, ἡ δ' ἐπαγωγὴ ἐκ τῶν κατὰ μέρος. (St. Thomas, lect. 30, 4). As we shall see later on, the attempts made by certain philosophers to reduce induction to the syllogism and to deny its essential originality as a type of reasoning, have all been futile.

This is true if we understand the word *inference* in an improper manner, simply as meaning the act of passing from one proposition to another proposition which follows from the first (the word *other* here refers only to the *disposition of the terms or concepts* in the proposition). Actually the proposition " no man is an angel " is not the same as " no angel is a man " and the mind sees immediately, without the need of having recourse to any intermediary, that if the first proposition is true the second is true also. But the fact is that these two propositions do nothing but *purely and simply signify the same truth ;* the mind *does not advance*, in passing from one to the other, for they are merely two different ways of saying the same thing, of constructing the same object of assent.

Therefore this in no respect constitutes an *inference properly so-called.* For in every inference properly so-called the mind passes from one proposition to an *other* proposition which follows from the first, the word *other* being here related *to the intelligible object itself which is presented to the mind.* The proposition " the human soul is indestructible," says *something else*, expresses *another truth*, than does the proposition, " Everything that subsists immaterially is indestructible." It is evident then that, when the word *inference* is taken in its proper sense, *there can be no immediate inference*.

When the word *inference* is taken in its proper sense (a passing from one truth to *another* truth) there is no such thing as an *immediate inference.*

For when the mind considers a single proposition, *e.g.*, " Everything that subsists immaterially is indestructible," it sees nothing else but this truth, therefore it cannot pass to a different truth. Only if it relates to this first known truth a second known truth—if, for example, it thinks the proposition " the human soul subsists immaterially " *under the dependence*, *and in the light of* the first truth : " Everything that subsists immaterially is indestructible "—may it proceed to a third truth by means of a vital act wherein the two premisses are seen together, and say " the human soul is indestructible "—a truth which it did not hitherto know as certain, and which it sees instantaneously *in the second truth as made fruitful by the first.* Therefore every inference properly so-called, every progressive act of the reason, every argumentation, supposes at least three propositions (two for the antecedent, one for the consequent), and therefore three terms.

*68. DISCUSSION OF THE INSTANCES OF SO-CALLED IMMEDIATE INFERENCE. Logicians ordinarily give as examples of immediate inference 1 simple and accidental conversion of propositions ; 2 subalternation ; 3 contraposition ; 4 passage from a proposition supposed as true to the negation of its contradictory or from a proposition supposed as false to the affirmation of its contradictory.

It is easy to see that in every one of these instances the mind employs the principle of identity or non-contradiction—but it does not do so to draw one truth from another, but, on the contrary, *to maintain one and the same truth* under two different logical formulations.

(1) In the case of simple conversion, the mind reflects on the manner in which the S. and Pr. are taken from the point of view of extension in the original proposition (it reflects on the *suppositio* of the extremes). In so doing it perceives that the SAME TRUTH (*e.g.*, There is a conformity between *man* and *liar* when each are taken particularly, or again there is no conformity between *man* and *angel* when each are taken universally), may be equally well expressed in a proposition *de inesse*, by assigning to the first term the logical function of S., and to the second term the logical function of Pr. (" some man is a liar," " no man is an angel "), or by assigning the function of S. to the second term and that of Pr. to the first (some liar is a man, no angel is a man). The mind grasps the same truth twice, for the same term is identified with the same term or separated from the same term in both cases, and the extension of these terms remains the same throughout.

(2) In the case of the accidental conversion of A, the mind sees likewise that THE SAME TRUTH (*e.g.*, there is conformity between *man* taken universally and *mortal* taken particularly) is equally well expressed in a proposition *de inesse* by taking the first term as S. (every man is mortal) or by taking the second term as S. (some mortal (being) is a man). The mind seized the same truth twice, although the second time it seized it in an implicitly partial or diminished manner, because Man, being the Pr. in the

second affirmative, is taken particularly therein. Having taken the universal *man* the first time according to all the singulars contained under it, in order to identify it with mortal, the mind took this same universal again in the second proposition to identify it with mortal, but this time it did not take it according to all the singulars contained under it.

(3) The accidental conversion of E comes into the case of subalternation, for, as we have seen, the partial converse of E is the subalternate of its simple converse.

(4) In the case of subalternation the mind sees immediately that once a certain truth has been constructed and stated, THE SAME TRUTH (*e.g.*, Every man is mortal) may be repeated in an explicitly partial or diminished fashion by taking the S. particularly instead of universally ; Some man is mortal.

The mind seizes the same truth both times ; having first seized the universal Man according to all its singulars in order to identify it with Mortal, it seizes it again for the same reason, but this time it takes it only according to some of its singular subjects (*individuum vagum*). It is of the very essence of this universal as such that its identification with Mortal according to all its singulars should also and by a single act be its identification with Mortal according to some of its singulars.

(5) In the case of contra-position the mind reflects on the extension of the extremes, and perceives that THE SAME TRUTH expressed by saying that everything included in A is also included in B (every A *is* B) may also be expressed by saying that everything exterior to B is also exterior to A (every non-B is non-A) ; just as it is the same to say that Paris is in France and to say that everything outside France is also outside Paris.[1]

[1] Likewise to say that a part of A is not included within the confines of B (" some A is not B ") is exactly the same as to say that part of that which is outside the confines of B is not outside the confines of A (" some not B is not not A," that is " some not B is A "). For example, to say that a part of Russia (namely Asiatic Russia) is not in Europe, is identical with saying that a part of that which is outside the confines of Europe (Asiatic Russia) is not outside Russia. Mr. Lachelier (*Études sur le syllogisme*, pp. 10–12, 16–17) has not understood that the true nature of contra-position consists in applying the negative particle *to the extremes* without changing the (affirmative or negative) quality of the copula.

(6) In the case of the opposition of contradiction the mind reflects upon the fact that one proposition flatly denies what the other affirms, and immediately sees that THE SAME TRUTH is expressed by the positing of the one (" every man is mortal ") and the destruction of the other (" it is false that some man is not mortal ") or by destruction of the one (" it is false that every man is sincere ") and the positing of the other (" some man is not sincere ").[1]

Consequently in none of these cases is there any *inference* properly so-called.

(*a*) However, this does not prevent us from *verifying* in every one of these cases that the change in logical structure does not affect the truth of the original proposition, but this matter of verification is the task of the logician, who would reason, for example, in the following fashion :

In the case of subalternation (Every man is mortal, therefore some man is mortal) :

That which is in every man is in some man
but mortal(ity) is in every man
therefore mortal(ity) is in some man.

In accidental conversion (Every man is mortal, therefore some mortal is man) :

That which is predicated, according to some one of its singular subjects, of every man, is identical, according to some one of its singular subjects, with man,
but Mortal is predicated of every man according to some one of its singular subjects,

[1] As Mr. Hamelin has remarked (*Syst. d'Arist.*, p. 166, note 1), it is begging the question to demonstrate the obvious fact that if a proposition is true its contradictory is false and *vice versa*, as Rondelet attempts to do in his *Theorie des propositions modales* (Paris, 1861, p. 141). On the other hand, in the case of the other two kinds of opposition, contrariety and sub-contrariety, it is by the intermediation of the opposition of contradiction that the mind passes from the affirmation of a true proposition to the negation of its *contrary* (Every man has a soul, therefore it is false that no man has a soul) or from the negation of a proposition supposed as false to the affirmation of its *sub-contrary* (it is false that some man is not mortal, therefore some man is mortal). In the former case the falsity of the (particular) contradictory : " some man has no soul," entails the falsity of the (universal) contrary : " no man has a soul " ; in the second case the truth of the (universal) contradictory : " every man is mortal " entails the truth of the (particular) sub-contrary : " some man is mortal."

therefore Mortal is identical with man according to some one of its singular subjects.

In simple conversion (no man is an angel, therefore no angel is a man) : that which is denied, according to all of its singular subjects, of all man, is separated, according to all of its singular subjects, from man, but Angel is denied, according to all its singular subjects, of all man, therefore Angel is separated according to all its singular subjects from man.

Such syllogisms are but verifications, subsequent explanations, or products of logical reflection, which must not be confused with the operation originally and naturally performed by the mind. As we have seen, this operation of which we have just been speaking is not an inference properly so-called, but is the simple passage, without progressive reasoning, from one logical structure to another expressing the same truth. The logician may subsequently develop this operation into a syllogism that is more *explanatory* than *illative* (a syllogism providing a formal verification but not a real proof),[1] but he does so by purposely taking as Major, a truth (*e.g.*, " that which is in all man is in some man ") to which the mind conforms *in actu exercito* without further explanation, because it seizes its application to the particular case immediately, even before it grasps its general truth (" Mortal(ity) is in all man, so it is in some man "). Actually this act does nothing but express that which is of the essence of universal terms as used by the mind.

(*b*) Drawing inspiration from the efforts of Ramus [2] and especially from those of Leibnitz,[3] Lachelier [4] asserts that subalternation, contra-position and (partial) con-

[1] The " demonstrations " of conversions, which proceed by reduction to the absurd, first proposed by Aristotle (*Anal. Pr.*, I, 2, 25 a, 14–26) and later by Theophrastus and Eudemus, and then by Alexander, are not proofs properly so-called but simple formal *verifications*. This point is understood neither by Rondelet in his *Theorie des Propositions modales*, nor by Ramus, who accuses Aristotle of circular reasoning because he " proves " syllogisms of the third figure by means of conversions, and " proves " conversions by means of syllogisms of the third figure.

[2] Ramus, *Animadvers. aristotelicae*, lib. XVII, ed. 1548, p. 373 *sqq*.

[3] Leibnitz, *New Essays on Human Understanding*, liv. IV, Chap. II, § 1.

[4] J. Lachelier, *Études sur le Syllogisme*, Part I.

version are in reality syllogisms of the first, second, and third figures, in which one of the premisses is understood by the mind but unexpressed.

Ingenious as this theory may be it must be rejected. It confuses the reasoning of verification constructed by the logician with the original operation of the mind thus verified. The former operation is neither a *mediate* inference or syllogism (on the contrary, the passage from one proposition to the other is immediate), nor an *immediate inference* (this passage, although immediate, consists in going from the same to the same).

Furthermore, this theory makes use of syllogisms in which one of the premisses (the one that is understood by the mind but not expressed) is an *identical* proposition. Thus, according to Mr. Lachelier, the partial conversion of the affirmative universal " All A is B, therefore some B is A " would in reality be this syllogism of the third figure (in Darapti) :

All A is A
but all A is B
therefore some B is A.

Likewise subalternation would be the following syllogism (in *Darii*) :

All A is B,
but some A is A,
therefore some A is B.

But, whatever Mr. Lachelier may say to the contrary, the propositions " All A is A," " Some A is A " (and all similar propositions which he uses in his theory, are *identical* propositions in reality as well as in appearance. All sane logic, that is to say all logic that works with concepts and objects of thought, not merely with words and signs, all logic that is really an art of thinking and not an algebra to dispense with thought, must absolutely refuse to use these purely tautological propositions which Leibnitz misused so grievously.

There will be no inconvenience in using the word " inference " in a broad sense, once it has been well established that, in the proper sense of the word, there is no such thing as an *immediate inference*, and that all the immediate passages from one proposition to another, generally given as examples of immediate inference are really two different formulations of one and the same truth. In this broad sense "inference" will be used to designate every passage from one proposition to a second proposition which is necessarily true if the first is true (even if these two propositions do nothing but state the same truth), and will also designate conversion, contraposition, etc., although in a more material than formal sense. Such is the traditional use made of this word by the ancients in their treatises *de consequentiis*.

SECTION 2. THE SYLLOGISM

A. THE CATEGORICAL SYLLOGISM

1. *General Notions*

In the syllogism, from an antecedent uniting two terms (T and t) to a third (M) a consequent is inferred, that unites these two terms to each other.

69. DEFINITION. What is the purpose of the syllogism? Not to order thought by ascending to the universal from the singular data of sense perception (for this is the task of induction), but to order thought *according to the connection between* (*universal*) *terms*.[1] Therefore syllogistic procedure consists essentially in inferring or deducing a proposition from an antecedent that reveals (in a third term) *the means* by which, *or the reason* for which, the two terms of this proposition must be united. The syllogism may be defined as [2]:

> *an argumentation in which,*
> *from an antecedent that unites two terms to a third,*
> *a consequent is inferred uniting these*
> *two terms to each other.*

The two terms united as S. and Pr. in the *conclusion* are

[1] The word *term* refers not only to the *oral term* here, but also to the concept itself signified by the oral term, and primarily to the *objective concept* or object of the concept.

[2] The definition given by Aristotle in the *Anal. Pr.* (I, 1, 24 b, 18): "Oratio in qua quibusdam positis, aliud quiddam diversum ab his, quae posita sunt necessario accidit, eo quod haec posita sunt." λόγος ἐν ᾧ, τεθέντων τινῶν, ἕτερόν τι τῶν κειμένων ἐξ ἀνάγκης συμβαίνει τῷ ταῦτα εἶναι, is undoubtedly true *par excellence* of the syllogism in the strict *sense* of the word, which is the perfect type of reasoning, but of itself it is applicable to *reasoning in general*, that is to the syllogism taken in *the broad sense* of the word as synonymous with argumentation (induction and the syllogism *stricto sensu*).

called *extremes.* Since the Pr. normally has a greater extension than the S., *the Pr. of the conclusion* is called the Major Extreme or the

MAJOR TERM (T).

T, t and M are the remote matter of the syllogism.

and *the S. of the conclusion*, the Minor Extreme or the

MINOR TERM (t).

The term to which each of these two terms, T and t, is united in the antecedent, and which is the means or reason of their union in the conclusion is called [1] the

MIDDLE TERM (M).

These three terms, T, t and M, are the *remote matter* of the syllogism.

As we have seen above (Chap. I, section 3, § 3, 24), in regard to the syllogism the *verb* in the proposition is not a term, but merely serves to *unite* the S. and Pr. When the syllogism is resolved into its elements, the verb is not *id in quod resolvitur*, but *id quod dissolvitur*.

The Major (prop. joining M and T) the Minor (prop. joining M and t) and the conclusion (prop. joining t and T) are the proximate matter of the syllogism.

The two propositions composing the antecedent, each of which unites one of the extremes to the Middle term, are called the

PREMISSES

of the syllogism. The premise containing the Major term (the term that becomes the Pr. of the conclusion) is called the

MAJOR.

The premise containing the Minor term (the term that becomes the S. of the conclusion) is called the

MINOR.

The Major, Minor and conclusion constitute the *proximate matter* of the syllogism.

From now on we may agree to designate the Minor term by the letter t, the Major term by the letter T, and the Middle term by the letter M. Thus, taking the classic example of

[1] The word *middle* should not be understood from the point of view of extension, in the sense that the extension of M is necessarily intermediary between that of T and t. This is true only in the *perfect moods* of the syllogism (see below, Nos. 77 and 78).

the syllogism, which logicians have chosen because of its excessive simplicity we have :

THE STRUCTURE OF THE SYLLOGISM

	M	T	
ANTECEDENT	Every man is	mortal	(*Major*)
	t	M	
	but Peter is a	man	(*Minor*)
	t T		
CONSEQUENT :	therefore Peter is mortal		(*Conclusion*)

(N.B.—In constructing a syllogism we must always take care to begin with the MAJOR, that is, with the premise containing the term (T) which will become the Pr. of the conclusion.)

It is evident now that the identification of Peter and Mortal with each other, by means of the M Man, is possible only because Man, which communicates Mortal to Peter, contains Peter in its extension. Whence is derived the property by which the syllogism is characterized : the syllogism is an argumentation in which, from the point of view of logical relations, we conclude from a more universal truth to a less universal truth contained in it.[1]

70. THE POINT OF VIEW OF EXTENSION AND THE POINT OF VIEW OF COMPREHENSION. As may be seen from the very names, Major term and Minor term, Major premise and Minor premise, we have designated the elements of the syllogism from the point of view of extension. Nothing could be more legitimate or more correct since this is merely a matter of assigning names, and the definitions of names are arbitrary.

Furthermore, logicians find that there are certain advantages to be gained by way of convenience and uniformity, in considering the syllogism *from the point of view of extension alone*. Especially does this enable them to give a geometrical representation of the syllogism. (Leibnitz and Euler are chiefly responsible for setting Logic off on this quest for visual schemas, such as were unknown to the ancient logicians.) This also is perfectly legitimate, since every proposition, whatever its nature, may be considered by logical reflection from the point of view of extension. Thus

[1] See below, No. 81.

we represent the extension of each of the terms of the syllogism by three circles (Euler's circles), and interpret the syllogism as follows :

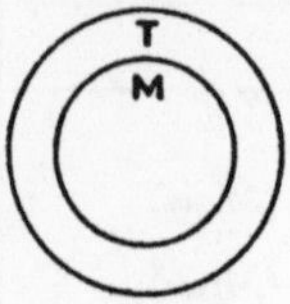

M T

(Maj.) Every man is mortal, *i.e.*, Man as a whole is a part of the extension of Mortal

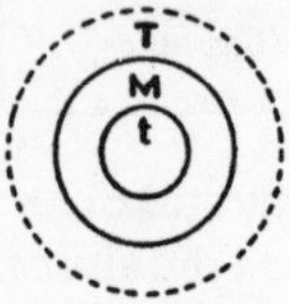

t M

(Min.) but Peter is a man, *i.e.*, Peter is a part of the extension of Man

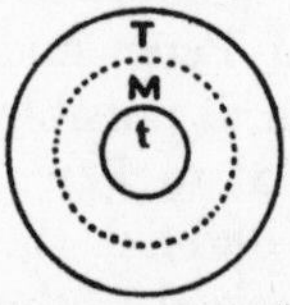

t T

(Concl.) therefore Peter is mortal, *i.e.*, Peter is a part of the extension of Mortal.

Since the middle circle is contained in the large one, and the small circle is contained in the middle one, the small circle is contained in the large circle.

This geometric representation is very convenient, yet it has some drawbacks. It risks substituting the *visual or sensible evidence of the relations of container to contained* for the *intelligible evidence* of the relation of *identification* of the two extremes to the middle term and consequently to each other. We must not forget that the judgment does not consist in declaring that one term is contained in the extension of another, but consists primarily in declaring that two terms, distinct as concepts, are *identical* in existence, and *only consequently* in making the one enter into the extension of the other. Nor should we think that the reasoning comes already made in the propositions presented to the mind, in such wise that the mind in reasoning simply ascertains that one drawer is in another which is in turn in a third. This ascertainment is the task of the logician reflecting upon the extension of the terms of the syllogism after the reasoning has been made. Reasoning is a vital act of the mind, for which the propositions grouped in the syllogism furnish but the matter. It is in seeing the identity of the t and the M in the Minor, under the dependence of the Major which identifies the M and the T, that the mind sees instantaneously that the t and the T are themselves identical *in re*. This is an act of intellectual perception which is in no way present beforehand in the materials of the syllogism; it reveals something new, and without it there would be only a series of words or concepts, only the matter of reasoning, but not the reasoning itself.

Note that in the case of *convertible* propositions (everything rational has the power of laughter, but man is rational, therefore man has the power of laughter) all three of Euler's circles coincide with each other from the point of view of the content of the propositions, and are included one within the other only from the strict point of view of the *logical relations* existing between the terms. (This latter is, however, the only point of view essential to the theory of the syllogism, see below, No. 81.)

Furthermore, it would be equally legitimate to consider the syllogism from the point of view of comprehension. That is to say that, although it is impossible [1] for logical reflection to dismiss all consideration of the extension of terms, yet it could very well consider affirmation in each proposition of the syllogism as including the Pr. in the comprehension of the S., and negation as excluding the Pr. from the comprehension of the S. (the while this Pr. and S. have certain logical properties from the point of view of extension). In this instance the logician would say, for example: Everything having human nature is mortal, Peter has human nature, therefore Peter is mortal. From this aspect the dispute between the *extensivists* (Leibnitz, Segner, Hamilton and the contemporary logisticians) and the *comprehensivists* (Lambert, Hamelin, Rodier) seems rather pointless.

But what is the actual procedure of the mind here? This question belongs to Psychology, not to Logic, and the confusion of these two points of view by many moderns has considerably obscured the issue. As we have said above, the mind, in judging, does but one thing directly, "explicitly," or in "signified act" (*in actu signato*) it identifies a Pr. and a S.; it is true, that simultaneously and by the same act it makes the S. enter into the extension of the Pr.,

[1] See above, No. 18.

or the Pr. enter into the comprehension of the S., but it does so only " in exercised act " (*in actu exercito*) and without saying it to itself. It is for this reason that he who has not *reflected* upon his act of reasoning does not know whether he has reasoned in extension or in comprehension. By making such a reflection, it becomes apparent that, as a matter of fact, everything depends upon the particular case, but that the more usual and natural procedure of the reason in making a judgment is to think that a certain note belongs to a certain subject. So, since the *logician* has the perfect right to develop the theory of the syllogism solely from the point of view of extension, the *psychologist* is equally justified in considering the reason as functioning ordinarily in comprehension.

To reason " in comprehension " is the more natural and fundamental procedure for the mind.

However, in many cases the reason alternates from the point of view of comprehension to that of extension. [This is clearly indicated in French, for ordinarily a Pr. thought from the point of view of extension is preceded by the indefinite article *a* (*un*). Thus everyday language says " Pierre est *un* homme " and not " Pierre est homme."] In the theory of the syllogism the logician may find it to his advantage to make use of a schema such as the following (wherein the Pr. is represented, as to comprehension, by the shading of the circle representing the S.).

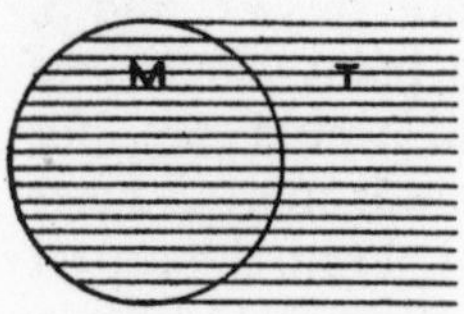

M T
(Maj.) Every man is mortal, *i.e.*, Every man has the attribute, mortality (from the point of view of comprehension).

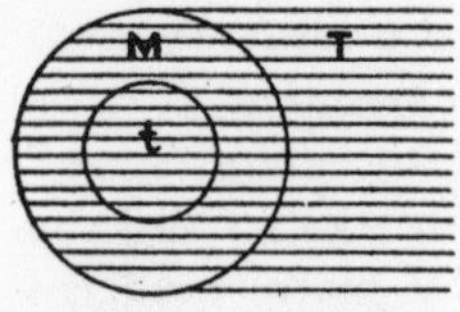

t M
(Min.) but Peter is a man, *i.e.*, Peter belongs to the human species (from the point of view of extension).

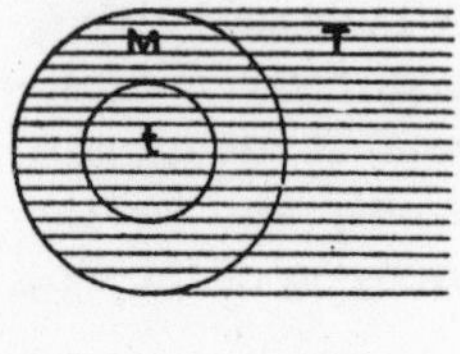

t T
(Concl.) Therefore Peter is mortal, *i.e.*, Peter has the attribute, mortality (from the point of view of comprehension).

Since the circle M is entirely shaded (T), the circle t which is contained in it is also shaded.

But let us not forget that it is one thing to reason and another to develop the theory of reasoning. Schemas, like Euler's circles, concern only the *reflection* which the art of Logic makes upon our reasonings in order to verify the conditions of legitimacy; they by no means pretend to impose a uniform type of procedure upon the *natural* movement of the reason. Those who accuse "classical Logic" of being a "Logic of extension"[1] err in failing to see that, whatever this procedure may be—whether we consider things "in extension" or "in comprehension" or alternately "in comprehension" and "in extension," the logical relations existing between the terms always remain the same and inevitably introduce conditions for legitimacy which depend upon extension, conditions which logical reflection cannot not take into account (nor does this make reasoning consist in enclosing boxes one within the other). The ancients were neither exclusively "extensivists" nor exclusively "comprehensivists." On the one hand, they emphasized the essential *rôle* played by the relations of "*extension*," in order to assure and guarantee the identification of the two extremes with the middle term, and in the theory of the syllogism they followed Aristotle in reflecting primarily upon the extension of terms. On the other hand, they said: *Praedicatum inest subjecto*, understanding thereby that the judgment has for its primary logical function the affirmation of the *inherence* of a Pr. in the comprehension of a S.; accordingly they called propositions *de inesse* inasmuch as they attribute a Pr. to a S. To indicate attribution, Aristotle says, not "A is B," but rather "to A belongs B" (τῷ *A* ὑπάρχει *β*) indicating that for him, as for his scholastic disciples, the judgment and the proposition are to be understood first and foremost from the point of view of *comprehension.*[2]

but whether the mind reasons "in comprehension" or "in extension" the logical properties of terms and propositions always remain the same.

71. THE SUPREME PRINCIPLES OF THE SYLLOGISM. All the

[1] Cf. Rodier *Les Fonctions du Syllogisme*, Année Philosophique, 1908. In truth, if Aristotelian logic has kept to the mean, "classical logic" among the moderns—especially since Leibnitz, seems indeed to have been impaired by exclusively extensivistic preoccupations.

[2] See above, No. 52.

force of the syllogism and the art of deduction depends upon this supreme, self-evident principle :

Principle of triple identity and the separating third.

> *Two things, identical with a same third thing are identical with each other ;*
> *two things, one of which is identical, the other not identical, with a same third thing, are different from each other.*[1]

This principle, which we may call the " principle of triple identity " in its positive form, and the " principle of the separating third " in its negative form, is but a particular expression of the principle of identity (a thing is what it is, every being has a determinate nature which properly constitutes it) or of the principle of contradiction (to be is not to not be, a thing cannot be both affirmed and denied at the same time and in the same respect.

Note that for the principle of triple identity : " two things identical with a same third thing are identical with each other " to be legitimate, the third thing must be THE SAME *re et ratione ;* not only in reality but also according to reason, lest it be taken under two different formal aspects, thus : " Nationality is an abstract notion, and my nationality is French, therefore an abstract notion is French " would be a defective reasoning, because nationality is identified with " abstract notion " and with " French " in two different senses. In the first instance " nationality " has a " logical " *suppositio* (substitutive value), in the second its *suppositio* is " real."

Likewise both the straight line $\overrightarrow{AB}$ and the straight line $\overleftarrow{BA}$ are identical with the same straight line $\overline{AB}$, in so far as this straight line contains these two different aspects virtually, but nevertheless we cannot identify $\overrightarrow{AB}$ and $\overleftarrow{BA}$ with each other. Similarly, as we shall see in natural philosophy, when two bodies interact, the *action* exercised by the one, and the *passion* undergone by the other, are each identical with one and the same *change*,

[1] *Principium identitatis et discrepantiae :* " *Quae sunt eadem uni tertio, sunt quoque eadem inter se : quorum unum cum tertio convenit, alterum ab eo discrepat, ea inter se diversa sunt.*"

but this change *proceeds from the agent* in one case, and is *received in the patient in the other*, so that this action and this passion are in no way identical with each other.

But the first principle of the syllogism may be applied to our reasonings—which have for matter abstract and universal concepts—only by means of two other equally fundamental principles which concern the relation of the universal concept with its subjective parts; to ignore them would be to destroy the syllogism:

1 *That which is universally affirmed of a subject is affirmed of everything contained under that subject.* ***Dictum de omni.***

This is called, after Aristotle, the *dictum de omni* (quidquid universaliter dicitur de aliquo subjecto, *dicitur de omni* quod sub tali subjecto continetur). To affirm universally of man that he is mortal, is by the same act to affirm the same of each individual human being.

2 *That which is universally denied of a subject is also denied of everything contained under that subject.* ***Dictum de nullo.***

This is called the *dictum de nullo* (quidquid universaliter negatur de aliquo subjecto, *dicitur de nullo* quod sub tali subjecto continetur). To deny universally of man that he is vegetal is thereby to deny the same of every individual human being.

These two principles are self-evident, since it is precisely the nature of the universal to be one and the same in all those things in respect of which it is universal—in other words, in all the things "contained under it." "Mortal," declared identical with "man," may be declared identical with "Peter" by means of this third term "man" only because the universal "man," which is one in the mind, is identified in reality with each human being, and therefore with Peter. Consequently what is affirmed of "man" must be also affirmed of each individual.[1] **The universal is the principle of the syllogism.**

Note that it is of the essence of the syllogism [2] that the third or middle term be a *universal* object of a concept.

[1] Cf. Aristotle, *Anal. Pr.*, I, 1, 24 b, 26.
[2] We are not speaking here of the *expository syllogism* (see below, No. 85) which is not a true syllogism.

For inasmuch as the middle term is the *cause* of, or *reason* for, the attribution of T to t, inasmuch as it communicates to a subject the predicate which is said of this subject in the conclusion, it must itself be *communicable* [1] to this subject; and whoso says "communicable to many" says "universal." That is why *the principle of the syllogism resides in the universal nature.*[2]

*Many modern logicians accuse the principle *dictum de omni* of considering only the *extension* of terms, and prefer to it a principle based solely on *comprehension* which they formulate as follows:

nota notae est nota rei ipsius,
repugnans notae repugnat rei ipsi.[3]

That which enters into the comprehension of a note (M) enters also into the comprehension of the subject possessing this note; that which is excluded from the comprehension of a note is also excluded from the comprehension of the subject possessing this note.

Thus in the syllogism "Every man is mortal, but Peter is a man, therefore Peter is mortal," "mortal" which enters into the comprehension of the note "man" also enters into the comprehension of the subject "Peter" which possesses this note.

This principle *nota notae* is assuredly true, but it is inadequate. 1 It does not make clear that which constitutes the essential force, the *raison d'être* of the syllogism,

[1] I say *communicable*. In a syllogism of the third figure: "Every man is fallible, but every man is an intelligent being, therefore some intelligent being is fallible," the M is the subject in both premisses, and therefore is not *communicated* to the t in the Minor. But it is *communicable* to the t (it suffices to *convert* the Minor to *communicate* it to the t, the truth expressed by the proposition remaining the same), and it is in virtue of this communicability of the M to the t that the T itself is communicated to the t. This is not the case in expository syllogisms (see below, No. 85); the converted Minor (*e.g.*, "some apostle was Judas") does not really communicate the M to the t here (for inasmuch as the M is singular it is incommunicable).

[2] Cf. Aristotle, *Eth. Nich.*, VI, 3, 1139 b, 28; ὁ δὲ συλλογισμὸς ἐκ τῶν καθόλου, *Anal Post.*, I, 18, 81 a, 40: ἔστι δ'ἡ μὲν ἀπόδειξις ἐκ τῶν καθόλου; *Metaph.*, M, 4, 1078 b, 24: ἀρχὴ δὲ τῶν συλλογισμῶν τὸ τί ἐστιν; Z, 9, 1034 a, 31: ὥσπερ ἐν τοῖς συλλογισμοῖς πάντων ἀρχὴ ἡ οὐσία. Ἐκ γὰρ τοῦ τί ἐστιν οἱ συλλογισμοί εἰσιν. Cf. *Anal. Post.*, II, beginning of 3. We shall meet this important thesis again in Major Logic.

[3] Cf. Kant, *über die falsche Spitzfindigkeit der 4 syll. Fig.*, § 2.—J. Lachelier, *Études sur le Syllogisme*.

viz., the *universal*. *Why* must the note Mortal which belongs to the note Man also belong to the subject Peter? . . . *Because* the note Mortal, like the note Man, is an objective concept communicable to many (a universal) and because, from the very nature of a universal, what is affirmed without restriction of Man must also be affirmed of all the subjects in which this universal is actualized. Thus the principle *nota notae* itself, presupposes the principle *dictum de omni*.[1] 2 By the very fact that it neglects the essential importance of the universal in the syllogism, the principle *nota notae* also neglects to make known the *conditions* which depend upon the *extension* of terms, and are indispensable for the validity of reasoning. "That which enters (by means of a judgment) into the comprehension of a note enters also into the comprehension of the subject possessing this note." By itself this principle does not tell us that this note (M) must be *taken universally* at least once in order for the syllogism to be valid. Given a defective syllogism, such as, "some man is a liar, but Peter is a man, therefore Peter is a liar"; were one to neglect to consider the extension of terms (and thus appeal implicitly to the *dictum de omni*), one might fancy that this syllogism satisfies the requirements of the principle *nota notae*; for the note Liar is certainly placed by the Major into the comprehension [2] of the note Man, which itself belongs to the subject Peter.

Thus the principle *nota notae* is not the true formulation of the supreme principle of the syllogism. The principle *dictum de omni*, on the contrary, is founded on the very nature of the universal (not that it considers extension

[1] Cf. T. Richard, *Philos. du Raisonnement dans la science*, Chap. VI.

[2] In the sense in which every judgment makes the Pr. enter into the "comprehension" of the S. See above, No. 52.—Undoubtedly *liar* does not enter into the comprehension of man taken in itself, but in constructing the theory of reasoning it is an error to consider the comprehension of concepts only as *taken in themselves*. The proposition and the judgment have the express power of making predicates that are not essential to it enter into the "comprehension" of the subject (whose concept is thus restricted or individualized). Since the proposition is the proximate matter of the reasoning, it is then absolutely necessary to take this fact into account in the theory of reasoning, and consequently to make clear the conditions for validity which depend upon the extension of terms, and which require that the Major in the first figure be universal.

exclusively, for the extension of a universal is a property that presupposes its comprehension, but what it does consider *directly* is the *communicability* of the universal to the subjects in which it is realized) ; and by that very fact it makes clear the *conditions* of validity which depend upon extension. Also, because it penetrates to the heart of the syllogism, this principle has universal jurisdiction over the syllogism, whereas the principle *nota notae* obtains only in regard to the first figure. To adopt the latter principle would entail the adoption of some other fundamental principle for each of the other two figures ; and we would have to say with Mr. Lachelier [1] that each of the three figures of the syllogism has a supreme principle proper to it, which would destroy the generic unity of the categorical syllogism. Mr. Lachelier is quite right in saying that syllogisms of the second and third figures are really valid by themselves and need not be *demonstrated*, even though they may be reduced to the first figure, as the imperfect to the perfect ; but the fact remains that they do not each have their proper supreme principle ; they simply require that the double supreme principle common to all three figures (*dictum de omni, dictum de nullo*) be particularized for each of them by a *special determination* (see below, No. 79, inset).

72. RULES OF THE SYLLOGISM. *But how must we proceed in order to apply* these supreme principles correctly? The answer to this question is contained in the *rules* or laws of the syllogism.

The principal rules which every valid syllogism must obey may be reduced to *three*.

Beware of reasoning with four terms,

1 *No syllogism may have more than three terms.* In the last analysis every syllogism defective on the side of the terms violates this rule.

Obviously if, instead of having T identical with M and t identical with M (three terms : middle term M), we have T identical with M and t identical with M′ (four terms : middle term M and M′) then T will not be identical with t.

[1] J. Lachelier, *Études sur le Syllogisme.*

2 *From two negative premisses no conclusion follows.*

or of using two negative premisses,

In order that T may be identified with t, T and t must be identified with M (in positive premisses).

In order that T may be declared non-identical with t, T must be said to be identical with M, and t non-identical with M (one positive premise, the other negative), or T must be said to be non-identical with M, and t identical with M (one negative premise, the other positive).

3 *From two particular premisses no conclusion follows.*

or of using two particular premisses.

As there is, in this case, *no term* (M) *which is taken universally* (*at least once*), so that this universal term, being itself identified with, or separated from, a T, may constrain the mind to affirm or deny this T of a t contained under it.

Logicians have laid down eight laws or rules of the syllogism, of which the *first four* concern *terms* and the *remaining four* concern *propositions*.

Rule I is the first one stated above and the following three may be reduced to it. Rules 5 and 8 are the last two stated above; and they are completed by rules 6 and 7, which are immediate applications of the supreme principles of the syllogism.

In order to facilitate the work of the memory logicians have had recourse to poetry and have formulated these rules in eight Latin lines:

1. *Terminus esto triplex: major mediusque minorque.*
2. *Latius hos quam praemissae conclusio non vult.*
3. *Nequaquam medium capiat conclusio oportet.*
4. *Aut semel aut iterum medius generaliter esto.*
5. *Utraque si praemissa neget, nihil inde sequetur.*
6. *Ambae affirmantes nequeunt generare negantem.*
7. *Pejorem semper sequitur conclusio partem.*
8. *Nil sequitur geminis ex particularibus unquam.*

1. *Only three terms, Major, Middle and Minor.*
2. They must never be broader in the Conclusion than in the Premisses.
3. The Middle Term must never enter into the Conclusion.
4. But it must be universal at least once.
5. *From two negative premisses nothing follows.*

6. When the premisses are affirmative, the conclusion must not be negative.
7. The Conclusion always follows the inferior Premise.[1]
8. *From two Particulars nothing follows.*

*(*a*) RULE 1. Do not say: "The *bull* bellows,
but the *bull* is a constellation,
therefore a constellation bellows."
Nor: "*Animality* [2] is a generic notion,
but man often cedes to *animality*,[3]
therefore man often cedes to a generic notion."

RULE 2. Do not say: "Birds fly,
but birds are *animals*,
therefore *every animal* flies."

(In the minor, *Animals* is taken *particularly*, being the Pr. of an affirmative proposition, in the conclusion it is taken *universally*. Therefore the syllogism really has *four terms* and violates the first rule.)

Nor: "The mind is *endowed with activity*,
but matter is not mind,
therefore matter *is not endowed with activity*."

(In the major the T is taken particularly, because it is the Pr. of an affirmative, but in the conclusion it is taken *universally* because it is the Pr. of a *Negative*.)

Nor: "Everything that thinks exists,
but no corporeal substance thinks,
therefore no corporeal substance exists."

RULE 3. Do not say: "Every plant is a *living thing*,
but every animal is a *living thing*,
therefore *every living thing* is a plant or an animal."

(This syllogism violates the second rule.)

[1] That which we are calling the *inferior* part or premise here is the *negative* or *particular* premise.

[2] Logical *suppositio*.

[3] Real *suppositio*.—A syllogism may in reality have four terms even though it apparently or verbally has but three, if a word is taken in two different senses, or if, having properly speaking the same *signification*, it "stands for" different things.

RULE 4. Do not say: "Some *men* are saints,
but criminals are *men*,
therefore criminals are saints."

(In the major, *men* is taken particularly and stands for *certain* (*good*) *men*; in the minor it is also taken particularly, but stands for *certain* (*bad*) *men*. Therefore t is identified with one part of M, and T with *another part* of M, and the reasoning thus has in reality four terms.)

Do not say: "Animals are irrational,
but man is an animal,
therefore man is irrational."

(In the major the indefinite term "*animals*" stands for *certain animals* (beasts).)

Nor: "Every plant is alive,
but every animal is alive,
therefore every animal is a plant."

RULE 5. Do not say: "The powerful are not merciful,
but the poor are not powerful,
therefore the poor are merciful."

(If neither of the terms is applicable to the third term, it is obvious that we cannot infer that the extremes are or are not united to each other.)

RULE 6. Do not say: "Everything that offends God must be hated,
but every lie offends God,
therefore some lie must not be hated."

RULE 7. Do not say: "Every sin against charity must be avoided,
but some severity sins against charity,
therefore all severity must be avoided."

(This syllogism violates rule 2.)

Nor: "No human device can be absolutely perfect,
but the social order is a human device,
therefore the social order can be absolutely perfect."

RULE 8. Do not say : " Some men are virtuous,
but some evil-doers are men,
therefore some evil-doers are virtuous." [1]

(This violates rule 4.)

Nor that : " Some intelligent creature is mortal,
but some corporeal living beings are not intelligent creatures,
therefore some corporeal living beings are not mortal."

(This syllogism violates rule 2. The Pr. is taken particularly in the major, universally in the conclusion.)

It is easy to see that these eight rules derive from the very nature of the syllogism, as more particular determinations of the supreme principle : *Two things identical with a same third thing are identical with each other, two things, one of which is identical, the other not identical with a same third thing, are different from each other*, and the two principles that are joined to it (*dictum de omni, dictum de nullo*).

They do not add anything new to these principles, but they are of practical utility because they regulate the syllogism at closer range.

*(*b*) EXERCISE. (1) Indicate whether or not the following syllogisms are defective, and, if so, which rules they transgress :

I Every great truth is difficult to understand,
but Schelling's System is difficult to understand,
therefore Schelling's system is a great truth.

II The Encyclopedists are poor philosophers,
but the Encyclopedists are French philosophers,
therefore French philosophers are poor philosophers.

[1] A syllogism such as :

some mushrooms are poisonous,
but some vegetables are mushrooms,
therefore some vegetables are poisonous,

is really defective and violates rule 4. The conclusion is true only by accident in virtue of the matter, because it so happens that the M is a part of the t. To reason correctly in such a case, we would have to say :

some mushrooms are poisonous,
but every mushroom is a vegetable,
therefore some vegetable is poisonous.

(Syllogism of the third figure, in *Disamis*.)

III Some French philosophers are good philosophers,
but the Encyclopedists are French philosophers,
therefore the Encyclopedists are good philosophers.

IV Delicate people are unfortunate,
but poets are delicate people,
therefore poets are unfortunate.

V Everything useful to man is good,
but sidereal astronomy is not useful to man,
therefore sidereal astronomy is not good.

VI Some fearlessness is virtuous,
but impudence is fearlessness,
therefore impudence is virtuous.

VII Everything that turns us away from God is evil,
but some joys turn us away from God,
therefore every joy is evil.

(2) Find examples of syllogisms that transgress the various syllogistic rules.

2. *Figures and Moods of the Syllogism*

73. THE FORM OF THE SYLLOGISM. Like every work of art the syllogism is made up of a *matter* and a *form*. As we have seen above (No. 69) the matter of the syllogism is double: *remote matter* (the terms) and *proximate matter* (the propositions).

The *figure* of a syllogism is the disposition of the terms in the premisses.

The form (in the broad sense) of the syllogism corresponds to this double matter, and is also double:

THE DISPOSITION OF THE TERMS in the premisses, according to which one is the S. and the other the Pr.[1] is called the *Figure* of the syllogism.[2]

THE DISPOSITION OF THE PROPOSITIONS themselves according to quantity and quality is called the *Mood* of the syllogism.

The *mood* of the syllogism is the disposition of the premisses themselves in the argumentation.

[1] "Dicitur figura ordo trium terminorum secundum subjectionem et praedicationem" (*Sum. Logicae*, X, 4). This definition is not taken from the simple *grammatical position* of the terms in the oral proposition, but from something much more fundamental,—namely from the *logical relations* implied *in thought* by the function of Pr. and S. In the strict sense the form of the syllogism is the *inference*.

[2] The word "figure" is used by analogy with the triangular "figure." In the triangle three points unite three lines, in a syllogism three terms unite three propositions. And just as there are three kinds of triangles (equilateral, isosceles, and scalene) so will there be three figures of the syllogism.

There are three syllogistic figures.

74. DIVISION OF THE SYLLOGISM BY REASON OF ITS FIGURE. In how many different ways may we dispose the terms in the premisses of a syllogism?

The M may be

Sub-prae.

(I) S. in the Major
and Pr. in the Minor,

or else

Prae-prae.

(II) Pr. in the Major
and Pr. in the Minor,

or

Sub-sub.

(III) S. in the Major
and S. in the Minor.

Thus there are three figures of the syllogism: they may be represented by the abbreviations: *sub-prae* [1] (first figure), *prae-prae* (second figure), *sub-sub* (third figure):

Sub-prae prima, bis prae secunda, tertia sub bis.

Finally the M may be

Pr. in the Major
and S. in the Minor.

This is the *indirect first figure, prae-sub*.

There are no other possible combinations. Thus we have the four following dispositions:

THE FIGURES OF THE SYLLOGISM

	First Figure *sub-prae*	Second Figure *prae-prae*	Third Figure *sub-sub*	Indirect First *prae-sub*
Maj. =	M. . T	T . . . . M	M. . . . T	T . . . . M
Min. =	t . . M	t . . . . M	M. . . . t	M. . . . t
Concl. =	t . . T	t . . . . T	t . . . . T	t . . . . T

The indirect first figure is also called the *Galenic* figure from the physician, Galen (A.D. 131–200), who is said to have considered it as a separate figure (a fourth figure). Aristotle and all the ancient logicians refuse to consider it as a distinct

[1] That is to say, the middle term is *sub*jectum (in the Major) and *prae*dicatum (in the Minor).

figure because it always concludes *indirectly*,[1] and thus to conclude directly must of its very nature be reduced to the first figure. It is in reality but the first figure concluding indirectly by the transposition of the premisses.

M T Every man is mortal t M but Peter is a man t T therefore Peter is mortal	First Figure

By inverting the premisses, that is by making T of t, and t of T, we have :

T M Peter is a man M t but every man is mortal t therefore some mortal is T Peter	Indirect First Figure

[1] A proposition is *indirect* or *unnatural* (*e.g.*, " some mortal is Peter," cf. No. 52, note 30) when the term to which the mind *really* applies a determination is not the subject of the proposition, as it should be, but the predicate. In this case, it is more a grammatical than a logical Pr., and seems to have a smaller extension than the S. of the proposition—(although as a matter of fact the extension of both S. and Pr. are equal because they both " stand for " exactly the same thing). Thus a syllogism of the fourth figure is said to conclude indirectly because the Conclusion of such a syllogism has for its S. the term which in the natural order would be the Pr. ; in other words, the t (of the direct figure) is the Pr. of the indirect figure, and the T (of the direct figure) is its S.

It is evident then that, although the fourth figure is a *grammatical* figure it is not a distinct *logical* figure : in that which concerns *thought* the grammatical predicate of the conclusion is in reality its *subject*. For this reason every true logician must reject the fourth figure and consider it only as the indirect first. The theory attributed to Galen by the Arabs (" although," as Leibnitz remarks —*New Essays on Human Understanding*, Bk. IV, Chap. II, § 1,—" we found nothing concerning it in the works of his remaining to us ") may be regarded as the first concession made by Logic in face of the temptation to consider words rather than thought, a *fatal* temptation which had already beset it for a long time (Alexander of Aphrodisus was already saying : *οἱ δὲ νεώτεροι ταῖς λέξεσιν ἐπακολουθοῦντες, οὐκέτι δὲ τοῖς σημαινομένοις*, *ad Anal. pr.* f. 154 A) and to which it has completely abandoned itself at the hands of many moderns. As Lachelier remarks (note written for Rabier's *Logic*, p. 66) : Galen's radically false idea " was combated by all the logicians of the Middle Ages, and began to come into favour only during the Renaissance." [N.B. This is not Lachelier's note, but Rabier's own statement, and is to be found in the text, not in a note, *Logic*, p. 66, Paris, 1886, Hachette. Tr.]

The conclusion is an indirect proposition.

Be careful not to mistake a syllogism such as : " Peter is a man, but every man is mortal, therefore Peter is mortal," for a syllogism of the indirect first figure. This is simply a *badly constructed* syllogism of the first figure ; for since Peter is the S. of the Conclusion, and consequently t, the premise " Peter is a man " is the Minor (the premise containing the t and the M) and should therefore come second (see above, No. 69 N.B.).

75. DIVISION OF THE SYLLOGISM BY REASON OF ITS MOOD. Let us consider the *mood*, that is, the disposition of the premisses themselves according to quantity and quality. From this point of view how many possible combinations are there? Each of the two premisses may be universal and affirmative (A), universal and negative (E), particular and affirmative (I), particular and negative (O) : thus we have four cases in which to consider the Major, and in each of them, four cases in which to consider the Minor ; in all—sixteen combinations *possible a priori*.

Major:	AAAA	EEEE	IIII	OOOO
Minor :	AEIO	AEIO	AEIO	AEIO

There are sixteen possible moods for each figure.

As each of these sixteen moods may be found in each of the four figures, the total number of possible combinations is $16 \times 4 = 64$.

But are all these combinations *legitimate* ? No, a great many of them violate one or more of the rules of the syllogism, as may easily be seen upon analysis.

For example, the combination A E in the first figure (wherein the M is the S. of the Major and the Pr. of the Minor).

(A) *Every* man *is* an animal,
(E) but *no* horse *is* a man,
therefore . . . , obviously no conclusion can follow ; the Conclusion, which should be negative (rule 7), " No horse is an animal," would violate rule 2.

The invalidity of each of the forty-five illegitimate moods of the syllogism may easily be verified in the same way.

As a matter of fact there are but *nineteen legitimate combinations :* **But of the sixty-four possible moods only nineteen are conclusive.**

4 for the first figurc
5 for the indirect first
4 for the second
6 for the third figure.

Logicians have grouped these nineteen legitimate moods of the syllogism in four famous lines that are truly a mnemotechnical masterpiece. The *first three vowels* [1] of the conventional words of which these lines are composed, represent in order [2] the *Major*, the *Minor*, and the *Conclusion*, which, as we know, may be either A, E, I or O. Certain *con-*

[1] When these conventional words have more than three syllables, *e.g.*, *Frisesomorum*, the extra syllables are but stopgaps, and have no symbolic meaning.

[2] An exception is made for the words relating to the moods of the indirect first figure, the *first* vowel of which stands for the MINOR, and the second for the MAJOR (due to the fact that the proposition which is the Major in the first figure is the Minor in the indirect first). Thus a syllogism in *Celantes* would be :

	M t	
CE	No philosopher is an angel,	(Min.)
	T M	
LAn	but Descartes is a philosopher,	(Maj.)
	t T	
TEs	therefore no angel is Descartes.	

This may be reduced to the first direct figure (*Celarent*) by purely and simply restoring to the first proposition its function as Major (that is by making angel the T, and Descartes the t).

	M T	
CE	No philosopher is an angel	(Maj.)
	t M	
lA	but Descartes is a philosopher	(Min.)
rEnt	therefore Descartes is not an angel.	

A syllogism in *Baralipton* (every artist is imaginative, but every poet is an artist, therefore some imaginative (being) is a poet) may likewise be reduced to a syllogism in *Barbara* (every artist is imaginative, but every poet is an artist, therefore every poet is imaginative). Note that the conclusion of the syllogism in *Baralipton* (affirmative, hence its Pr. has a *particular suppositio*) may be legitimately converted into the *universal* conclusion of the syllogism in *Barbara* only because *it already was this same universal conclusion* formulated in an indirect proposition (cf. Javelli, *Logicae compendium peripateticae*, Venetiis, 1541, tract. sextus, cap. II). Therefore the logicians who hold that the fourth figure is a distinct and separate figure should not consider the reduction of *Bamalip* to *Barbara* as valid.

sonants also have a meaning of their own, as we shall see further on. The figure of the syllogism, however, is not indicated in these lines. We have to remember that the first four words relate to the first figure, the next five to the indirect first, etc.

Here is the mnemonic formula [1]:

First figure. Barbara, Celarent, Darii, Ferio.//
Baralipton, Celantes, Dabitis, Fapesmo,
Frisesomorum.// . . . . First indir.

Second figure. Cesare, Camestres, Festino,
Baroco.//Darapti, Felapton, Disamis,
Datisi, Bocardo, Ferison . . . . Third figure

Remember that in the syllogism every singular term is equivalent to a *universal* term, in the sense that, since its extension is restricted to one determinate individual it evidently embraces the entire extent of the subject it signifies without having its own already restricted extension restricted the more. From this point of view " Peter is a man," " Descartes is a philosopher " equals an affirmative proposition (A), and the syllogism : " Every man is mortal, Peter is a man, therefore Peter is mortal " is a syllogism in *Barbara*. For this reason the theory of the syllogism takes into account only universal propositions (into which are assimilated singular propositions) and particular propositions.[2]

[1] The modern logicians, who hold that the fourth is a distinct figure, arrange the mnemonic formula of the legitimate moods of the syllogism in the following manner :

Barbara, Celarent, *primae* Darii Ferioque.
Cesare, Camestres, Festino, Baroco *secundae*.
Tertia grande sonans recitat : Darapti, Felapton,
Disamis, Datisi, Bocardo, Ferison, *Quartae*
Sunt Bamalip, Calemes, Dimatis, Fesapo, Fresison.

In this arrangement the words relating to the fourth figure, like those of the other figures (*Bamalip*, etc.) represent the Major by their first syllable, and the Minor by their second. Thus a syllogism in *Calemes*, for example, would be :

	T M	
cA	Descartes is a philosopher	(Maj.)
	M t	
lEm	but no philosopher is an angel	(Min.)
Es	therefore no angel is Descartes.	

[2] It is nevertheless obvious that a singular affirmative proposition used as Major would in no way equal an A proposition. A syllogism such as " *this man is a liar*, but Peter is a man, therefore Peter is a liar," is not a syllogism in *Barbara*, but a defective syllogism violating rule 4.

In order to construct one of the syllogisms to which each of those conventional words is a key, begin by constructing the schema of the *figure* which will indicate the place of M in the premisses ; then, with the help of the characteristic vowels of the key word, write in the quantity and the quality of each proposition (the *mood* of syllogism). Finally, fill in this framework with three suitable concepts.

For example, let us construct a syllogism in Baroco (a syllogism whose unnatural turn of expression clearly shows the derivation of the word *baroque*). Since this syllogism belongs to the second figure (*prae-prae*) we will have :

(Maj.)	T	M
(Min.)	t	M
(Concl.)	t	T

The characteristic vowels of the key word indicate the following quantity and quality :

(Maj.)	T	M
bAr	Every.................	is.........
(Min.)	t	M
Oc	But some...........	is not......
(Concl.)	t	T
O	therefore some......	is not......

Now it is easy to find appropriate terms with which to fill in this framework,[1] *e.g.* :

Bar Every bird has wings,
oc but some vertebrate does not have wings,
o therefore some vertebrate is not a bird.

N.B.—These are purely logical exercises which have as their purpose the familiarization of the mind with the *form* of the syllogism, abstracting from the intrinsic value

[1] It is easier to do this by beginning with the conclusion. For example, given " Some man is not a liar "—place the t (some man) and the T (liar) in their proper positions in the premisses : " Every liar is . . . , but some man is no. . . . Now there remains only to find a suitable M, for instance : " lazy."

of the content, which, on the contrary, is chosen from among the simplest and commonest things in order to facilitate this task. Therefore it would be utterly absurd to pretend to judge the value of the syllogism as an instrument of scientific progress from such exercises and examples.

We might add that these exercises are among the most useful of intellectual gymnastics, and, moreover, extremely fascinating to anyone interested in discovering the mechanism of his own thought. Playing at constructing syllogisms in different moods could be as entertaining a " parlour game " as anagrams—and we recommend it as such to students.

*76. LEGITIMATE MOODS OF THE FIRST FIGURE (*sub-prae*). The schema of this figure is :

M . . . . . . T
t . . . . . . M
———————————
t T

Legitimate moods of the first figure.

A < A—A, I—I

E < A—E, I—O

Special rule for the first (direct) figure : In the first (direct) figure, the Major can never be particular, nor the Minor negative.[1] (*If the Major* were particular, and the Minor affirmative, rule 4 would be violated. If the Minor were negative, we should have—rule 7—a negative conclusion, and then we would be violating rule 2 or 5.) In applying this special rule it is easy to see how, of the sixteen combinations that are *possible a priori* for the first figure, only four are valid : AAA, EAE, AII, EIO.

First Mood

M T
Bar EVERY LIVING BEING BREATHES,
t M
ba BUT EVERY PLANT IS A LIVING BEING,
t T
ra THEREFORE EVERY PLANT BREATHES.[2]

[1] *Sit minor affirmans, nec major particularis.*

[2] Despite appearances a syllogism such as " That which is not composed is of itself indivisible, but the soul is not composed, therefore the soul is of itself indivisible," is a valid syllogism in *Barbara*. For the Minor is only apparently negative ; it really means : " the human soul *is* a thing which is not composed."

From the point of view of *extension* this syllogism may be represented as :

Bar 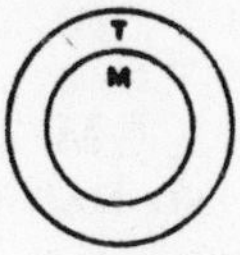

M is in T

ba 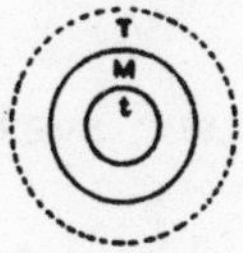

t is in M

ra 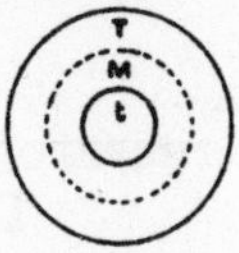

t is in T

Considering the Major and the Conclusion from the point of view of comprehension, and the Minor from the point of view of extension (see above, No. 70) we have the following schema (wherein the Pr. of the Major, in this case the T), is represented by the shading on the S. of the Major, in this case the M.

Bar 
M has the attribute T

ba 
t is in M

ra 
t has the attribute T

Second Mood

Schema in extension | Schema in comprehension and extension

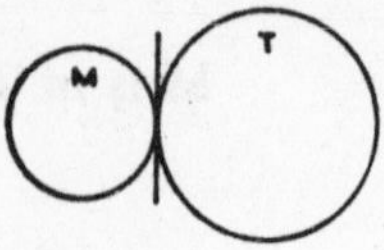

Ce M T
NO MAN HATES LIFE

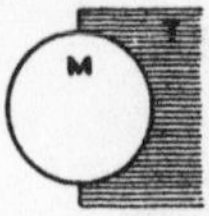

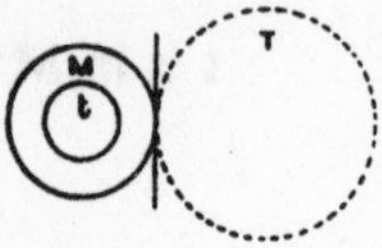

la t
BUT EVERY MANIAC IS
M
A MAN

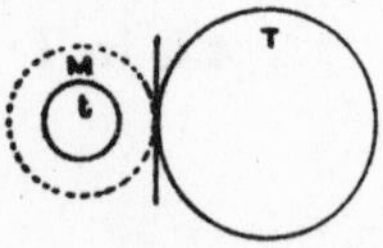

rent t
THEREFORE NO MANIAC
T
HATES LIFE

Third Mood

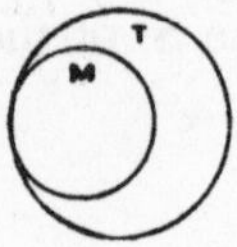

Da M
ALL THAT ENCOURAGES
T
EVIL IS PERNICIOUS

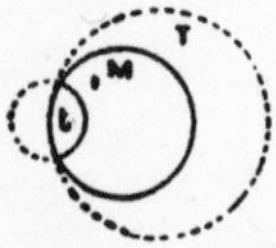

ri t
BUT SOME INDULGENCE
M
ENCOURAGES EVIL

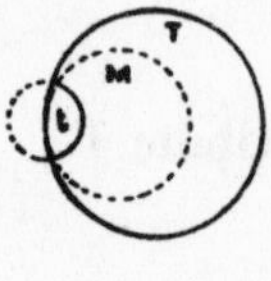

i t
THEREFORE SOME INDULGENCE
T
IS PERNICIOUS

Fourth Mood

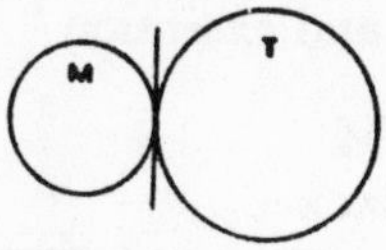

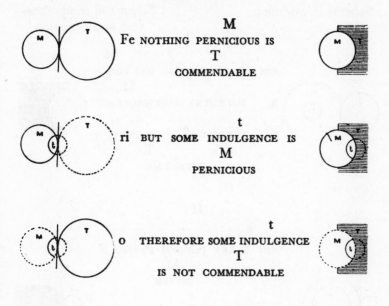

M
Fe NOTHING PERNICIOUS IS
T
COMMENDABLE

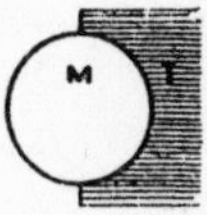

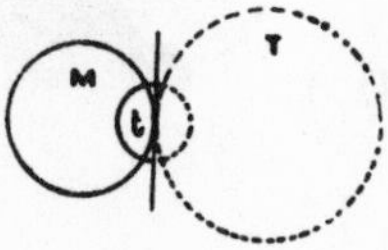

t
ri BUT SOME INDULGENCE IS
M
PERNICIOUS

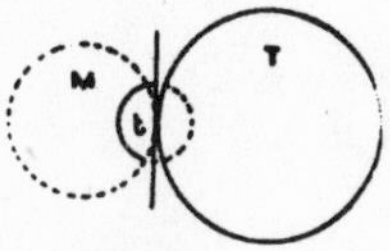

t
O THEREFORE SOME INDULGENCE
T
IS NOT COMMENDABLE

*77. LEGITIMATE MOODS OF THE SECOND FIGURE (*prae-prae*). The schema of this figure is :

T	M
t	M
t	T

Special rule for the second figure : In the second figure one of the premisses must be negative, and the Major cannot be particular.[1] (If the two premisses were affirmative, the M would be the Pr. in both premisses and we would violate rule 4. If the Major were particular, we would violate rule 2.) By applying this special rule, and the general rule 5, it is easy to see why, out of the sixteen combinations possible *a priori* for the second figure, only four are valid : E A E, A E E, E I O, A O O.

Legitimate moods of the second figure

A < E—E / O—O

E < A—E / I—O

[1] " *Una negans praeeat, nec major sit specialis.*"

I

Schema in extension	Schema in comprehension and extension[1]

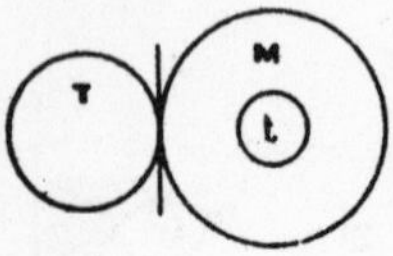

T M
ces NO BITTER MAN HAS PEACE
t M
a BUT EVERY SAINT HAS PEACE
t
re THEREFORE NO SAINT IS A
T
BITTER MAN

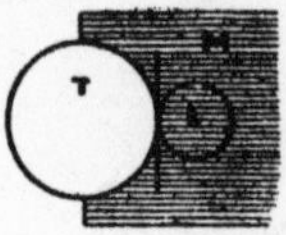

II

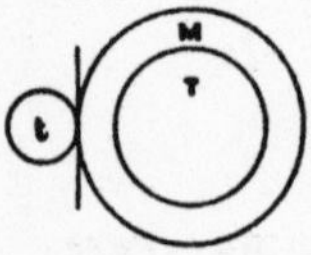

T
cam EVERY JEALOUS PERSON IS
M
BITTER
t M
es BUT NO SAINT IS BITTER
t
tres THEREFORE NO SAINT IS A
T
JEALOUS PERSON

III

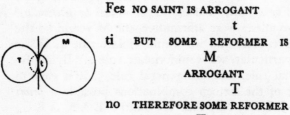

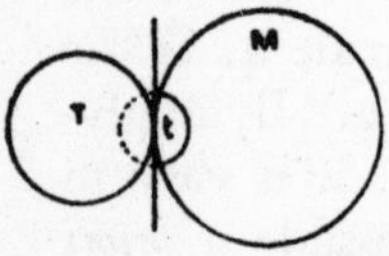

T M
Fes NO SAINT IS ARROGANT
t
ti BUT SOME REFORMER IS
M
ARROGANT
T
no THEREFORE SOME REFORMER
T
IS NOT A SAINT

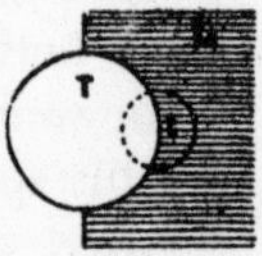

[1] Here the shading represents M (the Pr. of the Major).

IV

T M

Bar EVERY FOOL IS ANNOYING

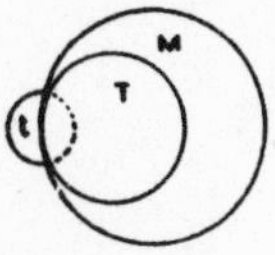

t

OC BUT SOME CHATTER-BOX IS

M

NOT ANNOYING

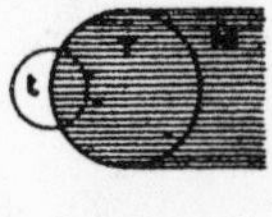

O THEREFORE SOME CHATTER-BOX IS NOT A FOOL

78. LEGITIMATE MOODS OF THE THIRD FIGURE (*sub-sub*). The schema of this figure is :

M . . . . . . T
M . . . . . . t
———————————
t T

Special rule for the third figure : In the third figure the Minor must always be affirmative and the Conclusion particular.[1] (If the Minor were negative, the Major would be affirmative—rule 5—and the Conclusion negative—rule 7—then the T would be taken particularly in the Major, and universally in the Conclusion, and we would violate rule 2. If the Conclusion were universal, the t would be broader in the Conclusion than in the Minor, which would also violate rule 2. In the Minor the t is, in fact, taken particularly, since it is the Pr. of an affirmative.)

Legitimate moods of the third figure
A < A—I, I—I
E < A—O, I—O
I—A—I
O—A—O

By applying this special rule and the general rule 8, it becomes apparent that, of the sixteen combinations possible *a priori* for the third figure, only six are legitimate : A A I, E A O, I A I, A I I, O A O, E I O.

[1] " *Sit minor affirmans, conclusio particularis.*"

I

Schema in extension

Schema in comprehension and extension.[1]

M
Da EVERY CENTAUR IS
T
HALF-MAN, HALF-HORSE

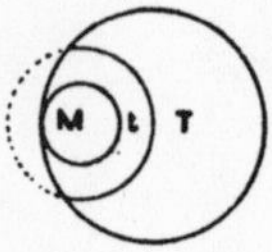

M
rap BUT EVERY CENTAUR IS
t
A FABULOUS BEING

ti THEREFORE SOME
t
FABULOUS BEING IS
T
HALF-MAN, HALF-HORSE

II

M
Fe NO ANIMAL IS
T
INCORRUPTIBLE

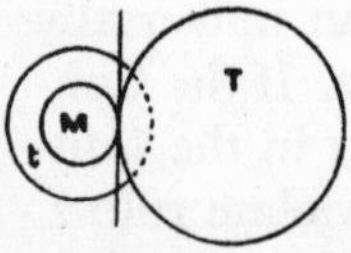

M
lap BUT EVERY ANIMAL IS
t
A LIVING BEING

ton THEREFORE SOME
t
LIVING BEING IS NOT
T
INCORRUPTIBLE

[1] Here the shading stands for T (the Pr. of the Major), as in the schemas of the first figure.

III

M
Dis SOME RICH MAN
T
IS MERCIFUL

M
am BUT EVERY RICH MAN
t
IS FEARED

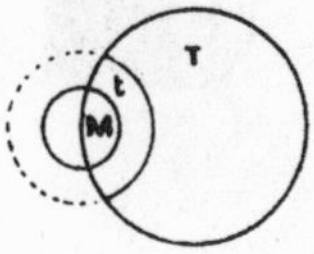

t
is THEREFORE SOME MAN
WHO IS FEARED IS
T
MERCIFUL

IV

M T
Da EVERY ANIMAL IS CORPOREAL

M
tis BUT SOME ANIMAL IS AN
t
INTELLIGENT BEING

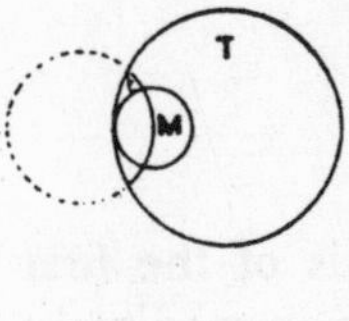

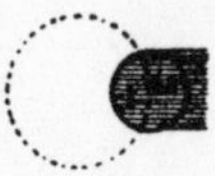

i THEREFORE SOME
t
INTELLIGENT BEING IS
T
CORPOREAL

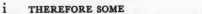

V

M

Boc SOME DIPLOMAT IS

T

NOT HONEST

M

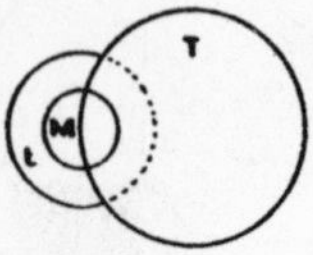

ar BUT EVERY DIPLOMAT

t

IS POWERFUL

do THEREFORE SOME

t

POWERFUL (man) IS

T

NOT HONEST

VI

Fe NO AMBITIOUS MAN IS

UNSELFISH

M

ris BUT SOME AMBITIOUS

MAN IS A

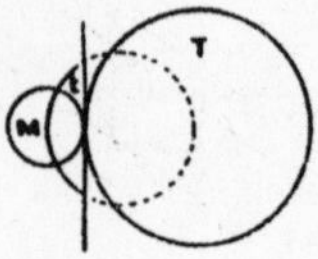

t

PHILANTHROPIST

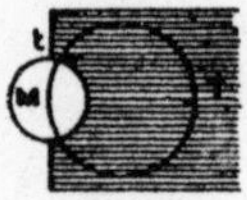

on THEREFORE SOME

t

PHILANTHROPIST IS

T

NOT UNSELFISH

*79. REDUCTION OF MOODS. The four moods of the first figure are said to be *perfect* because they are immediately regulated by the double supreme principle of the syllogism, *dictum de omni, dictum de nullo* (see above, No. 71) : for in these moods the extension of T is larger than that of M, which is in turn larger than that of t : T>M>t. Here the T is only the Pr., the t only the S., and the M itself, being S. in the Major and Pr. in the Minor, has the position of a *mean* in the premisses.[1]

All the other moods are said to be *imperfect*, because this double supreme principle is not so clearly evinced in them ; it regulates them only mediately, by means of some particular determination. If we wish to apply the *dictum de omni* or *de nullo* immediately, without the intermediation of these particular determinations, the imperfect moods must be *reduced* to perfect moods.[2]

In the second figure the extension of T is *smaller* than that of M, and greater than that of t : M>T>t. The double supreme principle is therefore applicable only under a special determination, which some authors call the " dictum de diverso." If a certain attribute (M) may be affirmed or denied of a universal subject (T), everything (t) of which this same attribute cannot be affirmed or denied is not contained under this subject. *Si aliquod attributum potest praedicari affirmative aut negative de quodam termino, non continetur sub illo termino omne de quo illud attributum praedicari nequit* (*affirmative aut negative*).

In the third figure the extension of T is greater than that of M, but the latter's extension is *smaller* than that

[1] Cf. Aristotle, *Anal. Pr.*, I, 4, 25 b, 32.

[2] We believe this to be Aristotle's true meaning.—To say that, in order to furnish conclusive evidence, imperfect syllogisms need something other than that which is made known by their premisses (cf. *Anal. Pr.*, I, 1, 24–26) is not equivalent to saying that in order to provide adequate evidence the M must, by suitable treatment, be given the same position that it has in the first figure, or in other words that these syllogisms must be *reduced* to the first figure, and thus be true syllogisms only on condition that they no longer be themselves. This statement signifies equally that : in order that imperfect syllogisms furnish conclusive evidence, it is necessary to distinguish in them not only the logical relations which, in the first figure, immediately manifest the supreme principle of the syllogism, but also those logical relations which suppose the application of a special principle particularizing this supreme principle.

If it is not true that the second and third figures each have their own supreme principle independent of the first principle of the first figure—as Mr. Lachelier would have it (see above, No. 71, inset). But this does not mean to say that the syllogisms of the second and third figure are not conclusive by themselves, do not produce conclusive evidence by themselves, or that they render the conclusion necessary, only in virtue of the first figure to which they may be reduced. On the contrary, they are valid in their own right, and, in certain cases, their use is to be preferred (see below, No. 80).

of t : T>t>M. The double supreme principle of the syllogism applies here only under a special determination which some authors call the "dictum de parte," and others—following A. Lambert (disciple of Leibnitz, contemporary with Kant) the "dictum de exemplo": two terms that contain a part in common (M) are partially alike ; but if the one contains a part that the other does not contain, they are partially different from each other. *Duo termini, qui continent aliquam partem communem, partim conveniunt ; si autem unus continet partem, quam alter non continet, partim differunt.*[1]

Reduction is *direct* or *per impossibile*.

Every imperfect mood has its perfect correspondent in one of the moods of the first figure : Every A conclusion is inferred in the most perfect manner in *Barbara*, every E conclusion in *Celarent*, every I in Darii, and every O in *Ferio*. How is this reduction of imperfect moods to perfect effected? We may distinguish here between two types of reduction : *ostensible* or *direct reduction*, wherein we draw the same conclusion from the perfect syllogism as was drawn from the imperfect syllogism under consideration ; or by *reduction per impossibile* wherein we prove the validity of the imperfect syllogism in question by showing, in a perfect syllogism, that if anyone deny the conclusion of this imperfect syllogism the while he accord its premisses, he contradicts himself. (All the imperfect moods may be reduced to perfect moods *per impossibile*, but two of them, *Baroco* and *Bocardo, do not admit of reduction by any other method.*)

In *direct* reduction we have recourse to two operations, 1 the *conversion* of one of the propositions of the imperfect syllogism in question, 2 the *mutation* or transposition of the Major into the Minor.

In reduction *per impossibile*, we *grant the premisses* and deny the conclusion. Then we form the contradictory of this conclusion, and substitute it for one of the premisses. From this there follows (in a perfect syllogism) a conclusion that is contradictory to this very premise (which had been granted by hypotheses).

[1] Cf. Gredt, *Elementa philosophiae aristotelico—thomisticae*, Logica formalis, cap. III.

The manner in which each imperfect syllogism should be reduced is indicated by certain *consonants* in the mnemonic words (Cesare, Camestres, etc.). These consonants indicate the operations to which the proposition represented by the *preceding* vowel should be submitted.

S. indicates that the proposition symbolized by the preceding vowel should be *converted simply*.

P. indicates that this proposition should be *converted per accidens*.

M. indicates that the premisses must be *transposed*.

C. indicates that reduction *per impossibile* is the only practicable method.

These symbols are summed up in the two following Latin lines :

S vult simpliciter verti, P vero per accid,
M vult mutari, C per impossibile duci.

Note that the *initial consonant* of a mood indicates that it must be reduced to the perfect mood beginning *with the same consonant*. For instance Festino should be reduced to Ferio.

For example, given to reduce a syllogism in *Camestres* to the perfect mood.

caM Every jealous man is bitter,
eS but no saint is bitter,
treS therefore no saint is a jealous man.

As the initial C indicates, this syllogism may be reduced to a syllogism in *Celarent*. To do this we must (1) (consonant M) transpose the premisses, and (2) (consonant S) convert the minor and the conclusion " simply."

ce No bitter man is a saint,
la but every jealous man is bitter,
rent therefore no jealous man is a saint.

Or, again, let us reduce a syllogism in *Felapton* to a perfect mood :

fe No animal is incorruptible,
laP but every animal is a living being,
Ton therefore some living being is not incorruptible.

This is reducible to a syllogism in *Ferio*, initial F. To do this we need only (consonant P) convert the minor *per accidens* " by accident."

fe No animal is incorruptible,
ri but some living being is an animal,
o therefore some living being is not incorruptible.

Finally, let us reduce a syllogism in *Baroco* to a perfect mood :

bar Every fool is annoying,
oC but some chatterbox is not annoying,
o therefore some chatterbox is not a fool.

This syllogism may be reduced to *Barbara* (initial B). As the consonant C indicates, we shall have to proceed *per impossibile*,[1] that is to say, we shall have to, 1 suppose that some adversary, in declaring this syllogism invalid, *denies* the Conclusion but *grants* the premisses ; 2 replace one of the premisses (the *Minor* here, since it is followed by C), by the contradictory of the conclusion ; 3 reason in a syllogism in Barbara :

bar Every fool is annoying,
ba but every chatterbox is a fool,
ra therefore every chatterbox is annoying.

[1] *Baroco* and *Bocardo* which are reducible *only per impossibile*, are reduced to the perfect mood starting with the same consonant in the mnemonic lines, viz. : *Barbara*. But the same is not true of the reduction *per impossibile* of the other moods (for the first consonant of the symbolic word was chosen in relation to the perfect mood to which these moods may be reduced *directly*).

The *vowels* in the following lines indicate the *conclusion* of the *perfect mood* to which the imperfect moods may be reduced *per impossibile :*

Ind. First Fig.	Second Fig.	Third Fig.
Febiferaxis	*Obit Terras*	*Spheramque quotannis*

Other logicians propose the following :

Nesciebatis	*Odiebam*	*Laetare Romanis*

For example, given the third mood of the second figure (*Festino*) to reduce *per impossibile ;* it would have to be reduced to the perfect mood whose conclusion is E (third vowel of the symbol obit terras), that is to *Celarent.*

Fes No saint is arrogant,
ti but some reformer is arrogant,
no therefore some reformer is not a saint.

Supposing that we admit the premisses but deny the Conclusion ; by replacing the Minor by the contradictory of the Conclusion we have :

Ce No saint is arrogant,
la but *every reformer is a saint*
rent therefore no reformer is arrogant,

which contradicts the Minor, " some reformer is arrogant," which had been admitted by hypothesis.

This conclusion is the *contradictory of the Minor* of the syllogism in *Baroco*, which our adversary *had admitted by hypothesis*. Thus the adversary's position is reduced to the absurd, for in granting the premisses of this syllogism, and denying its Conclusion, he contradicted himself.

*80. THE COMPARATIVE VALUE OF THE THREE SYLLOGISTIC FIGURES. The first figure contains the perfect moods of the syllogism, and consequently it deserves to come first. The ancients granted second place to the second figure and last place to the third, because in the second figure the M is twice Pr., and in the third it is twice S. and it is " nobler " to be Pr. than to be S., for the S. has the *rôle* of matter and the Pr. the *rôle* of form in the proposition.[1]

Although the first figure is the most perfect, the second and third have their advantage according to circumstances : the second, whose conclusion is always negative, in the refutation of an adversary ; the third in showing that a thesis could not be universally true because an example of the contrary may be encountered.

(*a*) The theory of the figures and moods of the syllogism is set forth in detail in the *Prior Analytics*. Moreover, Aristotle states [2] that no one had ever studied the question before him. Here we have the extremely rare case of a scientific doctrine being constituted in all its perfection by its discoverer. For since Aristotle, whatever additions Logic may have received from other sources, especially from the Stoics and the scholastics, and whatever variety of aspects may have been brought out by certain modern philosophers, especially in the nineteenth century, no one has ever been able to improve upon the *theory itself of the categorical syllogism*, and every effort to reform it has been unsuccessful (see below, Nos. 82, 83, 84).

(*b*) EXERCISE. (1) State the conclusion of the following syllogisms, and indicate their figure and mood :

No wise man is garrulous, but some old men are garrulous, therefore—

[1] Cf. the tracts attributed to St. Thomas, *De Natura Syllogismorum* and *Summa totius Logicae* (X, 4) (opusc. 47 and 48, rom. edit). Although apocryphal their doctrine is excellent.

[2] *De. Soph. elench.*, Chap. XXXIV, 184 b 1.

Everything that is poisonous is harmful to man, but certain fruits are poisonous, therefore—

No mammal is a bird, but some mammal is a flying animal, therefore—

Everything that is beautiful is rare, but virtue is beautiful, therefore—

Some fish has wings, but every fish has scales, therefore—

No mammal is oviparous, but the bat is a mammal, therefore—

Every mammal is viviparous, but every mammal is a warm-blooded animal, therefore—

No lie is praiseworthy, but some praise is a lie, therefore—

Every ambitious man is uneasy, but no wise man is uneasy, therefore—

(2) From among these syllogisms, reduce those that are in imperfect moods to perfect moods.

(3) Find examples of each of the syllogistic moods.

3. *Explanations and Discussions of the Syllogism* [1]

In a perfect syllogism the major is *always* more universal than the conclusion from the point of view of *logical relations*, and very often so from the point of view of *the content* of the *propositions*.

*81. THE TRUE NOTION OF THE SYLLOGISM. Having studied the moods and figures of the syllogism, and familiarized ourselves with its logical mechanism, we are better able to understand what constitutes its essence and its force. The syllogism *consists essentially* in identifying two terms with a middle term, and in inferring from this the identity of these two terms with each other.[2] It does not consist essentially in descending from a more universal term to a less universal term contained under it. All the treatises on Logic undoubtedly teach that *in the syllogism the mind concludes from a more universal truth to a less universal truth contained in the first*, and this is true, at least *as to logical relations*, or as to the logical functions of the S. and Pr. in the proposition. But the essential force and merit of the syllogism lies, not in the passage

But that which essentially constitutes

[1] The criticisms of the syllogism from the point of view of its demonstrative value (Sextus Empiricus, Descartes, Stuart Mill, Goblot—) will be studied in Major Logic. We are interested here only in that which pertains to the syllogism as it enters into Minor or Formal Logic.

[2] See above, Nos. 66, 69, 71.

from the universal to the particular, but *in the identification of the two extremes with a same third term.* When we said above [1] that the principle of the syllogism resides in the *universal* it was only to stress the fact that this third term must necessarily be universal if an inference is to be *drawn* by means of such an identification.

the syllogism is not the passage from the universal to the particular but the identification of two terms by means of a same third term.

(1) The passage of the mind in the syllogism from a more universal truth to a less universal truth is not the *essence* of the syllogism, but merely a *property* that springs from this essence. Nevertheless, it is very important that this property be correctly understood—property which the earlier logicians did not emphasize as much as do the moderns, but which they understood *formally* and *as logicians.* Since the decadence of Scholasticism in the fifteenth and sixteenth century, however, this property has been understood *in a material way* which has completely falsified its meaning. The addition of this misinterpretation to the ever-increasing tendency to reduce all reasoning to the mere establishment of the relations of extension,[2] has resulted in the serious distortion of Logic in modern times. It is therefore advisable to emphasize this point in order that any ambiguity may be avoided.

To say that the syllogism goes from the more universal to the less universal, or from the universal to the particular, is true only *from the point of view of logical relations*, or, in other words, it is true only in regard to the logical structure of propositions, considering things from the point of view of the *being of reason* (in the order of concepts) which constitutes the proper object of the logician.

For in a syllogism of the first figure the M is Pr. in the Minor, and we know that, *from the point of view of logical relations, considering only the logical function of the Pr. in reference to the S.,*[3] the Pr. has a greater extension than the S. Therefore in the Minor t<M, that is, functionally *as Pr. of the Minor*, M contains t in its extension. Furthermore, since M in the Minor is communicated to t as the subject of the

[1] See above, No. 71.

[2] Thus for Hamilton the syllogism consists in "inferring that the part of a part is the part of a whole." J. S. Mill, *Hamilton's Philosophy*, Vol. II, p. 196, Spencer, 1866.

[3] See above, No. 52.

Major, from the point of view of logical relations, or of the form of the syllogism, M must also contain t in its extension in the Major. Consequently, from the point of view of logical relations, the Conclusion " t is T " is a less universal proposition than the Major " M is T."

Moreover, all the moods of the second and third figure, and also those of the indirect first, may be reduced to the moods of the first figure.

Therefore, in so far as logical relations taken in themselves are concerned and in the measure in which every syllogism is reducible to a syllogism of the first figure, it is indeed true that the mind in the syllogism concludes from a more universal truth to a less universal truth contained in the first.

But does this mean that the essential *force* of the syllogism consists in this property ?—Not at all. This property does nothing but make manifest to us a *sine qua non condition* for the validity of the syllogism. If we were not sure of the legitimacy of the identification of the two extremes in virtue of their mutual identification with the middle term, that is, if the logical functions of the Pr. and S. in the propositions did not guarantee that the middle term, in being identified with T, *is no smaller* than it is when identified with t, the syllogism would not be absolutely foolproof, and might sometimes lead us into error.

This guarantee of legitimate identification is the only thing manifested by the property in question.

(2) The proof of this lies in the fact that, considering the contents of the proposition and not its logical structure, there are many instances in which the Conclusion is *just as universal* as the Major :

> Every rational being is made to live in society,
> but every man is a rational being,
> therefore every man is made to live in society.

Or again :

> If a parallelogram is divided into two isosceles triangles by its diagonals, these diagonals are perpendicular to each other,

but a rhombus is a parallelogram divided into two isosceles triangles by its diagonals,
therefore the diagonals of a rhombus are perpendicular to each other.

All the propositions in these syllogisms are convertible, and the Conclusion has THE SAME UNIVERSALITY as the Major. Only from the pure point of view of the logical relations, considering the *logical functions* of t and M (t, the subject of the conclusion, stands to M in the minor as S., *as* a term of less extension, and M is subject in the Major) is there any passage here from a more universal to a less universal truth. Nevertheless, these are valid syllogisms in *Barbara ;* moreover, as we shall see in Major Logic, Aristotle and the Scholastics considered such examples as the *perfect type* of the syllogism from the point of view of demonstration.[1]

Furthermore, it is evident that in a syllogism in *Darii*, such as :

Every man has the power of thought,
but some corporeal creature is a man,
therefore *some corporeal creature* has the power of thought,

or again in a syllogism of the third figure in *Darapti* or *Disamis :*

Every man is mortal,
but every man is a thinking being,
therefore *some thinking being* is a mortal,
Some thinking being is mortal,
but every thinking being wants to live for ever,
therefore *some being who wants to live for ever* is mortal,

the Conclusion, from the point of view of the content of the propositions, is not less universal than the Major.

Consequently if, instead of considering propositions from the formal point of view of logical relations, we consider them materially from the point of view of their contents (which is not the point of view proper to Minor Logic), we cannot say that the Major, of itself, contains the Con-

[1] If Minor Logic has recourse to examples such as " Every man is mortal, but Peter is a man, etc.," it is only in order to make sensibly manifest, in the very matter of the propositions, the logical relations existing between terms.

clusion as a more universal proposition contains a less universal proposition. We may only say that the Major contains this Conclusion as a cause, reason, or *principle*, contains its effect virtually; from this point of view the Major appears, not as a proposition that is necessarily and always *more universal*, but indeed as a proposition that is necessarily and always of *greater range*.

(3) Therefore when it happens, as it very frequently does, that the Major is actually more universal than the Conclusion from the point of view of material contents, *e.g.*, "All that subsists immaterially is indestructible, but the human soul subsists immaterially, therefore the human soul is indestructible," we do not draw our Conclusion *because* "human soul" is a subjective part of "that subsists immaterially," but *because* "that subsists immaterially" is a *middle term* which serves to unite the term "human soul" to another term. In saying: "Every man is mortal, but Peter is a man, therefore, etc.," we do not draw our Conclusion *because* "Peter" is a subjective part of "man," but *because* "man" is a *middle term* by means of which the term Peter and the term mortal are identified. The argumentation in question is a syllogism *not because* it proceeds from a universal term to one of its subjective parts (see below No. 96, 3), *but because* it proceeds in virtue of the connection between terms or concepts, or more definitively, because it proceeds entirely upon the intelligible plane, upon the plane of concepts and self-evident principles.

The true, the essential characteristic of the syllogism is that it proceeds *from one universal to another universal* (be it equally or less extended than the first). In any event the axiom that *the syllogism proceeds from the more universal to the less universal* is true only from the formal point of view of the *logical relations* existing between terms and concepts.

(4) Many more or less nominalistic authors, who confound the *extension* of a concept with *its resolution into a simple collection of individuals*, that is, with its pure and simple *destruction*,[1] and consequently entirely misunderstand the meaning of the axiom "the syllogism proceeds from the universal to the particular," interpret the syllogism from a

[1] See above, No. 12 *d*.

purely *collective* point of view. In other words, they think it consists merely in passing on *to one or several individuals* a predicate that has been proven true *of all the members* of the collection in which these individuals are a part. This is a basic error and deals a veritable death-blow to all Logic ; it is not at all surprising that these authors, beginning by gratuitously forming so crude a conception of the syllogism, should consider it useless tautology, or a vicious circle.[1]

Indeed there are exceptional cases in which, by reason of its matter, a universal proposition signifies absolutely nothing except a fact common to all the individuals in a collection taken as such, and tells us nothing of the requirements of a universal nature or reason—*e.g.*, " All the inhabitants of this town perished in the tidal wave," but in this event it is evident that such a proposition can be true only if the truth of each particular instance has been verified ; the truth of the conclusion " therefore this or that particular inhabitant of this town perished in the tidal wave " had to be known before the major could be held as true ; hence the *reasoning* in question goes around in a circle. But, precisely in such cases *there is neither reasoning nor inference*, and no true logician has ever regarded them as valid examples of the syllogism.

We have recourse to the exterior form of the syllogism in such instances, only that we may proceed to some sort of *verification or sensible identification* of a fact recorded in a proposition which presupposes it as known, but which we know only because we remember it or are told by someone else. For example : upon hearing a news-flash to the effect that " none of the passengers on train 22 were injured in yesterday's accident," we could exclaim : " therefore our friend X, who was travelling on that train was not killed." Or, in recalling that " all Verlaine's works were published by Vanier," we could say : " therefore *Sagesse* was published by Vanier." But the fact remains that in such examples (even in expository syllogisms, see below, No. 85) we make no real inference, we do not really reason at all. It is not

[1] Cf. Sextus Empiricus, *Hypotyp. Pyrrh.*, Bk. II, Chap. XIV, § 196 ; Stuart Mill, *System of Logic*, Bk. II, Chap. III, § 2.—A more detailed examination of these criticisms of the syllogism will be given in Major Logic.

a little remarkable that these exceptional cases wherein there is no reasoning, and which offer us but a sterile verbal form, an appearance, a mere corpse of a syllogism, should be regarded by certain logicians as the " only true categorical syllogisms of the first figure," [1] syllogisms which we will very willingly agree are unquestionably " tautological."

In reality, the syllogistic inference owes its entire value and its very existence not to a collection of individuals, but to the *universal nature* which is communicable to these individuals and taken as the syllogism's middle term. It is not from the point of view of a *simple collection of individuals*, but from the point of view of the *universal essence* that we must look upon the syllogism if we wish to understand it, for the syllogism consists in passing on to an (individual or universal) subject, a predicate that we know to be true of the universal nature to whose laws this subject submits. This is a legitimate operation and furthers knowledge; for to know that " every triangle has the sum of its angles equal to two right angles " is not the same as to know that " the sum of the angles of the figure inscribed in a semicircle is equal to two right angles." It is no more necessary to know the second truth in order to establish the first, than it is to know that Peter is mortal in order to know that every man, being corporeal, is mortal.

So we may say that in the syllogism we do not proceed from *all* to *several* but from *all* to *every* or to *some*. In order to avoid ambiguity, therefore, the logician must formulate his examples of the syllogism by saying " *Every man is mortal*," " *Some man is sincere* " and not: " *All men are mortal*," " *Some men are sincere*." The latter expressions signify the individuals in a group *before* signifying the universal nature of which they partake; nevertheless (aside from exceptional cases such as those mentioned above) they do signify this universal nature itself, though only secondarily.[2] Everyday language risks the creation of a good deal of confusion by the careless substitution of " all men " for " every man." But it would hardly be edifying for a logician, a specialist

[1] E. Goblot, *Logique*, p. 222.
[2] See above, No. 51 *c*.

in the technique of reasoning, to be taken in by the inexactitudes of common speech.

*82. ON THE REDUCTION OF MOODS. The reduction of moods as treated in Scholastic Logic has been criticized on the pretext that it makes use of the *conversion* of propositions, and that conversion itself is, in reality, a syllogism of the second or third figure (see above, No. 68 *b*) whence it follows that this reduction of imperfect syllogisms to perfect syllogisms is merely circular reasoning.

This criticism is absolutely inoperative, for, as we have seen, conversion constitutes neither an *immediate inference* nor a *syllogism*; it is simply the immediate passage, without inference or reasoning of any kind, from a truth expressed in one way to *the same truth* expressed in another way.

*83. THE QUANTIFICATION OF THE PREDICATE. The English philosopher, Hamilton, last great representative of the Scottish School, thought he could completely revolutionize the theory of the proposition and the syllogism, and carry it to unsuspected peaks of perfection by means of his doctrine of the *quantification of the predicate*—In what does this doctrine consist?

1. Hamilton starts from the principle that Logic should "state explicitly what is thought implicitly," that is, that it should replace the expressions of ordinary speech by expressions in which everything implicitly contained in thought should be explicitly signified.

Hamilton demands that in every proposition, the quantity of the Pr. be indicated by a sign.

2. As a consequence he declares that the Pr. in every proposition must be modified by a sign expressly manifesting its quantity.

3. But in reality his proposed reform goes much further. He considers every proposition as an *equation* between two concepts of a certain determinate extension, let us say between two *logical quantities*. (According to him to say "Every man is mortal" is to think: "the whole expanse of man = a certain definite portion of the expanse of mortal.") Hence he distinguishes as many propositions as there can be possible combinations *a priori* between one (universal or particular) logical quantity and another.

4. Which is to say that, instead of the *four* kinds of propositions (A, E, I, O) treated in the theory of the proposi-

tion (opposition and conversion) and the syllogism, Mr. Hamilton distinguishes *eight* kinds of propositions—four affirmative (a—a a—i, i—a, i—i) and four negative (e—e, e—o, o—e, o—o) :

Affirmatives
- (1) toto-total (a—a) : "*All* man is ALL rationality."
- (2) toto-partial (a—i) : "*All* man is SOME animal."
- (3) parti-total (i—a) : "Some animal (viz., man) is ALL rationality."
- (4) parti-partial (i—i) : "*Some* animal (viz., man) is SOME thinking being."

Negatives
- (5) toto-total (e—e) : "*No* man is NO angel." [1]
- (6) toto-partial (e—o) : "No man is SOME animal" (viz., irrational animal).
- (7) parti-total (o—e) : "*Some* animal (viz., man) is NO angel."
- (8) parti-partial (o—O) : "Some animal (viz., man) is not SOME thinking being (viz., angel)."

According to Hamilton classical Logic is at fault because it has not recognized propositions of the a—a, i—a type, for it has not seen that there are affirmative propositions in which the Pr. is taken universally (the convertible propositions "all man is rational," "some animal (namely, man) is rational"), and because it has not recognized propositions of the e—o, o—o type : "men are not some mammals," "some animals (men) are not some mammals." In his eyes his reform has a number of important advantages of which he enumerates eighteen in particular,—the reduction of the conversion of propositions from three species to one : simple conversion (the simple transposition of the two extremes without changing their quantity : $x = y$, therefore $y = x$; every man = some animal, therefore some animal = every man) ; "the reduction of all the general

[1] Or according to the more correct formulation of the ancients : πᾶς ἄνθρωπος οὐδεὶς λίθος, omnis homo nullus lapis est.

rules of categorical syllogisms to a single canon" and "the abrogation of all the special laws of the syllogism." In fact in this doctrine the syllogism, which from now on admits of thirty-six legitimate moods, consists solely,—given that $y = z$ (*Major*),—in substituting z for its equivalent, y, in the proposition $x = y$ (*Minor*), with the result $x = z$ (*Conclusion*); in other words, the syllogism rests solely upon the principle of the substitution of similars (Stanley Jevons). From this it follows that "the figure is a non-essential variation in the syllogistic form, and in consequence it is absurd to reduce the syllogisms of other figures to the first."

Criticism.—Stuart Mill has shown at some length the vanity of the claim that progress has been made in formal logic owing to the theory of the quantification of the Predicate; but this theory had already been summarily criticized by St. Thomas Aquinas in his commentary on the *Perihermeneias* (lib. 1, Cap. VII, lect. 10, Nos. 23 and 24). This important text, the inspiration of the following remarks, is given in a note.[1]

[1] "Deinde cum dicit: *in eo vero quod*, etc., removet quoddam quod posset esse dubium. Quia enim posuerat quamdam diversitatem in oppositione enunciationum ex hoc quod universale sumitur a parte subjecti universaliter vel non universaliter, posset aliquis credere quod similis diversitas nasceretur ex parte praedicati, ex hoc scilicet quod universale praedicari posset et universaliter et non universaliter; et ideo ad hoc excludendum dicit quod in eo quod praedicatur aliquod universale, non est verum quod praedicetur universale universaliter. Cujus quidem duplex esse potest ratio.

"Una quidem, quia talis modus praedicandi videtur repugnare praedicato secundum propriam rationem quam habet in enunciatione. Dictum est enim supra quod praedicatum est quasi pars *formalis* enunciationis, subjectum autem est pars *materialis* ipsius: cum autem aliquod universale profertur universaliter, ipsum universale sumitur secundum habitudinem quam habet ad singularia, quae sub se continet; sicut et quando universale profertur particulariter, sumitur secundum habitudinem quam habet ad aliquod contentorum sub se; et sic utrumque pertinet ad *materialem determinationem universalis;* et ideo neque signum universale neque particulare convenienter additur praedicato, sed magis subjecto: convenientius enim dicitur, *nullus homo est asinus,* quam *omnis homo est nullus asinus;* et similiter convenientius dicitur, *aliquis homo est albus,* quam *homo est aliquid album.*

"Invenitur autem quandoque a philosophis signum particulare appositum praedicato, ad insinuandum quod praedicatum est *in plus* quam subjectum, et hoc praecipue cum, habito genere, investigant differentias completivas speciei, sicut in II *de Anima* dicitur quod *anima est actus quidam.*

"Alia vero ratio potest accipi ex parte veritatis enunciationis; et ista specialiter habet locum in affirmationibus, quae falsae essent si praedicatum universaliter praedicaretur. Et ideo manifestans id quod posuerat, subjungit quod *Nulla affirmatio est in qua,* scilicet vere, *de universali praedicato universaliter praedicetur,* id est in qua universali praedicato utitur ad universaliter praedicandum; ut si diceretur, *omnis homo est omne animal.* Oportet enim, secundum

1. Let us examine the eight varieties of proposition recognized by Hamilton. We shall find (*a*) *that those only are legitimate* which correspond to the four types of classical Logic (A, E, I, O), and (*b*) that even in these propositions *there is no question of quantifying the Predicate.*

(*a*) *Toto-total and parti-total affirmatives* (a—a, i—a). "All man is all rational being," "some animal (*i.e.*, man) is all rational being."

These propositions are *absolutely illegitimate*, for the very good reason that an affirmative proposition in which the

---

praedicta, quod hoc praedicatum *animal* secundum singula quae sub ipso continentur, praedicaretur de singulis quae continentur sub homine ; et hoc non potest esse verum, neque si praedicatum sit *in plus* quam subjectum, neque si praedicatum sit convertibile cum eo. Oporteret enim quod quilibet unus homo esset animalia omnia, aut omnia risibilia : quae repugnant rationi singularis, quod accipitur sub universali. . . .

"Signum autem universale negativum, vel particulare affirmativum, etsi convenientius ponantur ex parte subjecti, non tamen repugnat veritati etiam si ponatur ex parte praedicati. Contingit enim hujusmodi enunciationes in aliqua materia esse veras : haec enim est vera, *omnis homo nullus lapis est ;* et similiter haec est vera *omnis homo aliquod animal est.* Sed haec, *omnis homo omne animal est*, in quacumque materia proferatur, falsa est. Sunt autem quaedam aliae tales enunciationes semper falsae ; sicuti ista, *aliquis homo omne animal est* (quae habet eamdem causam falsitatis cum hac, *omnis homo omne animal est*) ; et si quae aliae similes, sunt semper falsae : in omnibus enim eadem ratio est. Et ideo per hoc quod Philosophus reprobavit istam, *omnis homo omne animal est*, dedit intelligere omnes consimiles esse improbandas."

(St. Thomas *in Perihermeneias*, lib. I, Chap. VII, lect. 10, Nos. 23 and 24.) In the text upon which St. Thomas is commenting here (*Perihermeneias*, 17 b 12, 16) Aristotle has clearly foreseen the theory of the quantification of the predicate. This is also the text upon which the most important observations concerning this theory were made by the ancients, by Ammonius in particular and, among the Latins, by Boethius (*Commentarii in librum Aristotelis Periherm.*, p. 439 ; ed. Meiser, Teubner. *Secunda editio* II, Chap. VII, pp. 162–163), and by Albertus Magnus (lib. I, *Periherm.*, tract. V ; Vivès, t. I, p. 413). But the most complete and profound treatment of this question has been given by St. Thomas.

It is peculiar that none of the modern critics of Hamilton's theory should have perceived that this question had been definitely settled over six hundred years ago. Hamilton himself, a man of great learning, quotes Aristotle, Alexander, Ammonius, Boethius, Averroes, Albert the Great, Levi Ben Gerson, the masters of Louvain, etc., but ignores St. Thomas' text.

We may further point out the thesis upheld here by St. Thomas should be considered as classic in the School. Apparently the Terminists were the first to attempt to shake it. Cf. Occam, *Summa totius Logicae*, Chap. IV, f. 26, v. A : "Secundo sciendum, quod omnis propositio universalis, in qua praedicatum sumitur universaliter, est falsa, si praedicatum et subjectum verificentur de pluribus contentis ; si autem praedicatur praecise de uno solo contento et similiter subjectum, tunc posset esse propositio vera, sicut si non esset nisi unum animal, puta unus homo, haec esset vera *omnis homo est omne animal*" (quoted by Prantl, II, p. 583, note 908). Occam's thesis here conforms with his general doctrine on universal propositions, which, in his eyes, always have an existential meaning, even in necessary matter.

Pr. is *universally* attributed to the S. is under every circumstance *false*. Had Hamilton understood the nature of the proposition and of attribution (*praedicatio*), he would have seen that in every universal or particular affirmative the Pr., being attributed to a universal subject (taken universally; "all man" or particularly, "some animal") is by that very fact declared to be communicable to the individuals contained under this universal subject. He would also have immediately perceived that if the Pr. is taken *universally*, as it is in the propositions in question, it is taken as communicable to the S. (and therefore to the individuals for which the S. stands) *according to all the singulars contained under it, secundum singula quae suo ipso praedicato continentur.* Thus the proposition "all man is all rational being" necessarily infers that "Peter is all rational" and that "Peter is all rational beings," which is absurd.

Thus the complaint that Hamilton brings against classical Logic concerning convertible propositions turns back upon him. The logicians of antiquity were well aware that the extension of the Pr. in convertible propositions ("Every man is rational") coincides with that of the S. (*praedicatum non est in plus*), but they were also aware that it is only by reason of the matter of the proposition that this is so.[1] And they were especially careful to add that, even in this case, the Pr. ("rational") always continues to be *taken particularly*, that is, it continues to have a particular *suppositio* (*suppositio confusa tantum, seu disjuncta*), and to stand

[1] See above, n. 52, § 2.—For this reason, as de Morgan and Mill have remarked, it is not sufficient to consult the proposition "every man is a rational animal" in order to know that the Pr. rational belongs exclusively to the S. Man, for of itself this proposition does not tell us this. To know this fact we must either add another proposition to the first, viz., "every rational animal is a man," or we must have recourse to the *occultly compound* proposition: "man alone is a rational animal," which really combines the import of two different propositions (see above, n. 45).

Hamilton's error, so vigorously denounced by John Stuart Mill, consists in attempting to make one and the same proposition *affirm two different things* (*An Exam. of Hamilton's Philosophy*, Vol. II, p. 209 (Spencer, 1866)). On this point Mill quotes (after Grote) a passage from Levi Ben Gerson, a Jewish philosopher of the fourteenth century: "We do not ordinarily add a quantitative sign to the predicate, for were we to do so we would state two *quaesita* at the same time: namely—that the predicate is affirmed of the subject, and that it is denied of everything else" (J. S. Mill, *An Exam. of Hamilton's Philos.*, p. 489 (French translation, Cazelles, Paris, 1869)). [I have been unable to find the English edition from which this translation was made. Tr.]

in the proposition for an *individuum vagum* in which the universal concept " rational " is realized.[1]

Toto-partial and parti-partial negative propositions (e—o, o—o). " No man is some mammal (viz., irrational), " Some animal (viz., man) is not some mammal." [2] As we have just seen, toto-total (and parti-total) affirmatives are artificial and *necessarily false* formulations (" all man is all rational (being) ") of true propositions that are used in ordinary language (convertible propositions : " all man is rational "). Toto-partial and parti-partial negative propositions are entirely artificial and exist only because of the exigencies of Hamilton's classification. They, too, are *illegitimate* and *inadmissible* for, being essentially amphibological, they are both *true and false at the same time*, which is repugnant to the very nature of the proposition. For example, given the expression " No man is some mammal " ; in so far as " some mammal " signifies " irrational mammal " in this proposition this expression is *true*. But a proposition is false if its contradictory is true ; the contradictory proposition " some man is some mammal " (viz., rational mammal) is true ; therefore from this aspect " no man is some mammal " is *false*. This expression is essentially amphibological from the fact that it declares what a thing is not precisely by the aid of what it is.

In reality, the addition of the particle *some* to the Pr. of a negative proposition—if we understand this addition as

[1] As soon as we begin to lose hold of the true notion of the *suppositio* of terms, and consider only Euler's schemas, and the circles that represent the extension of concepts, we also begin to lose sight of the true nature of the proposition. We should note that the expression " to be taken in all its extension " or " in a part of its extension," which replaces the expression " to be taken universally or particularly " is equivocal, and may lead us into Hamilton's error. In a convertible proposition the extension of the Pr. is not restricted *in the sense* that the Pr. concept has the same extension as the S. concept and that the extension of the Pr. coincides entirely, and not only in part, with that of the S. (praedicatum non est in plus). But the extension of the Pr. is restricted *in this sense*, that the Pr. has a particular *suppositio*—or, in other words, that *it is not taken in all its universality* to be attributed to the S. (non praedicatur universaliter).

[2] In the text cited above, St. Thomas does not speak of toto-partial and parti-partial negatives. Our criticism of these propositions is drawn from other sources, especially from remarks made by the ancient logicians on the nature of the categorical proposition, which necessarily admits of but *one* affirmation or of *one true* or *false negation*.

Hamilton does,[1] does not give a *particular suppositio* to the Pr. taken as such. It merely carves out of the latter's extension a more restricted concept that continues to be *universally separated* from the subject, or, in other words, a concept that continues to be taken *according to all its universality* to be denied of the subject (and therefore according to all the singulars contained under it). Thus the expression, " no man is some mammal " is but a defective formulation of a proposition such as " No man is an irrational mammal " or " man is not a mammal of any kind," propositions in which the Pr. is not simply determined in relation to the singulars it contains under it by a quantitative sign, but is, on the contrary, intrinsically modified by a connotative term which excludes from it the specific difference proper to the subject. The Pr. of these propositions is taken universally, following the usual rule of negative propositions, and their contradictory: " Some man is an irrational animal," " Man is any kind of mammal " is false.

This innovation is *illegitimate* for four types of proposition.

Therefore the four types of proposition (a—a, i—a, e—o, o—o) which Hamilton thought to add to those already recognized by Aristotelian Logic, represent an *absolutely illegitimate* innovation.

(*b*) *Toto-partial and parti-partial Affirmatives, toto-total and parti-total Negatives.* There remain to be considered the four classic types of proposition (A, E, I, O), which become a—i, i—i, e—e, o—e propositions in Hamilton's classification. In their case it is not *illegitimate* to express the quantity of the Pr. by a sign, but it is *absolutely useless* to do so, since it

***useless* and *awkward* for the other four.**

[1] This addition may be understood in another manner—the only one in which the expression " no man is some mammal " is not amphibological and may be held as a true proposition. But in this case this proposition is false. For to say that " no man is some mammal " is in this sense equivalent to saying that no identity ever exists between a man and a mammiferous *individuum vagum*, or to denying the affirmative proposition that posits this identity (some man is (some) mammal). In this sense the proposition " no man is some mammal " is far from being toto-partial, for its Pr. is taken universally (that is, it is so denied of the S. that none of the singulars contained under it could be attributed to the S.) and it purely and simply signifies that " No man is a mammal." Similarly to say " no man is *some* angel " is the same as saying " no man is an angel."

Hence it follows that, considered as real propositions (and not as amphibological), Hamilton's toto-partial negatives are always false, for from this aspect they really signify that *no A is B*, whereas Hamilton always so constructs his propositions and so chooses his terms A and B, that *A is some B.*

is of the very nature of the affirmative proposition that its Pr. always be taken particularly, and of the very nature of the negative proposition that its Pr. always be taken universally. Furthermore, although this quantification is not incompatible with the truth of the enunciation, as it is in the preceding cases, yet, as St. Thomas has profoundly remarked, it is incompatible with the proper function of the Pr. in the enunciation (*videtur repugnare praedicato secundum propriam rationem quam habet in enunciatione*). Consequently it constitutes not only a superfluous but an awkward innovation (*non convenienter dicitur*). For the Pr. is as the *formal* part, and the S. as the *material* part of the enunciation. Now when a universal is quantified (that is, when we show by a sign that it is taken universally or particularly), it is explicitly considered according to its relation to the singulars which it contains under it. But this relates to the *material determination of the universal ;* consequently it is proper to quantify the S., which has the function of the material part, but not the Pr., which has the function of the formal part in the proposition.

2. The errors pointed out above spring from a fundamental error, due to which Hamilton completely misunderstands the nature of the proposition.

Considering the signs more than the objects of thought, he substitutes for the identification of a S. and Pr. by means of the copula *is*—which identification is of the very essence of the proposition and the judgment (" man is mortal ")—an entirely different relation. This relation, belonging to the mathematical and not to the logical order, is simply that of an *expressed equality* between an extension A (the concept " man ") and an extension B (the concept " some mortal ").

Thus the proposition " Man is mortal " is reduced to the expression, " Man = some mortal," which is no longer a logical enunciation and no longer functions as a proposition to be thought, but rather as an algorism to be used without thinking.

Hamilton is thus led to regard the proposition " all A is B " as signifying that " all the genus A " (later on it will be called the " class " A) " is all the genus B " or " a part of the genus B" ; or that " all the genus man is all the genus rational," or " all the genus ox is a part of the genus ruminant." But this is absurd, for what ruminates is not the *genus ox*, which has only logical being, but *the ox* concretely realized in this or that individual. As a matter of fact Hamilton confuses the universal terms which are the S. and Pr. of the proposition, with *collective wholes*, and Stuart Mill (who for his own part reduces the universal to a collection of individuals taken one by one) is justified in telling him that " to affirm that, when we judge every A to be a B, we always, and necessarily, recognize in thought a fact which is not true of every, or even of any A, but only of the aggregate composed of all A's, seems to me as baseless a fancy as ever implanted itself in the intellect of an eminent thinker." [1]

3. This false notion of the proposition, naturally entails a false notion of the syllogism (which will henceforth consist, not in *thinking* according to a certain linking together of concepts, but in *performing certain operations upon signs*, as in algebra). It is also accompanied by a false notion of logic itself. Undoubtedly, in reflecting as a technician, the logician should take into explicit account that which is implied in the play of thought,[2] but he cannot—as Hamilton would have him do—transform the natural play of thought into an artificial system in which everything should be explicit, and which would usurp the function of thought itself. The logical art, *ars cooperativa naturae*, must direct this play of thought and verify its laws, but it cannot take its place.

4. We have dealt at length with the theory of the quantification of the predicate because it presents in their embryonic stage and as yet in continuity with Logic, certain notions which claim to perfect Logic but in reality

[1] John Stuart Mill, *An Examination of Sir William Hamilton's Philosophy*, Vol. II, Chap. XXII, p. 205 (Spencer, 1866).

[2] Hamilton's expression " what is thought implicitly " is equivocal. When I think a proposition, even " in extension," for example, " the ox is a ruminant, this plant is not a dicotyledon," the *suppositio* of the Pr. (particular in the first case, universal in the second) is indeed a logical *property* of my thought. But this *property*—the object of the logician's reflection—is not contained in my thought *as something which I would think*, as something which would be the object of my thought, even *implicitly*.

lead it astray. The systematic development of these conceptions in another field has erected in the face of Logic a totally different discipline, namely Logistics.[1]

It was also necessary to show here how very far was the Logic of the Schools from paving the way for the theory of the quantification of the predicate, as some ill-informed thinkers would have us believe. Classical Logic, while taking into account the quantity of the Pr. conformably to the nature of things, is, on the contrary, radically opposed to Hamilton's doctrine, not only as it concerns the quantification of the Pr., but also in its notion of the proposition, of the syllogism and of Logic itself.

*84. THE LOGISTICIANS, OPPONENTS OF THE THEORY OF THE SYLLOGISM, OF SUBALTERNATION AND OF PARTIAL CONVERSION. In Major Logic we shall examine several problems concerning *Logistics*, a system of ideographical calculus apparently originated by Leibnitz, which made great strides during the nineteenth century, thanks to the mathematico-logical labours of several Italian and English authors (de Morgan, 1806–1871; Boole, 1815–1864; Schroeder, 1841–1902; MacColl, Peirce, Macfarlane, Peano, Russell, Padoa).

Logistics is an art concerned not with thought but with the signs of thought, and which proposes to dispense with thought.

We shall see that Logistics *differs essentially* from Logic. For, whereas the latter bears upon the act of reason itself in its progress towards the true, and thus upon the order of concepts themselves and of thought, Logistics is concerned with the *relations between* ideographic *signs* and therefore with these signs themselves which, once determined, are taken as sufficient.

Consequently Logistics proposes to *dispense with thinking*, to do away with rational and properly *logical* operations such as distinction, argumentation, etc., and to *suppress* every difficulty in reasoning by means of an excessively complicated algebra which the intelligence need only apply. Logic, on the contrary, proposes to *teach us to think*, to teach us to effectuate correctly the rational and properly *logical* operations such as distinction, argumentation, etc., and to *surmount* the numerous difficulties of reasoning by means of an art (an intellectual virtue) which should

[1] See Major Logic.

intrinsically perfect the very life of the intelligence and co-operate with its natural activity.

In any event, aside from the question of whether or not the former is a legitimate and viable method, Logistics and Logic remain separate disciplines, entirely foreign to one another. Correctly understood they cannot contradict each other, since in reality they do not have the same object.

The Logisticians, however, do not always view the situation so soberly and have formulated high-flown criticisms of some theories of "classical Logic" concerning which it would not be amiss to speak here.

I. *The Syllogism in General.* Padoa,[1] for example, says that if we translate the nineteen legitimate moods recognized by classical Logic into logistic formulas, we perceive that,

[1] Alessandro Padoa, *La Logique déductive dans sa dernière phase de développement*, Paris, Gauthier-Villars, 1912, p. 78. For example, a syllogism in *Datisi* would be represented by the formula

$$b \supset c : \exists\,(b \frown a) : \supset : \exists\,(a \frown c)$$

which means: If b is contained in c, and if there exists a part that is common to class b and class a, then there is a part common to class a and class c. A syllogism in *Darii* would be represented by the formula:

$$b \supset c\ \exists\,(a \frown b) : \supset : \exists\,(a \frown c)$$

which means: If b is contained in c, and if there exists a part that is common to class a and class b, then there exists a part common to class a and class c.

And granted the equation $a \frown b = b \frown a$ (which is nothing but the symbol of the simple conversion of particular affirmatives), the first "syllogism" is reducible to the second, which procedure is in conformity with classical logic. (But it could be said with equal right that the second is reducible to the first.)

Similarly a syllogism in *Celarent* would be represented by the formula

$$b \supset -\ c : a \supset b : \supset : a \supset -\ c$$

which means: If b is contained in the contrary class of c (that is, in the group of individuals that are not in the class c) and if a is contained in the class b, then a is contained in the contrary class of c. A syllogism in *Barbara* would be represented by the formula:

$$b \supset c . a \supset b : \supset : a \supset c$$

that is: If b is contained in the class c, and if a is contained in the class b, then a is contained in the class c. Granting that

$$d = -\ c . = . c = -\ d$$

(to say that the class d is the contrary class of c is equivalent to saying that the class c is the contrary class of d), the first "syllogism" is reducible to the second —by merely calling the term d, c. But this is no longer conformable to classical logic, and is valid only for the laws of the algebra of signs, not for those of the logic of thought, for (1) we do not think a syllogism in *Celarent* in this way:

Every man is a non-angel,
but every philosopher is a man,
therefore every philosopher is a non-angel.

and (2) the substitution of *non-angel* by a term d (such as "corporeal") signifying the "contrary class" of the class "angel," would cause a change in the very *matter* of the syllogism.

by a series of transformations which reduce such and such a mood to such and such another, there finally remain but three original moods: *Barbara*, *Darapti* and *Bramantip*.[1] Therefore the whole theory of the syllogism is an " illusion due to the imperfect means of expression used by the Scholastics."

Signor Padoa, shocked at " the great number of moods " admitted by the ancients, seems to be unaware that Aristotle and the Scholastics were acquainted with the reduction of moods long before his time, and that they allowed only the four moods of the first figure to subsist as *perfect* moods.

To criticise the syllogism in the name of Logistics is to sin through ignorance of the question.

Especially does he appear to ignore the fact that the nineteen classical moods of the syllogism are in no sense *formulas of logical algebra* constituting a ready-reckoner of signs comparable to those of Logistics, but are in truth types of *rational operations* effected naturally by the intelligence in the actual course of thinking. Nor does he advert to the cardinal point, that the principles and object of Logistics are *essentially different* from those of Logic and that it is consequently as absurd to apply a logistic treatment to the nineteen moods of the syllogism as it would be to apply a musical method to the construction of houses or the commanding of armies.

There is no common measure, only pure equivocity, between the logistical " reduction " and the " logical " " reduction " of the moods of the syllogism. The operations by which the logistician " reduces " one mood to another are altogether different from *logical* operations (they are not operations of the *reason*, of thought, concerned with the order of intellectual objects, but *algebraic* operations concerned with signs, abstracting from every intellectual operation). For the logistician the reduction of one formula to another implies the pure and simple suppression of the first in favour of the second (there is no reason for keeping an algorismic symbol when another is its equivalent), whereas, for the logician, reduction in no way prevents the

[1] *Bramantip* (or *Bamalip*) is the mnemonic word substituted for *Baralipton* to designate the first mood of the first indirect figure by those logicians who consider the latter as an independent (fourth) figure. See above, Chap. III, Section 2, § 2, note 27.

first formula from continuing to be valid in its own right as a natural and primary operation of the reason.

In view of this it is not surprising that the logician and the logistician should achieve different results in reducing the moods, nor that Signor Padoa's method should recognize as primary moods only *Barbara*, *Darapti* and *Bramantip* (the latter two considered as *false*, as we shall see below) in place of the four moods of the first figure which " classical Logic " allows to subsist as " perfect." The logistic result remains absolutely foreign to Logic itself, and cannot be considered as a criticism of the syllogistic theory except in the eyes of a *barbarus in arte logica*.

II. *Subalternation, Partial Conversion, Syllogisms in Darapti and Baralipton* (*Bamalip*). Several logisticians (MacColl, Miss Ladd, Shroeder, Nagy, Peano, etc.) followed in France by Couturat [1] and Rougier,[2] believe that they have discovered the *falsity* or illegitimacy of subalternation, of partial conversion (*conversio per accidens*) and of syllogisms in *Darapti* and *Baralipton* (Bamalip).[3] Their claims may be summarized as follows: (1) Every particular affirmative (I) implies the *existence* of subjects having such and such a Pr.: " some men are learned " implies that there exist certain subjects possessing human nature who are learned. (2) Universal affirmative propositions (A) on the contrary, contain *no affirmation of existence* whatsoever: in the proposition: " every centaur is half-man, half-horse " the affirmation is concerned exclusively with the conformity of the Pr. " half-man half-horse " to the object of thought " centaur," or, as these authors would say, it concerns only the inclusion of the " class " centaur in the " class " half-man half-horse, independently of all existence.[4]

The logistician's criticism of inferences in A I or in A A I.

It follows, then, that if we conclude from A to I, I will contain an affirmation of existence that A did not contain,

[1] Cf. Couturat, *La Logique de Leibniz*, pp. 9 and 19.

[2] Cf. Louis Rougier, *La Structure des théories déductives*, Paris, Alcan, 1921.

[3] This criticism applies also to syllogisms in *Fapesmo* (*Fesapo*) and *Felapton*, if what is said here of affirmatives be extended also to negative propositions.

[4] As we have seen above (No. 23), even in this case the verb *to be* continues to signify existence, but *ideal* existence. The copula signifies the relation of the Pr. *half-man half-horse* to the S. centaur, inasmuch as they are *identified with each other in a certain existence*, in the existence which beings of reason have *in the mind*.

and we will have performed an *illegitimate* operation. But this is what we do in subalternation, in partial conversion, and in the syllogistic moods (*Baralipton* and *Darapti*) wherein from two A premisses we infer an I conclusion. Therefore these operations taught by classical Logic, are in reality illegitimate. This, says Padoa,[1] is " one of the first and most remarkable results of adopting an ideographic logic."

It is also in truth a perfect example of the errors to which the adoption of an ideographic logic can lead in the absence of a preliminary and profound investigation of logical problems and clearly shows the disadvantages resulting from an ignorance of the works of the ancients. The logicians of the Middle Ages had long since probed into all the elements of the problem which the logisticians claim to have unearthed and had very clearly indicated its solution.[2] The theory of the *suppositio* and the *ampliatio*,[3] especially as developed by the Aristotelio-Thomist school in its controversy with the " Terminists " (the school of Occam), contains, among many other remarks, all that is needed to answer the difficulties raised by MacColl and his emulators. We shall try to set forth this answer here by assembling the pertinent information scattered here and there among the works of the ancients.

(1) First let us observe that this problem exceeds the limits of Lesser or Formal Logic and encroaches upon the realm of Greater Logic. For the existential or non-existential signification of a proposition depends upon its *matter*, and not upon its *form* alone. The fundamental error of the logisticians lies in their failure to distinguish between the form and the matter of propositions and in their belief that

[1] Alessandro Padoa, *La Logique Deductive*, Paris, 1912, p. 79, note 2.

[2] Cf. Javelli, *Logicae compendium peripateticae*, Venetiis, 1541, tract. VII, *de suppositionibus*, Chap. IV and VI ; tract. IX, *de consequentiis*, Chap. IV, § 2.—John of St. Thomas, *Logica*, pp. 32–33, 72, 170.—The reason that no specific discussions of the case of syllogisms in A A I are to be found in the works of these authors is that they were careful to add to their treatises on the syllogism : " Tu autem adverte novitie, *quod praedictas defensiones servare non poteris, donec intellexeris tractatum suppositionum et ampliationum et appellationum et probationum terminorum* " (Javelli, p. 168). Thus the application of these rules to *Baralipton* and *Darapti* followed as a matter of course. However, Messrs. MacColl, Schroeder, etc., may be granted the honour of having made the discussion centre explicitly upon this point.

[3] See above, Nos. 27 and 28.

considerations bearing exclusively on the form suffice to explain the entire discourse.

(2) From the point of view of matter we must distinguish between *propositions in necessary matter*, that is, those in which the Pr. is *essential* to the S. (in which case we say that the S. has *suppositio naturalis*) and *propositions in contingent matter*, that is, those wherein the Pr. is *accidental* to the S. (*the S. has a suppositio accidentalis*).

In the first case the proposition expresses an eternal truth and affirms only the relation (of identification) between the object of thought signified by the Pr. and the object of thought signified by the S. (*habitudinem praedicati ad subjectum*). Thus it does not require the actual existence of the subject in order to be true (*non requiritur existentia subjecti ut praedicatum verificetur de subjecto*) and has not necessarily and of itself an " existential " sense.

In the second case the proposition expresses a contingent truth, and for this reason, that is, inasmuch as it does not express an eternal truth, it requires the (actual) existence of the subject in order to be true. It has an " existential " sense (*dicit et habitudinem et existentiam*) ; since the Pr. does not follow from the nature of the subject, it could not be verified except of a subject posited in existence.

(3) But it is false both that the first case is realized only in *universal* affirmative propositions and is always realized therein, and that the second case is always realized in *particular* affirmatives and nowhere else. Each of these cases may be realized both for A and for I.

An I proposition may attribute an essential Pr. to the S.

Every man is mortal,
Some man is creable,
Some animal (viz., man) is rational.

These three propositions express eternal truths and remain equally true even if no man exists.

An A may attribute an accidental Pr. to the S.

Some angel is damned,
Every man is born in sin,
All were taken prisoners.

These three propositions express contingent truths and would be false if no angel or man existed.

(4) Moreover, when a proposition, for example an A, states an essential Pr. it is not necessarily and of itself concerned with anything except the relation of the Pr. to the S., that is, with the simply ideal existence of this S. with this Pr. But there is nothing to prevent the mind from adding an existential sense to it (the truth expressed ceasing in this case to be an eternal truth) as it does in all the universals obtained by *induction* in the experimental sciences.

Every acid makes litmus paper turn red.
Every mammal is viviparous.

Taken in themselves these propositions would, no doubt, remain true even were there neither acids nor mammals, but actually we never think of them without understanding that there are acids and that there are mammals.

An A proposition whose Pr. is essential to the S. may have an "existential" signification.

The first principle to which the logisticians appeal is therefore doubly false : not only are there A propositions whose Pr. is *accidental* to the S. and which for this reason have an existential signification, but A propositions, whose Pr. is *essential* to the S., may also be understood as having an existential signification.

(5) On the other hand, when a proposition, for example an I, states an accidental Pr., it implies, as we have seen, the actual existence of its subject in the same measure in which the *suppositio* is *accidentalis*, that is to say, in the measure in which the proposition does not of itself express an eternal truth. But the mind is always free to vary the *suppositio*, while the form of the proposition remains the same, and to make the affirmation bear upon simply *possible* or ideal existence, and in this manner render the proposition necessary and eternally true (called by the ancients *ampliatio in ordine ad tempus*). Thus the proposition

Some man is sincere

is *amplified* if we understand it in the sense that

Some man (as a possible creature) is sincere.

In other words, " human nature is not exclusive of sincerity " (it was in this sense that Lachelier understood all I propositions). This proposition remains true even if no man exists.

In mathematics this *absolutio a tempore*, this transfer to simply possible existence, occurs of itself :

> Some magnitudes are incommensurable.
> Some angles are obtuse.

That is, there are (in possible existence) obtuse angles and magnitudes that lack a common measure.

An I proposition whose Pr. is accidental to the S. may receive an ideal signification.

Thus the second principle invoked by the logisticians is doubly false. Not only do there exist I propositions whose Pr. is *essential* to the S. and for this reason do not necessarily have an existential sense, but also the I propositions whose Pr. is *accidental* to the S. may be freed from the temporal order by thought and elevated by *ampliatio* to the order of ideal existence, and in this case they no longer imply the actual existence of their S.

(6) Furthermore, *it is always possible for the thinking mind* (for which Logic is constructed) to keep *the same kind of suppositio* in passing from an A to an I proposition, whether it attaches an existential sense to A, and consequently does the same in thinking I, or whether it abstracts from actual existence in thinking A and does likewise in thinking I. And from the fact that the kind of *suppositio* (that is, in this case the mode of existence in relation to which the *suppositio* is taken) [1]—is not changed, the sequences in question are legitimate. For example :

(*a*) *Subalternation.* If we say, in abstracting from actual existence in the A proposition :

> Every man has imperfections (whether or not men exist)

we conclude rightly that :

> Therefore some man (even for example a saint) has imperfections

Inferences in A I.

for the subalternate also abstracts from actual existence. (But we would conclude wrongly were we to say : therefore some man has imperfections, in the sense that : there exist in the world men who have imperfections ; for were

[1] See above, pp. 62–63.

there no men in the world this proposition would be false, although the subalternant would still be true.)

On the other hand, if we attach an existential sense to A, and say:

Every man has imperfections (and men exist)

then we conclude rightly in saying: therefore some (existing) man has imperfections.

(β) *Partial Conversion.* If we attach an existential sense to A and say:

Every bat is a mammal (and bats exist)

we conclude correctly that: therefore some (existing) mammal is a bat.

If, in abstracting from actual existence in A, we say:

Every philosopher is a man (whether or not there are philosophers)

we conclude correctly that: therefore some man is a philosopher, on condition we understand by means of an *ampliatio* that: therefore some man (as a possible creature) is a philosopher.

and in A A I. (γ) *Syllogisms in Baralipton and Darapti.* If we reason in *Baralipton* and say, attaching an existential sense to the Major [1]:

Every visionary is a dangerous man,
but every Utopian is a visionary (and Utopians exist),

we conclude quite legitimately that

Therefore some dangerous (existing) man is a Utopian.

And if, keeping the Major in the order of eternal truth, we say:

Every cowardly act is despicable,
but every lie is a cowardly act (whether or not lies exist),

[1] In the construction of a syllogism of the first indirect figure we start with the Minor. For those, on the contrary, who look upon the fourth figure as autonomous (represented therefore by *Bamalip* or *Bramantip*, and not by *Baralipton*) the same syllogism is constructed, in the same way as all the others, with the Major as the first premise.

we also conclude legitimately : therefore some despicable act (taken in possible existence) is a lie.

Likewise, in reasoning in *Darapti*, we conclude in a perfectly valid manner :

Every bat has wings (and bats exist),
but every bat is a mammal,
therefore some (existing) mammal has wings.
Every poet is an artist (whether poets exist or not),
but every poet is a man,
therefore some man (as a possible creature) is an artist.
Every square has four right angles,
but every square is a rhombus,
therefore some rhombus has four right angles.

The additions which we have placed in parentheses in these examples in order to make manifest the unexpressed thought, need not be explicitly stated,[1] for they introduce no necessary statement on the side of the form, but serve only to specify the manner in which the mind should make use of sequences that are in themselves valid. In short, they simply indicate certain *conditions of legitimacy* among the multitude of similar conditions which concern the *suppositio* of terms and which ancient Logic treated in great detail. Thus subalternation, partial conversion, and syllogisms in AAI, are of themselves just as legitimate for the logician as any other valid logical sequences.

(7) If the logisticians claim the contrary, and congratu-

[1] This would not be true in passing from an A to a *singular*, for in that case, even if we attached an existential sense to the A proposition, the singular consequent might be false (if its subject did not exist) the while the universal antecedent remained true :

Every man is mortal (and men exist),
therefore Peter is mortal.

In the supposition that Peter did not exist, the consequent would be false and the antecedent would remain true. The rule set forth by the Scholastics for similar cases stipulates that in order for the sequence to be valid an explicit statement must be added, viz., the affirmation of the existence of the subject (called the *addere constantiam* by John of St. Thomas) : " Every man is mortal, *and Peter exists*, therefore Peter is mortal."

They required that the same addition be made in the passage from a singular negative to a particular negative. " Peter is not bald. Therefore some man is not bald " ; supposing that Paul alone existed in the world, and that he were bald, then every man would be bald and the consequent " some man is not bald," would be false, the while the antecedent, " Peter is not bald " remained true, since Peter does not exist. That is the reason why we must say " Peter is not bald, *and Peter exists*, therefore some man is not bald."

late themselves upon a discovery that is neither new nor true, it is because the very principle from which their method proceeds requires that *everything be expressed*, and that there be nothing in the reasoning that is not in the *signs* of the reasoning, for once the latter signs have been ascertained they are supposed to be self-sufficient.

But in this very principle, Logistics, if it professes to be a system of logic, is the negation of Logic. For Logic is an art made to *serve* the intelligence, not to replace it ; the task of formal Logic is to teach those modes of procedure which entail no risk of error on the side of the form (that is, the disposition of terms), and which do not betray the intelligence *on the condition* that it perform an act of thought, that the mind really move. It is not its function to provide us with formulas that suffice for their own development, an algorismic machine that is self-operative the while the intelligence remains at rest or exerts itself only to superintend this movement.

Language cannot be system of mechanically determined signs.

This lengthy discussion will not have been unprofitable if it has shown us the precision and depth of the notion of Logic that was held by the ancients. From the very fact that language is a system of material signs destined to express the life of immaterial thought, they saw that it must necessarily be a system that is *neither rigid nor mechanical*, nor independent of the activity of the mind. They saw also that it entails the possibility of various procedures ordered by thought (whence the imperfections, the inevitable dangers and difficulties the *mastery of* which it is Logic's precise duty to teach us), and entailing the possibility of varying within certain limits *the intelligible sound* conveyed by one and the same combination of signs, a possibility which is strikingly manifested in the scholastic theory of the *suppositio*.

Because they have failed to take this theory into consideration, modern logicians have become involved in many futile quarrels, each one claiming to attribute forever to certain propositions a sense that corresponds in reality to a contingent *suppositio*, in which he has arbitrarily and unconsciously fixed his thought. Thus for Lachelier [1]

[1] Lachelier, *Études sur le Syllogisme*, pp. 53–57.

every particular affirmative proposition (as opposed to those which he calls "partial collectives," see above, No. 51, *e*) of itself has no existential sense, but only a sense *de jure*, whereas for the logisticians affirmative particulars have, on the contrary, nothing but an existential sense. For Whitehead [1] every affirmative universal implies a judgment of existence, whereas for MacColl [2] and the logisticians cited above, no affirmative universal could ever have an existential sense.

We may conclude therefore that the so-called demonstration of the invalidity of inferences in A I proves but one thing : the danger of adopting too summary an ideographic Logic. Especially does it reveal the fundamental falsity of every alleged Logic that aims at fixing the work of the intelligence once and for all in ideographic symbols and requires, not that these symbols *signify* the diverse inflections and the nice edge of thought more exactly than ordinary language—a perfectly legitimate ambition—but that they *substitute* a certain regulated manipulation of algebraic signs for the work of thought itself. An ideographic Logic, thus conceived, could never be adequate to its object unless it were to replace the difficulties of rational labour by an infinite material complication. In truth it could not *fix* thought except as in the way that most stains used in histology *fix* living matter—by killing it.

§ 4. *The Expository Syllogism*

*85. NOTION OF THE EXPOSITORY SYLLOGISM. In the ordinary categorical syllogism, which we have just studied, the M is an universal term. In the expository syllogism (syllogism "*of exposition*," *syllogismus expositorius*) the M is a *singular term*. Example :

> *Judas* turned traitor,
> but Judas was an apostle,
> therefore an apostle turned traitor.

The expository syllogism is a syllogism whose M is a singular term.

[1] Whitehead, *Universal Algebra*, Cambridge, 1898, Vol. I, p. 104.

[2] MacColl, *The Calculus of Equivalent Statements*, ap. Proceedings of the Mathematical Society, Vol. IX, June 13th, 1878. Cf. *Symbolical Reasoning*, ap. *Mind*, No. 17, January, 1880.

This singular M [1] makes evident or "exposes" the union of T and t to each other, hence the name "expository" syllogism.

But it is not really a syllogism.

We must note, however, that this form has only the exterior appearance of a syllogism, for it is not one in reality : it is not an *inference*, it is simply a *sensible representation* or an *exposition* to the senses. Undoubtedly it conforms to the principle of identity, but this principle does not regulate a movement of the intelligence here, nor does it cause any passage from one truth to another truth. To know that the apostle Judas turned traitor to his master is to know already in act that an apostle turned traitor. The syllogistic form has no *rôle* here other than that of rendering materially or sensibly evident to me (in the order of sensible representations which I use to think), of making me "put my finger on," a truth of which I already possessed intellectual knowledge.[2] For this reason the expository syllogism is immediately ruled by the principle of triple identity or of the separating third, without the intermediation of the

[1] Obviously this M must be *absolutely singular*, that is to say incommunicable, otherwise we would be reasoning with four terms (cf. above, No. 51, inset), as in saying :

> The straight line $\overline{AB}$ is identical with the straight line $\overrightarrow{AB}$,
>
> but the straight line $\overline{AB}$ is identical with the straight line $\overleftarrow{BA}$,
>
> therefore the straight line $\overleftarrow{BA}$ is identical with the straight line $\overrightarrow{AB}$.

In the Major AB stands for AB *taken under the aspect* $\overrightarrow{AB}$, and in the Minor it stands for AB *taken under the aspect* $\overleftarrow{BA}$.

[2] Cf. the opuscula *De Natura Syllogismorum* . . . "Syllogismus expositorius non est vere syllogismus, sed magis quaedam sensibilis demonstratio seu quaedam resolutio facta ad sensum, ad hoc ut consequentia quae vera erat secundum intellectualem cognitionem, declaretur in sensibili." "In this case," adds P. Richard (*Phil. du Raisonnement*, p. 361), the syllogistic form plays the same *rôle* as does the material object or the diagram drawn upon the blackboard as a help in certain demonstrations."

It could be objected (cf. Lachelier, *Études sur le Syllogisme*, p. 56), that an expository syllogism such as, "Peter is sincere, but Peter is a man, therefore some man is sincere" is a true reasoning inasmuch as the conclusion does not express the simple *fact* (already expressed in the Major) that a certain man is sincere, but signifies this *general truth* that human nature is not exclusive of sincerity. In reality, however, this last meaning, far from being inferred by the pseudo-syllogism in question, is communicated by the mind to the conclusion in virtue of an inductive *ascensus* (*ascensus disjunctivus* : a certain man is sincere, therefore some man is sincere—see above, No. 17 and below, No. 96). The conclusion as presented in the expository syllogism signifies only this *fact*, that a certain determinate man is sincere.

dictum de omni or *de nullo* (which is necessarily implied in every genuine syllogistic inference by the very fact that it has a universal objective concept as its middle term).

The expository syllogism may be constructed in all the figures, but the third figure is most naturally suited to it, since what is proper to the individual is not to be attributable to a subject but to be itself the subject.

In the second figure, besides the ordinary negative moods, it has four affirmative moods (premisses A A, I I, A I, I A). On the other hand, in the third figure it may have only two moods (premisses A A and E A)—the letter A designating here, not a universal affirmative but a singular affirmative and the letter E a singular negative.

DIVISION OF THE SYLLOGISM

SYLLOGISM	Categorical	True (*syllogism* in the pure and simple sense of the word)	First figure Second figure Third figure
		(expository)	
	Hypothetical	Conditional Disjunctive Conjunctive	

B. THE CONDITIONAL SYLLOGISM

§ 1. *Hypothetical Syllogisms in General*

86. HYPOTHETICAL SYLLOGISMS. In the categorical syllogism (the syllogism in the pure and simple sense of the word) which we have just studied, the Major was a *simple* or categorical proposition.

HYPOTHETICAL syllogisms are those in which the *Major* is a *hypothetical* or *compound* proposition, and the *Minor* posits or destroys one of the parts of the Major.

The hypothetical syllogism has for its Major a *hypothetical* proposition one of whose members is posited or destroyed by the Minor.

This second condition is indispensable to a truly hypothetical syllogism.[1] Even though its Major and even all of its propositions (proximate matter) be hypothetical, a syllogism

[1] Cf. Gredt, *Elementa*, I, No. 67.

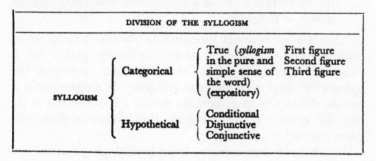

such as : " If Peter is rational he has the power of laughter ; but if Peter is a man he is rational ; therefore if Peter is a man he has the power of laughter," is in reality a categorical syllogism. In this case we have three conditional propositions united to one another *in the same manner* as are the propositions of an ordinary categorical syllogism (by the identification of two extreme terms to a middle term). In other words we have a categorical *syllogism* whose *terms* are *propositions :*

> Everything inferring that Peter is rational infers that Peter has the power of laughter,
> but that Peter is a man infers that Peter is rational,
> therefore that Peter is a man infers that Peter has the power of laughter.

This is a categorical syllogism in *Barbara* having as its middle term the complex term " inferring that Peter is rational." Evidently then, the difference between the categorical and hypothetical syllogism is deeper than a simple difference in proximate matter : it is the *very structure*, the essence of the syllogism that differs in these two cases (see below, No. 89).

As we have seen above, hypothetical propositions are either *conditional*, *disjunctive*, *conjunctive* [1] or *copulative*. From the latter type nothing can be inferred. Therefore we have but three kinds of hypothetical syllogisms to consider :

> *Conditional.*
> *Disjunctive.*
> *Conjunctive.*

As the last two types are reducible to the first, it is to this first type—*the conditional syllogism*—that we shall give special attention.

(*a*) THE DISJUNCTIVE SYLLOGISM. The Major is a disjunctive proposition (copula, *or*) ; the Minor *posits* or *destroys* one of the members of the disjunction, the Conclusion *destroys* or *posits* the other.[2]

[1] See above, p. 101, note 1.
[2] For the cases in which the Major is an *improperly* disjunctive proposition, see above, No. 46, 2, *c*, pp. 103–104.

TWO FIGURES, accordingly as the Minor *posits* (in which instance the Conclusion *destroys*), or *destroys* (in which instance the Conclusion *posits*), and four MOODS in each, accordingly as the parts of the MAJOR are (1) *both affirmative*, (2) *affirmative and negative*, (3) *negative and affirmative*, (4) *both negative* (see the table below).

The disjunctive syllogism may be reduced to the conditional syllogism : " If we have a leader we shall not be powerless, but we have a leader, therefore, etc." " If we do not have a leader, we shall be powerless, but we have no leader, therefore, etc." (It may also be reduced directly to a categorical syllogism—at least when the two members of the Major have the same subject : " those who have a leader are not powerless, but we shall have a leader, therefore, etc.")

FIGURES AND MOODS OF THE DISJUNCTIVE SYLLOGISM

	First Figure (*ponendo-tollens*)	Second Figure (*tollendo-ponens*)
1ST MOOD	We shall either have a leader or *be* powerless. But we shall have a leader, Therefore we shall *not be* powerless.	We shall either have a leader or *be* powerless. But we shall not have a leader, Therefore we shall *be* powerless.
2ND MOOD	We shall either have a leader or *not* co-operate, But we shall have a leader, Therefore we *shall* co-operate.	We shall either have a leader or *not* co-operate, But we have no leader, Therefore we *shall not* co-operate.
3RD MOOD	We shall either have no leader or *obey*, But we shall have no leader, Therefore we *shall not obey*.	We shall either have no leader or *obey*, But we shall have a leader, Therefore we *shall* obey.
4TH MOOD	We shall either *not* have a leader or *not* all be able to command, But we shall not have a leader, Therefore we *shall* all be able to command.	We shall either not have a leader or *not* all be able to command, But we shall have a leader, Therefore we *shall not all* be able to command.

(*b*) THE CONJUNCTIVE SYLLOGISM. The Major is a conjunctive proposition (A *cannot* at the same time be B and C) which denies that two propositions (having the same S) can be at the same time true.

Only one figure (*ponendo-tollens*), in which the Minor *posits* one of the two members of the Major, and the Conclusion *destroys* the other member : " No man can serve both God and Mammon at the same time ; but Judas serves Mammon, therefore he does not serve God (but John serves God, therefore he does not serve Mammon)."

The figure *tollendo-ponens* is not valid, for both members of the Major can be false at the same time.[1]

The conjunctive syllogism may be reduced to the conditional syllogism : " If a man serve God, he does not serve Mammon, but John serves God, therefore, etc." (it may also be reduced directly to a categorical syllogism : " He who serves God does not serve Mammon, but John serves God, etc.")

(*c*) Aristotle does not speak of the hypothetical syllogism. The expression συλλογισμὸς ἐξ ὑποθεσέως does not signify a *hypothetical syllogism* to him, but signifies a categorical syllogism the *conclusion of which depends upon some postulate.*[2] The theory of hypothetical syllogisms was first treated by Theophrastus, a disciple of Aristotle, and was developed principally by Chrysippus and the Stoics. It was studied in great detail during the Middle Ages through the influence of Boethius who, using Greek sources, expounded it in a very detailed, precise and " remarkably complete " manner (Prantl, *Geschichte der Logik*, p. 700).

§ 2. *The Conditional Syllogism*

87. THE CONDITIONAL SYLLOGISM. When the MAJOR is a conditional proposition (copula *if*), one of whose members is either *posited* or *destroyed* by the MINOR [3] the syllogism is

CONDITIONAL,

e.g., if the earth turns, it moves, but it does turn, therefore it moves.

[1] Nevertheless, by accident, and by reason of the matter (if there is no middle term), we may reason in this figure : " No one can be dead and alive at the same time, but Peter is not dead, therefore he is alive."

[2] Cf. Waitz, I, 427, *ad Anal. Pr.* I, 23, 40 b 25 ; Hamelin, *Le Syst. d'Aristote*, p. 181, note 1.

[3] See above, No. 86.

The entire theory of the conditional syllogism rests upon the assertion formulated above,[1] that in conditional propositions the affirmation bears uniquely upon the necessary connection between the propositions (with the *sequence* or *inference* itself). Consequently that which is stated by the Major of a conditional syllogism (granting that the conditional proposition is true) is simply a *valid sequence.*

The conditional syllogism has for its Major a *Conditional* proposition, one of whose members is posited or destroyed by the Minor.

Thus we see that the *supreme principle of the conditional syllogism* is the very same as the one which we have said above to be *the essential law of all argumentation*, and which is but an immediate determination of the principle of identity or non-contradiction.[2] *In every valid sequence, it is impossible that the antecedent be true and the consequent false;* in other words, *by the very fact that the antecedent is true the consequent is also true* (and therefore if the consequent is false the antecedent is false). Note carefully however that the inverse is not true, and that it is possible that a true consequent follow from a false antecedent : if the antecedent is false the consequent may be true ; and therefore if the consequent is true the antecedent is not for that reason true (my pocket-book is in the moon, but the moon is in my pocket, therefore my pocket-book is in my pocket).

Supreme principle

Whence are derived the special rules for the conditional syllogism : I. *To posit the condition is to posit the conditioned.* (If Peter is speaking to me he exists ; but he is speaking to me, therefore he exists.)

and the special rules for the conditional syllogism: to posit the Condition is to posit the Conditioned.

II. *But to posit the conditioned is not to posit thereby the condition.* (If Peter is speaking to me, he exists ; but he exists, therefore he is speaking to me : this is an *illegitimate conclusion*, for he can exist without speaking to me.)

To posit the Conditioned is not to posit the Condition.

III. *To destroy the conditioned is to destroy the condition.* (If Peter is speaking to me he exists : but he does not exist, therefore he is not speaking to me.)

To remove the Conditioned is to remove the Condition.

IV. *But to destroy the condition is not to destroy thereby the conditioned.* (If Peter is speaking to me he exists ; but he is not speaking to me, therefore he does not exist : this is an *illegitimate conclusion*, for he may very well exist without speaking to me.)

But to remove the Condition is not to remove the Conditioned.

[1] See above, No. 46, 3 *sqq.* Only Majors that are conditional *in the strict sense* are treated in the theory of the conditional syllogism.

[2] See above, No. 65.

Many errors and sophisms arise from the neglect of these rules. It often happens, particularly in the natural sciences, that a hypothesis be looked upon as "*demonstrated*" because certain conclusions drawn from it are verified by facts. Such an hypothesis may nevertheless be merely probable (for example Newton's hypothesis in astronomy) or even entirely false (*e.g.*, the Darwinian hypothesis in biology).

FIGURES AND MOODS OF THE CONDITIONAL SYLLOGISM

	First Figure (*ponendo-ponens*) [1]	Second Figure (*tollendo-tollens*) [2]
1ST MOOD	If Peter died a martyr's death he is in heaven, But Peter died a martyr's death, Therefore he is in heaven.	If Peter died a martyr's death he is in heaven, But Peter is not in heaven, Therefore he did not die a martyr's death.
2ND MOOD	If Peter died a martyr's death he did not deny his faith. But Peter died a martyr's death, Therefore he did not deny his faith.	If Peter died a martyr's death he did not deny his faith. But Peter did deny his faith, Therefore he did not die a martyr's death.
3RD MOOD	If Peter does not love his neighbour he lacks charity, But Peter does not love his neighbour. Therefore he lacks charity.	If Peter does not love his neighbour he lacks charity. But Peter does not lack charity, Therefore he loves his neighbour.
4TH MOOD	If Peter does not love his neighbour whom he sees, he does not love God whom he does not see, But Peter does not love his neighbour whom he sees, Therefore he does not love God whom he does not see.	If Peter does not love his neighbour whom he sees, he does not love God whom he does not see. But Peter loves God whom he does not see, Therefore he loves his neighbour whom he sees.

There are *two legitimate* FIGURES [3] for the conditional syllogism accordingly as the MINOR *posits the* CONDITION

[1] That is to say, which *in positing* (the Condition in the Minor) *posits* (the Conditioned in the Conclusion).

[2] That is, which, *in destroying* (the Conditioned in the Minor) *destroys* (the Condition in the Conclusion).

[3] The word *figure* is used here by *analogy*. In the categorical syllogism the figure depends upon the function of the *mean* of the argumentation (the *middle* TERM) in the premisses. In the conditional syllogism it depends equally upon the *rôle* of the *mean* (but which is in this case a PROPOSITION) in the premisses (the first figure: *condition* in the Major, *posited* in the Minor; second figure, *conditioned* in the Major and *destroyed* in the Minor).

(in which case the Conclusion posits the Conditioned) or *destroys* the CONDITIONED (in which case the Conclusion destroys the Condition). In each of these figures there are four MOODS, accordingly as the parts of the MAJOR are 1 both affirmative, 2 affirmative and negative, 3 negative and affirmative, 4 both negative.

The figure (*ponendo-ponens*) wherein to posit the Conditioned would be to posit the Condition is *illegitimate ; e.g.*, " if Peter died a martyr's death he is in heaven, but he is in heaven, therefore he died a martyr's death. . . ."

The figure (*tollendo-tollens*) wherein to destroy the Condition would be to destroy the Conditioned is likewise *illegitimate :* " if Peter died a martyr's death he is in heaven, but he did not die a martyr's death, therefore he is not in heaven."

88. THE RESOLUTION OF CONDITIONAL SYLLOGISMS INTO CATEGORICAL SYLLOGISMS. It is often said that the conditional syllogism may be *reduced* to the categorical syllogism by taking, as the Major, a universal proposition that has for its S. the Pr. of the Condition and for its Pr. the Pr. of the Conditioned. Thus the syllogism : " If Peter is a martyr he is a saint, but he is a martyr, therefore he is a saint," becomes : " Every martyr is a saint, but Peter is a martyr, therefore Peter is a saint."

The conditional syllogism may be resolved into a categorical syllogism the Major of which has for S. the Pr. of the Condition and for Pr. the Pr. of the Conditioned.

But this categorical Major expresses another truth than does the conditional Major. For the fact is that the conditional syllogism is not *reducible* to the categorical syllogism as the moods of the second and third figure [1] are reducible to those of the first, that is, as the imperfect to the perfect in the same genus. It constitutes a *distinct type of argumentation*, an original manner of procedure and, as such, is properly irreducible. The proof of this will be evident if we consider a conditional Major whose two members do not have the same subject ; for example in the syllogism :

If the world exists, God exists,
but the world exists,
therefore God exists,

the reduction indicated above is impossible.

[1] Nor, for even better reasons, as the moods of the fourth figure are reduced to the moods of the first, from which they differ only apparently.

Nevertheless, it constitutes a distinct type of reasoning.

Therefore let us say rather that we can *translate*, or better, *resolve* a conditional syllogism into a categorical syllogism either in the manner shown above, when the conditional Major has but one S., or, in the contrary case, by first resolving the syllogism under consideration into two conditional syllogisms each of whose Majors has but one subject, for example :

(I) If the world exists it was created by God, But the world exists, Therefore it was created by God.	which is in turn resolvable into	That which exists (without being God) was created by God, But the world exists (without being God), Therefore the world was created by God.
(II) If God created the world, God exists, But God did create the world, Therefore God exists.	which is in turn resolvable into	He who created the world exists, But God created the world, Therefore God exists.

True, in proceeding thus, we have destroyed both the unity of the conditional syllogism, and that which constituted its proper nature. But this is so whenever a whole is resolved into its parts ; that which constitutes the unity of the whole as such is by that very act dissolved. The conditional syllogism is a syllogism of a type apart that contains virtually in its unity either one or two categorical syllogisms.

This is the direct consequence of the thesis established above (No. 46, 3, *a*) that the conditional proposition expresses a truth *of another type*, constructs an *other* object of assent than does the categorical proposition. It follows then that the argumentation founded upon a categorical Major must itself be necessarily *other* than the argumentation founded upon a conditional Major.

But this by no means signifies that the conditional syllogism indicates our possession of another logic and of other laws of thought than those upon which the categorical syllogism depends. In fact, on the contrary, the conditional syllogism presupposes the categorical syllogism just as the conditional proposition *presupposes* the categorical proposition. The reason that it does not consist in establishing the union or connection of a Pr. to a S. by means of a third term is, that this union or connection is already made, already given, in one of the members of the compound proposition which acts as the Major in the conditional reasoning. Therefore there are no grounds for seeing in the conditional syllogism a mode of reasoning that escapes the Logic of " inherence " or " predication," that is to say, the Logic which recognizes that we can neither judge nor reason without attributing or refusing a Pr. to a S. The categorical proposition *consists* in this attribution itself, and the hypothetical or compound proposition which unites two categorical propositions, *supposes* this attribution as already made.

*89. THE NATURE OF THE CONDITIONAL SYLLOGISM. We saw above [1] that the categorical syllogism orders discourse according to the *connection* of TERMS. From an antecedent that reveals *in a third term* the *means by which, or the reason for which*, two terms should be united to (or separated from) each other, it deduces or infers the proposition that unites these two terms to one another (or separates them). Thus it concludes, at least in so far as logical relations are concerned, from a more universal truth to a less universal truth contained in it.

In order that these notions be applicable as such to the conditional syllogism, the latter must be resolved into the categorical syllogism, or the categorical syllogisms, which it contains virtually. But these notions as such are not applicable to the conditional syllogism considered in itself and in its proper nature. So we may say that the conditional syllogism and the categorical syllogism are alike in this : that both have as their object the *manifestation of the truth of a conclusion by the resolution of the latter* into the *first principles* of *intelligibility*,[2] but that they differ in the following characteristics : in conditional reasoning the mind does not apprehend a Minor under the dependence of another proposition as it does in categorical reasoning ; it appre-

The conditional syllogism infers a conclusion from a previously formed and affirmed conclusion.

[1] See Nos. 69 and 81.
[2] See above, No. 66.

hends a Minor under the dependence of a *connection of propositions* of which this Minor is one of the members. The conditional syllogism orders discourse according to the connection of PROPOSITIONS ; from an antecedent which sets forth (in the conditional Major) the *connection of two propositions* (the sequence), and which presents one of these two *propositions* as *the means* or *the reason* for positing (or destroying) the other, it deduces or infers the position (or destruction) of this other. Hence it is no longer a question of manifesting the union (or separation) of two terms to each other by means of a third term or concept, but of manifesting by means of one of the members of the Major the necessity of positing or destroying the other member. Consequently the conditional syllogism does indeed conclude from the *whole* to the *part ;* but not, as in the categorical syllogism, from a more universal (from the point of view of the logical relations that exist between the connected terms) to a less universal truth, but from a compound proposition to one of the members which it contains. The mind, in the conditional syllogism, does not infer one proposition from another, it infers a proposition from an *inference that has already been made and affirmed* between two propositions. The need is not to see by a *new light* and in virtue of an inference which the mind discovers while it affects it, rather is it to affirm or deny something by a *renewed application* of an already existing light and by the use of a previously made inference.

It must be borne in mind, however, that the conditional syllogism may be resolved into the categorical syllogism, and that just as the union of propositions to each other presupposes the union of terms, so does the logical mechanism of the conditional syllogism presuppose the logical mechanism of the categorical syllogism.

Logically it presupposes the categorical syllogism.

And that is the fundamental reason for which Aristotle neglected to treat of the theory of the conditional syllogism and why those modern logicians, who think to have found in this theory the means of renovating Logic, are completely mistaken. The conditional syllogism is not a primary process of the reason ; this manner of inferring a proposition, not from another proposition, but from a previously affirmed sequence between two propositions is, so to speak, a reasoning in the second degree, grafted upon the categorical syllogism which is the sole truly primary form of rational *discursus :* " If this figure inscribed in a semicircle is a triangle, the sum of its angles is equal to two right angles, therefore, etc."—Granted.—But why is this conditional Major true ? Because *the sum of the angles of a triangle is equal to two right angles.* " If the human intelligence is independent of matter in its specific operation, it is independent of matter in its being ; but, etc."—Why is this conditional Major true ? Because independence of matter in the order of operation necessarily implies independence of matter in the order of being ; in other words, because this categorical Major is true : " *Everything independent of matter in its specific operation is independent of matter in its being.* In order to give the *reason* for a conclusion we must always definitively attain to an essence or a universal nature, that is, to a categorical syllogism (or to an induction in the experimental sciences).[1]

[1] This important point did not escape Boethius : " *Praedicativa simplex est propositio,*" he wrote, " *conditionalis vero esse non poterit, nisi ex praedicativis propositionibus conjungatur. . . . Necesse est categoricos syllogismos hypotheticis vim conclusionis ministrare* " (*De Syll. hyp.*, p. 607, cf. Prantl, *Gesch. der Logik*, I, 701). It has, however, escaped the author of a recent treatise who completely reverses the true order of things on this count and gratuitously turns Logic upside down (cf. E. Goblot, *Traité de Logique*, Nos. 98, 112, 118, 120, 153–159).

Because he misconceives the nature of the universal, the author, followed in this by Rougier (*Structure des théories déductives*, p. 6 and *sqq.*), 1 believes that the *subject* of every categorical proposition is in reality necessarily *singular*. In so doing he confuses, as do many modern logicians, the *real* subject, which is indeed always *singular*, with the *logical* subject, which may very well be a universal nature communicable to individuals (" Every man is mortal ").

2 Consequently he completely destroys the theory of the categorical syllogism, whose Major has, in his eyes, merely a collective signification (see above, No. 81).

3 As a consequence he takes, as hypothetical syllogisms, syllogisms which are, in reality, *true categorical syllogisms* disguised under a hypothetical form, *e.g.*,

> Two triangles having their sides parallel are similar,
> but *the two triangles ABC and DEF* have their sides parallel,
> therefore they are similar.

This is but an authentic categorical syllogism *camouflaged* as a conditional :

> Two triangles having their sides parallel are similar,
> but the triangles ABC and DEF are two triangles having their sides parallel,
> therefore they are similar,

for the whole force of the inference in question comes from the identification of the minor term, " the triangles ABC and DEF " with the major term,

THE QUANTITY OF THE PREMISSES IN THE CONDITIONAL SYLLOGISM

A conditional proposition is always universal in this sense that its affirmation concerns only the *sequence* itself which is declared to be always and everywhere valid. However we may agree to designate as universal, particular, or singular, a conditional wherein the proposition expressing the conditioned is itself universal, particular or singular.[1]

From this agreement results a remarkable property of the conditional syllogism. Since the Major affirms the connection not of two terms but of two propositions, and the Minor states the position or destruction of one of them, from which follows the position or destruction of the other, the premisses of the conditional syllogism may not only be both universal or one universal and the other particular, but they may *both be singular* (if Peter is a martyr he is a saint, but Peter is a martyr, therefore he is a saint) or *both particular* (if some animal is rational, he has an immortal soul, but some animal is rational, therefore some animal has an immortal soul).

"similar," by means of the middle term, "two triangles having parallel sides," and not from the positing, by the Minor, of the condition expressed in the Major (since a minor term was introduced in the Minor and the latter thus expresses *something other* than the *simple condition*). But we know (see above, No. 86) that the true conditional syllogism differs from the categorical syllogism because of the *very nature of the inference*. Whatever the form in which we may wish to express it, the reasoning given in the illustration above is founded upon *the* union *of the terms* and the identification of the extremes through the mean; it is a categorical syllogism.

Therefore, since Goblot is really working with categorical syllogisms, it is not surprising that he should have rediscovered all the known moods of the categorical syllogism in his "hypothetical syllogisms." Because the scholastic logicians did not make this same mistake, he upbraids them for their "negligence" and reproaches them for having omitted the minor term in the theory of the conditional syllogism (*Logique*, No. 98, p. 158). He does not perceive that, in introducing this minor term, he himself disregards the proper nature of the conditional syllogism and wholly destroys its distinctive character.

The theory of Demonstration proposed by this same author will be examined in Major Logic.

[1] If we agree to call "*negative*" those conditional propositions (see above, No. 48 *b*) wherein the proposition expressing the conditioned is itself negative, then we shall say that the Major: "If Peter does not love his neighbour he does not love God" is negative, and that the conditional syllogism: "If Peter does not love his neighbour he does not love God, but he does not love his neighbour, therefore, etc.," has two negative premisses.

Because of this property, the conditional syllogism is principally and most frequently used to establish the truth of facts concerning particular events: "If the criminal had escaped through the window, the window would have been open, but the window was not open, therefore, etc."

C. DIVISION OF THE SYLLOGISM (both categorical and conditional)

90. PRELIMINARY REMARKS. The following divisions are "accidental" (*i.e.*, unlike the preceding divisions they do not relate to the very essence of the syllogism considered in its form, *see the schema, No.* 85). They are concerned first and foremost with the pure and simple, or categorical syllogism, but they may be analogically applied to the hypothetical, and particularly to the *conditional*, syllogism. In order to avoid useless complications, however, we shall draw our examples from the categorical syllogism alone, except for the dilemma.

§ 1. *Demonstrative, Probable, Erroneous and Sophistic Syllogisms*

91. By REASON OF THE PROXIMATE MATTER OF THE SYLLOGISM (THE PROPOSITIONS) CONSIDERED AS TO ITS VALUE we may have the following cases: 1 the premisses of the syllogism cannot be false, in other words, they are

necessary.

In this case the Conclusion is the object of KNOWLEDGE and the syllogism is "apodeictic" or

DEMONSTRATIVE

2 The premisses may be false, in other words they are

contingent.

The Conclusion is then the object of OPINION and the syllogism is

Demonstrative, probable, erroneous and sophistic syllogisms.

PROBABLE

3 The premisses *cannot be true*, in other words they are

impossible.

In this case the Conclusion is necessarily an ERROR and the syllogism is

ERRONEOUS.

4 The syllogism *violates the rules* and is consequently defective on the side of form, but, at the same time, because its matter disguises this defection, it

appears to be conclusive.

The conclusion is in this instance *illusory*—or FALLACIOUS and the syllogism is said to be

SOPHISTIC.

DIVISION OF THE SYLLOGISM BY REASON OF THE PREMISSES CONSIDERED AS TO THEIR VALUE

		SYLLOGISM
PREMISSES	necessary	*demonstrative*
	contingent	*probable*
	impossible	*erroneous*
	apparently correct (but not really so)	*sophistic*

(*a*) Sophisms may be studied in Lesser Logic because they violate the formal *rules* of the syllogism (they are, in other words, pseudo-syllogisms). But since it is their *matter* that conceals their defective form and makes them seem conclusive, and since sophisms are classified according to the different ways in which the matter of a pseudo-syllogism may disguise this defection, the study of sophisms really belongs to Greater Logic.[1]

(*b*) BY REASON OF THE PROXIMATE MATTER CONSIDERED AS TO THE QUALITY[2] OF THE CONCLUSION, that is according as the conclusion is *affirmative* or *negative*, the syllogism is divided into affirmative and negative.

(*c*) BY REASON OF THE PROXIMATE MATTER OF THE SYLLOGISM CONSIDERED ACCORDINGLY AS THE PROPOSITIONS ARE MODAL OR SIMPLY ATTRIBUTIVE[3] the syllogism is either ABSOLUTE or MODAL. In the first case its pre-

[1] Cf. Sanseverino, *Elementa Philosophiae Christianae*, Vol. I.
[2] See above, No. 48.
[3] See above, No. 49.

misses are propositions *de inesse ;* in the second either one or both of them are modal propositions. For example :

It is necessary that every animal be corruptible,
but it is possible that an intelligent living being be an animal,
therefore it is possible that an intelligent living being be corruptible.

When the two premisses are modal *de necessario* or *de impossibili*, the conclusion is of the same mood and the rules of the syllogism are easily applicable. But the other possible combinations give rise to such complications that the theory of the modal syllogism (treated in detail by Aristotle in the first book of the *Prior Analytics*) [1] has been called the " logician's cross," *crux logicorum*.

§ 2. *Incomplete Syllogisms*

92. BY REASON OF THE PROXIMATE MATTER OF THE SYLLOGISM (THE PROPOSITIONS) CONSIDERED AS TO ITS INTEGRITY—the syllogism is *complete* when the two premisses are explicitly formulated. In the contrary case, that is, when one of the premisses is *not expressed*, the syllogism is *incomplete* or truncated, and is called an

The *Enthymeme* or truncated syllogism.

ENTHYMEME.[2]

Example : Peter is a man, therefore he is mortal.[3]

The enthymeme is much more frequently used in current language—scientific as well as common—than is the complete syllogism.

§ 3. *Oblique Syllogisms*

93. BY REASON OF THE REMOTE MATTER (THE TERMS) OF

[1] A summary of this theory may be found in Chap. XII of *Le Système d'Aristote* by Hamelin. It is also extremely well presented in the *Summa totius logicae*, attributed to St. Thomas (opuscula 48, rom. ed.).

[2] Aristotle uses the word enthymeme (ἐνθύμημα) in an altogether different sense—in the sense of " rhetorical syllogism proceeding from probable premisses and from examples." Cf. *Anal. Pr.*, II, 27, 70 a, 10 ; *Rhetor.* I, 1, 1355 a, 6.

[3] Or, for example, in the conditional syllogism : " The world exists, therefore God exists "—the Major is understood : " If the world exists, God exists."

Direct and *oblique* syllogisms.

THE SYLLOGISM CONSIDERED ACCORDINGLY AS THE TERMS ARE DIRECT OR OBLIQUE—the syllogism is either

DIRECT

or

OBLIQUE

In the latter case *one of the syllogistic terms itself*, t, T or M, is in an oblique case, that is to say that the term is not itself the subject or predicate of the proposition wherein it figures, but that it determines this subject or predicate *according to a certain relation* which it has to it. For this reason the word signifying this term is in an oblique case in Latin, and is preceded in English by a preposition or some sign indicating a relation. Example :

M T
Christ is God

t M
but Mary is the *Mother* of Christ,

t T
therefore Mary is the *Mother* of God.

The M, direct in the Major, is oblique in the Minor, and the T, direct in the Major, is oblique in the Conclusion. [1]

M T
Every son of my father is my brother,

t M
but Paul is my father,

t T
therefore *every son* of Paul is my brother.

The M, oblique in the Major, is direct in the Minor, and the t, direct in the Minor, is oblique in the Conclusion. The same is true in the following syllogism :

[1] We may also say *by analogy* that a *conditional* syllogism, such as : " If Peter is a martyr he is a saint, but it is probable that Peter is a martyr, therefore it is probable that Peter is a saint " is an oblique syllogism.

Everything greater than $\overbrace{\text{greater than B}}^{\text{M}}$ is
$\overbrace{\textit{greater}\text{ than B}}^{\text{T}}$

but $\overset{\text{t}}{\text{A}}$ is $\overbrace{\text{greater than B}}^{\text{M}}$

therefore *everything greater than* $\overset{\text{t}}{\underline{}}$A is $\overbrace{\text{greater than B}}^{\text{T}}$.

(*a*) Certain difficulties concerning the "Logic of Relation" which beset logicians even as well informed as Lachelier,[1] and which we shall examine in Major Logic, are easily solved by taking into consideration oblique syllogisms. Thus it is very certain that a formula such as

A>B
B>C
Therefore A>C

does not at all represent a true syllogism, for the syllogism

$\overset{\text{M}}{\text{B}}$ is $\overbrace{\text{greater than C}}^{\text{T}}$

but $\overset{\text{t}}{\text{A}}$ is $\overbrace{\text{greater than B}}^{\text{M}}$

therefore $\overset{\text{t}}{\text{A}}$ is $\overbrace{\text{greater than C}}^{\text{T}}$

is incorrect and is true only by accident or by reason of its matter, for the middle term is not the same in the Major as it is in the Minor ("B" in one, "greater than B" in the other). The fact is that, far from being related to an autonomous type of proposition and reasoning, and positing a properly *logical* question, the formula under consideration is nothing but an algebraic abbreviation of discourse, such as is often met with in everyday language. The practical use of the relation "is greater than" as a copula is legitimate only because a pseudo-syllogism of this kind (the Stoics called it λόγος ἀμεθόδως

[1] Cf. J. Lachelier, *Études sur le Syllogisme*, Paris, 1907.

περαίνων) *implies or supposes the following* syllogisms which are *true syllogisms* and into which it may easily be resolved.

(I) Everything greater than $\overbrace{\text{greater than C}}^{\text{M}}$ is $\overbrace{\text{greater than C}}^{\text{T}}$

But $\overset{\text{t}}{\bar{B}}$ *is* $\overbrace{\textit{greater than C}}^{\text{M}}$

Therefore everything greater than $\overset{\text{t}}{\bar{\text{B}}}$ is $\overbrace{\text{greater than C}}^{\text{T}}$.

(II) Everything greater than B is greater than C,
but *A is greater than B*,
therefore *A is greater than C*.

Both of these syllogisms are perfectly correct, but the first one is an oblique syllogism.

(*b*) It is always possible to transform an oblique syllogism into a direct syllogism. For example—using the examples given above, we have: "The Mother of Christ is the Mother of God, but Mary is the Mother of Christ, therefore, etc." "Every son of my father is my brother, but every son of Paul is a son of my father, therefore, etc." "Everything greater than greater than B is greater than B, but everything greater than A is greater than greater than B, therefore everything greater than A is greater than B." But in effecting this transformation something has been changed in the logical process of the thought; from the point of view of the movement of reason itself, as Leibnitz has remarked (*Nouveaux Essais*, livre IV, Chap. XVII, § 4), the oblique syllogism constitutes a distinct manner of procedure. Nevertheless, the very fact that it is reducible to the direct syllogism shows that Leibnitz was wrong in calling it an "asyllogistic" sequence; it is a true syllogism founded essentially upon the identity of two terms with a same third term (for one of the two terms and the third is once identically modified).

§ 4. *Compound Syllogisms*

94. BY REASON OF THE SIMPLICITY OR THE COMPLEXITY OF THE ARGUMENTATION—the syllogism is either SIMPLE or COMPOUND (*i.e.*, made up of *several* implicitly or explicitly formulated syllogisms). There are *four* kinds of compound syllogisms :

(1) THE EPICHEIREMA [1] in which one premise or the other, or even both, are *conjoined with their proof* (causal propositions). Example :

The *Epicheirema* or syllogism with a causal premise.

> Every martyr is a saint because every martyr possesses heroic charity,
> but Peter is a martyr,
> therefore Peter is a saint.

The Major is itself resolvable into a complete syllogism : " Every man possessing heroic charity is a saint, but every martyr possesses heroic charity, therefore every martyr is a saint."

(2) THE POLYSYLLOGISM which links together *several syllogisms* in such a way that the conclusion of one serves as a premise of the next.

The *Polysyllogism*, in which the conclusion of one serves as a premise of the next.

Bar	Every spiritual substance is a simple substance,	
ba	but the human soul is a spiritual substance,	
ra	therefore it is a simple substance,	*ba*
	but every simple substance is incorruptible,	*Bar*
la	therefore the human soul is incorruptible ;	*ra*
ce	but that which is incorruptible cannot cease being,	
rent	therefore the human soul cannot cease being. [2]	

[1] Aristotle used the word *epicheireme* (ἐπιχείρημα) in an altogether different sense, to mean a " dialectical syllogism " proceeding from probable propositions and ordained to invention, not demonstration. Cf. *Topic.*, VIII, 2, 162 a, 15.

[2] The conditional syllogism would be : " If the human soul is a spiritual substance it is a simple substance, but it is a spiritual substance, therefore it is a simple substance ; but if it is a simple substance it is incorruptible, therefore it is incorruptible ; but if it is incorruptible it cannot cease being, therefore it cannot cease being."

The *Sorites*, in which the t is united to the T by a series of subordinate m's.

(3) THE SORITES,[1] which links several propositions together in such a way that the Pr. of the first becomes the S. of the second, and the Pr. of the second the S. of the third, and so on, until a conclusion is reached which unites the S. of the *first* with the Pr. of the *last*.

The Sorites *implicitly* contains several syllogisms (the same number as the premisses less one). Cicero justly called it the most deceptive of arguments, and it is, in truth, the one into which error may most easily creep.

t M^1
Peter is a man
M^1 M^2
Every man is an animal
M^2 M^3
Every animal is endowed with instincts
M^3 T
Every being endowed with instincts has spontaneous reactions,
t T
Therefore Peter has spontaneous reactions.[2]

This is the *Aristotelian sorites*. The logician, Goclenius,[3] gave his name to another type of sorites (the Goclenian sorites) in which the Conclusion unites the S. of the *last proposition* to the Pr. of the *first*.

M^1 T
Every being endowed with instincts has spontaneous reactions,
M^2 M^1
Every animal is endowed with instincts
M^3 M^2
Every man is an animal

[1] Aristotle does not use the word *sorites* (σωρείτης), but he indicates this type of reasoning in the *Anal. Pr.* I (41 a 18 and 25 (42 b 1)).

[2] The conditional syllogism would be :
If Peter is a man he is an animal.
If he is an animal he is endowed with instincts.
If he is endowed with instincts he has spontaneous reactions.
But Peter is a man, therefore he has spontaneous reactions.

[3] The sorites in question was proposed in his *Isagoge in Organum Aristotelis* (Frankfort, 1598).

t M[3]
Peter is a man
t T
Therefore Peter has spontaneous reactions.[1]

In the *Aristotelian sorites* the series of M's has an increasing extension, whereas in the *Goclenian* sorites the series has a decreasing extension.

(4) THE DILEMMA, the "two-horned" or "two-edged" argument (*syllogismus cornutus*), presents in the antecedent a disjunction of such a kind that whether one or the other of its members be posited, the *same conclusion* follows.

The dilemma is most frequently constructed according to the *conditional* type. For example if a man had, through his own fault, so vitiated his conscience that it commanded him to do a crime, we could reason that :

Either this man will commit this crime or he will not.
If he does commit it he will act against eternal law (and he will be guilty).
If he does not commit it he will act against his conscience (and he will be guilty).
Therefore whether or not he commits it he will be guilty.

Or again, the famous dilemma of Tertullian against the decree of Trajan :

The Dilemma states a disjunction such that the same conclusion follows in either case.

The Christians are either guilty or innocent.
If they are guilty why should it be forbidden to search for them? (The decree is unjust.)
If they are innocent why should they be punished? (The decree is unjust.)
In either event the decree is unjust.

The dilemma may also be constructed in the *categorical* type :

Every just man needs grace in order to persevere,
Every sinner needs grace in order to be converted.
But every man is either just or a sinner,
Therefore every man needs grace.

[1] The conditional syllogism would be :
If Peter is endowed with instincts he has spontaneous reactions.
If he is an animal he is endowed with instincts.
If he is a man he is an animal.
But he is a man, therefore he has spontaneous reactions.

(*a*) Rules for the dilemma : (1) The disjunction must be complete. Because this rule is so easily broken this form of reasoning lends itself very readily to sophisms. For example in the following syllogism: Every philosopher is an " innatist " or a sensist ; if he is an " innatist," he falls into idealism, if he is a sensist, he falls into materialism ; in either event error cannot be avoided ; the disjunction is not complete. The philosophers in the Aristotelian tradition are neither innatists nor sensists.

(2) The partial consequent inferred by each member must follow *legitimately*. The dilemma of the Caliph Omar, for example, violates this rule :

> The books in the library of Alexandria are either in conformity or not in conformity with the Koran.
>
> In the first case they are superfluous (and should be burnt).
>
> In the second case they are pernicious (and should be burnt).
>
> Therefore in either case they should be burnt.

(3) The common conclusion declared to be inferred by one or the other of the members must follow *exclusively*, that is, it must be the only one that can be drawn. If not, the dilemma can be *retorted*,[1] as in the familiar example :

> You will conduct public affairs either honestly or dishonestly.
>
> If you conduct them honestly you will please God (*and it will be to your advantage to go into politics*).
>
> If you conduct them dishonestly you will please men (*and it will be to your advantage to go into politics*).
>
> Therefore in both cases it will be to your advantage to go into politics.

To this argument it may be retorted :

> If you conduct them honestly you will displease men.
>
> If you conduct them dishonestly you will displease God.
>
> Therefore in either event it will not be to your advantage to go into politics.

[1] To *retort* an argument is to draw the opposite conclusion from one of its own premisses.

(*b*) Do not confuse the *disjunctive syllogism* with the *dilemma*, as is so frequently done. In the dilemma the conclusion follows from *both of the members* of the disjunction. In the disjunctive syllogism, on the contrary, one of the members of the disjunction is excluded. Orators very often confuse the two, and when they say that they " have their adversary in a dilemma " they are usually talking about a disjunctive syllogism. " How, gentlemen, shall the Prime Minister escape this dilemma? either he has been deceived by his officials and should therefore act immediately, or else he has known what was going on and should himself be put under suspicion. But he assures us that his officials have not deceived him, he protects his minions ! Therefore, etc."

(*c*) EXERCISES. (1) Find examples of all the different types of syllogism enumerated in this section.

(2) To which category of syllogisms do the following reasonings belong :

" Qui prudens est, et temperans est ; qui temperans est, et constans est ; qui constans est, et imperturbatus est ; qui imperturbatus est, sine tristitia est ; qui sine tristitia est, beatus est ; ergo prudens beatus est, et prudentia ad beatam vitam satis est " (Seneca, *Epist.* 85).

You are a liar, therefore you are a coward.

Every flatterer lives at the expense of those who listen to him, but every man who lives at the expense of another is a parasite, therefore every flatterer is a parasite, but every parasite is unable to support himself, therefore every flatterer is unable to support himself, but every man who is unable to support himself is unfortunate, therefore every flatterer is unfortunate.

Every rational creature is free by the very fact that he is endowed with intelligence, but man is a rational creature, therefore he is free.

Every mammal is viviparous, therefore the bat is mammiferous.

Montaigne's fox reasons in the following way (*Essays*, II, 12) : " This stream is noisy, that which is noisy moves, that which moves is not frozen, that which is not frozen is liquid, that which is liquid gives way under a weight, therefore this river will not bear me."

Bias reasoned in this way: "If you marry, you marry either a beautiful woman or an ugly one. If she is beautiful you will be tortured by jealousy, if she is ugly you will not be able to stand her, therefore you should not marry."

SECTION 3. INDUCTION

A. INDUCTIVE REASONING

95. NOTION OF INDUCTION. As we have already indicated, Induction is a type of reasoning that *differs essentially* from the syllogism. This difference has its root in the very nature of our mind, which cannot attain to truth except it base itself upon two kinds of essentially different principles:

(1) upon sense data and singular facts known through sense experience—*material principle* of all our knowledge (*from which* all our knowledge is derived);

Induction is a reasoning in which we infer a universal truth from a sufficient enumeration of singular or partial facts.

(2) upon self-evident self-known intelligible truths—*formal principles* of all our knowledge ("first principles" *by which* all our knowledge is demonstrated).[1]

To show how a conclusion derives from previously known universal truths, or in the terminology of the ancients, to "resolve" a conclusion into the intelligible truths upon which it depends (and finally into the first self-evident truths) is to proceed by the *deductive* or *syllogistic* method (*resolutio formalis*). To show how a conclusion is disengaged, so to speak, from sense experience, in other words, to resolve a conclusion into the facts from which our mind extracts it as from a matter (*resolutio materialis*) is to proceed by the *inductive* method. In the syllogism we remain upon the intelligible plane, we move from one point of this plane to another, as a submarine that navigates horizontally upon the surface of the ocean. By induction we attain to the intelligible plane, we move from the sensible plane to the intelligible plane, as a submarine that navigates vertically upwards from below.

[1] See above, No. 66.

It is in this sense that Aristotle and St. Thomas teach that we have but two means of acquiring knowledge : viz., the syllogism, which proceeds from universal truths, and induction which proceeds from singular data ; for all our knowledge depends formally upon first self-evident truths, and derives its origin materially from the singular and concrete reality perceived by the senses.

Thus we may define induction as :

> *an argumentation in which the mind infers an universal truth from sufficiently enumerated singular cases ;*

" a singularibus sufficienter enumeratis ad universale progressio."

This amount of water boils at 100°, and so does this amount, and this other, and this other also . . . , therefore water boils at 100°. Note that, in virtue of the same ascensional process, induction goes not only from *individuals* to the universal whole of which they are the subjective parts, but also from all subjective parts whatever they may be to their universal whole. For example : copper conducts electricity, and gold, iron, zinc and silver do also. . . . Therefore *metal* (that is, every metal) conducts electricity. Like many other excellent definitions formulated by the ancients, the definition of induction given above is a definition according to its *principal* or absolutely first function. The following definition is broader but less typical : an argumentation in which we ascend to a universal truth from a sufficient enumeration of *partial* data.

96. STRUCTURE OF INDUCTION. (1) Because the syllogism remains upon the plane of the universal, upon the plane of concepts as such, the entire force of syllogistic argumentation resides in the connection between terms or concepts. To say syllogism is equivalent to saying *the identity of two terms or concepts* WITH A SAME THIRD TERM.

M T
Everything that subsists immaterially is indestructible,
t M
But the human soul subsists immaterially,
t T
Therefore the human soul is indestructible.

Induction, on the contrary, moves from the plane of the concrete singular to the plane of ideas, the plane of the universal; the whole force of inductive argumentation will reside then in the connection between individuals and the universal concept. To say induction is equivalent to saying the *conformity of two concepts* WITH ONE SAME SERIES OF SUFFICIENTLY ENUMERATED INDIVIDUALS.

The structure of inductive argumentation is therefore evident; to formulate it suitably we should say, for example:

This fossil equidae
and this one
and that one
and this other
} T — has a very distinctive dentition.

And the universal subject which represents [1]
{ this fossil equidae
and this one
and that one
and this other }
in relation to the predicate "having a very distinctive dentition."
} t — is the *hipparion.*

Therefore the hipparion (t) has a very distinctive dentition (T).

M { This amount of water a^1
and this amount a^2
and this amount a^3 }
} T — boils at 100°

And the universal subject which represents
M { a^1
and a^2
and a^3 }
in relation to the predicate "which boils at 100°"
} t — is water

[1] In more precise terms: the universal subject which *stands for* these (individuals).

t T
Therefore water boils at 100°

M {copper
and iron
and gold
and silver
and zinc} T
is a conductor of electricity

and the universal subject
which represents
{copper
and iron
and gold
and silver
and zinc}
in relation to the predicate
"conductor of electricity" t
is *metal*

t T
Therefore metal is a conductor of electricity.

We have taken apart the logical mechanism of inductive inference in this way in order to make clear the ascension which the mind effects from singular terms to the universal quiddity.

As a matter of fact in everyday language, induction is formulated in a much simpler manner. We would say, for example : this hipparion molar, and this one (found elsewhere) and that one, and that one, are very distinctive, therefore the hipparion has a very distinctive dentition. This amount of water boils at 100°, and this one, and this one likewise, therefore water boils at 100° ; copper, iron, gold, silver, zinc are conductors of electricity, and copper, iron, gold, silver, zinc, etc., are metals, therefore metals are conductors of electricity. But the reason for this is precisely that the *passage to the universal*, essential to inductive inference, is not verbally formulated in speech, because it is not one of the *materials* of reasoning (as are the terms of a syllogism), it is *an operation performed and exercised* by the mind *at the moment in which it passes from the Major to the Minor*, an operation which it belongs to logical reflection alone to signify in a formula. The task of the mind in induction is not to signify induction but to effect it. This observation also explains why inductive reasoning is verbally expressed in a less invariable and fixed fashion than is syllogistic reasoning.

(2) Let us compare induction and the syllogism by means of any two examples, such as :

	Induction		Syllogism	
	M	T	M	T
MAJOR	*Peter* and *James* and *Paul* and *John*	is endowed with speech.	Every rational being	is endowed with speech.
			t	M
MINOR	And the universal which is realized in : M { *Peter* and *James* and *Paul* and *John*	is man	But man	is a rational being
	t		t	T
CONCLUSION	Therefore man	is endowed with speech	Therefore man	is endowed with speech.

The difference is immediately apparent : in both cases the conclusion expresses a general truth and unites two concepts to each other. But in the syllogism the Major expresses the conformity between a concept (Pr. : endowed with speech) and *another concept* (S. : rational being) ; in induction, on the contrary, the Major expresses the conformity between a concept (Pr. : endowed with speech) and *a series of individuals* taken one by one (Peter, James, Paul, John).

Induction passes from the sensible to the intelligible plane. The *mean* in induction is not a universal *term*, but an *enumeration of individuals or of parts.*

In the syllogism the Minor expresses the conformity between a concept (Pr. : rational being) and *another concept* (S. : man) : in induction, on the contrary, the Minor expresses the conformity between a concept (Pr. : man) and this same concept taken in relation *to the individuals which are its parts* (S. : the universal which is realized in Peter, James, Paul, John, etc.). Further, in the Minor of the syllogism, the predicate-term (rational being) is taken particularly, in accordance with the ordinary rule of affirmative propositions. In the Minor of the induction, on the contrary, the predicate-term (man)—which is said, not of each individual, Peter, James, Paul, John, etc.,[1] but of the universal subject itself of which Peter, James, Paul, John, etc., are the subjective parts [2]—is taken neither particularly nor universally, since it is not considered according to the manner in which it passes to the individuals in the real. It is taken, as is the subject-term itself, according to the unity which it has in the mind. This Minor does not indeed express the existence of a predicate in the comprehension of a subject, but expresses the *ascension* that the mind makes from the individuals to the universal term which represents them.

To say this briefly in another way, *in induction there is no middle* TERM. *That which takes the place of the middle term, which is the* MEAN *of argumentation, is not a term or a concept, but an* ENUMERATION OF INDIVIDUALS OR OF PARTS.[3] In the Major these individuals are taken one by one; in the Minor they are taken in the unity of the universal concept which represents them.

SCHEMATIC STRUCTURE OF THE SYLLOGISM AND OF INDUCTION		
INDUCTION		SYLLOGISM
a^1 and a^2 and a^3 and a^4	is B	C is B
And that which, in relation to B, has for subjective parts a^1 and a^2 and a^3 and a^4	is the universal A.	But A is C
Therefore A	is B	Therefore A is B

[1] As was the case for the Pr. of the Major (endowed with speech) which is said of each individual or of each part distributively.

[2] In this case the *suppositio* is *simplex*. See above, No. 27.

[3] Aristotle said (*Anal. Prior.*, II, 23) in this sense, that the term which serves as the *mean* uniting the two extremes *in the syllogism* is, *in induction*, the subject of which an extreme is proven by means of a third thing (the enumeration of individuals or parts).

INDUCTION: The monkey, the cat, the hedgehog, the ox, the rat are viviparous; and who says monkey, hedgehog, ox, rat . . . says mammal; therefore every MAMMAL is viviparous.

SYLLOGISM: Every MAMMAL is viviparous; but the bat is a MAMMAL; therefore the bat is viviparous.

Such is the essential and absolutely irreducible difference which distinguishes the syllogism and induction.

Whence this consequence : whereas the syllogism or deductive reasoning proceeds, at least from the pure point of view of logical relations, from a more universal truth to a less universal truth contained in the first, induction proceeds from the less universal to the more universal, from the parts to the whole.

*(3) Such is the property generally designated as differentiating induction from the syllogism. But there are certain pitfalls to be avoided. *Induction proceeds from the singular (or from the particular)* : this is true if we consider the first point of departure of induction, and thus consider its *principal* function and *characteristic* movement : *ascensional* movement going from the parts to the whole. But contraries belong to the same genus, as black and white to the genus colour. Therefore the movement of *descent*, by which the mind goes from a universal to its subjective parts, and to the singular data of experience, *must also belong to the inductive process.*

To return to the simile we used above, the mind in inductive reasoning is as a submarine (whose first point of departure is the bottom, not the surface of the ocean). Since it can raise itself from the bottom to the surface, it can also descend again from the surface to the bottom, and this coming and going constitutes for it the same kind of movement. This point did not escape the sagacity of the scholastic logicians, who made of the *ascensus* and *descensus* two particular cases of the same *inductive process.*[1]

Induction ascends from the parts to the whole, and descends from the whole to the parts.

Inductive reasoning is a reversible mechanism because, as we pointed out above, its Minor always affirms the identity of a universal whole considered in itself (" metal " for example), and of the same universal considered in relation to its parts ; consequently this Minor is a convertible proposition.

> Iron, and copper, and gold, and silver, each conduct electricity.
> And to say iron, and copper, and gold, and silver, is to say metal.
> Therefore metal conducts electricity.

[1] Cf. John of St. Thomas, *Log.*, I, *P. Sum.*, lib. III, Cap. II, p. 52. The ancients had analysed and formulated in detail the rules of the *ascensus* and *descensus*. Cf. John of St. Thomas, *op. cit.*, pp. 53–54.

The mind moved itself from the particular to the universal : *ascensus.* Now, considering the inverse procedure :

Metal conducts electricity.
To say metal is to say iron, and copper, and gold, and silver, etc.
Therefore iron conducts electricity.

Here the mind moved itself from the universal to the particular, from the whole to the part as such : *descensus.*[1]

It proceeds in virtue of the connection of the parts with the universal whole,

If the mean ("*nerf*"—the heart, core) of the argumentation were metal taken as *the middle term which identifies the other terms with each other* (every metal conducts electricity, but iron is a metal, therefore) this reasoning would be a syllogism. But as formulated and thought here, the mean of the argumentation is metal taken as a *superior universal dividing itself into its subjective parts,* and the reasoning is an inductive *descensus.* The difference may appear to be a subtle one because it belongs to the entirely formal order, but it is nevertheless of cardinal importance.

In the syllogism it is impossible to reverse the direction of the movement in this way. The syllogistic mechanism is not reversible. Indeed, in virtue of its structure, syllogistic argumentation proceeds necessarily from the principle to the conclusion, and therefore, at least as to logical relations, from a more universal truth to a less universal truth contained in the first.

But we must be at great pains to remember that this property of the syllogism, which is a *consequence* of its essential structure (an argumentation founded upon the connection of terms or concepts) concerns the universality of a truth (or connection of concepts) in relation to another truth from the precise point of view of the *logical relations* maintained by the connected terms or concepts—and does not concern, from the point of view of the *content* of the concepts, the universality of a concept in relation to the subjective parts which it contains. If we reason in *Darii* for example :

Every man is rational,
but some substance is a man,
therefore some substance is rational,

[1] See above, No. 27 (3), A, 6, inset, and No. 81 (3).

the concept *substance* is evidently not a subjective part of the concept *man*.

whereas the syllogism proceeds in virtue of the connection between terms and concepts.

We have already given considerable attention to this point (No. 81): the essential constitution of the syllogism does not consist in proceeding from a universal term to its subjective parts, but *in proceeding in virtue of the connection between terms or concepts*, that is, in proceeding from a truth (principle) to a truth (conclusion) which, from the point of view of logical function, is always less universal than the first, but which may in fact, considering the content of the propositions, be *equally universal*. Induction, on the contrary, considers the universal concept, not in its logical connection with other universal concepts, but in its relation with the subjective parts which are to it as matter.

(*a*) It is evident from the foregoing that a same singular conclusion, for example: Peter is mortal, may be inferred *either* in virtue of a syllogism, *or* in virtue of an inductive *descensus*. In saying:

> Every man is mortal,
> but Peter is a man,
> therefore Peter is mortal,

we construct a syllogism, we base ourselves upon the connection of three terms or concepts: Mortal, Peter, Man, and we draw our conclusion not *because* Peter is a subjective part of Man, but *because* the term Peter is identified with another term by means of the term Man. In saying:

> Man is mortal,
> and to say man is to say Peter, and Paul and James, etc.,
> therefore Peter is mortal,

our method of inference, the core of our reasoning is altogether different; we make an *inductive descensus*, we base ourselves upon the identity of the universal whole "man" considered in itself with this same whole considered in relation to its parts, and we draw our conclusion *because* Peter is a subjective part of man.

Or again, a conclusion such as: "iron conducts electricity" may be inferred *either* in virtue of an inductive *ascensus*, starting from actual facts: "this piece of iron, and this one, and that one, each conduct electricity," *or* in virtue of an inductive *descensus*, starting from the universal "metal," for example: "metal conducts electricity, and to say metal is to say iron, and silver, and copper, etc.," *or* in virtue of a syllogism starting from the same universal "metal" but proceeding by the force of an altogether different kind of inference: "every metal conducts electricity, but iron is a metal, therefore, etc."

(*b*) It should now be apparent how great is the too frequently committed blunder of representing the opposition of the syllogism and induction as the simple opposition of two movements proceeding in contrary directions on the same road. Such a representation betrays a complete misunderstanding of the true nature of this opposition and even risks confusing the syllogism with inductive *descensus*. The opposition between the syllogism and induction is much deeper: it is a fundamental opposition. The very paths which they pursue are different. One moves entirely upon the intelligible plane; the other leads from the plane of sense experience to the intelligible plane, from the plane of the particular or the singular to the plane of the universal (or inversely). The syllogism is based entirely upon the connection of two terms with a same third term (the middle term). Induction replaces the middle term by an enumeration of parts and is entirely based upon the connection of individuals or of parts with the universal whole.

Because certain authors have not understood the nature of induction, they have thought that it could be reduced to the syllogism.

Thus the disciples of Wolff considered induction as an enthymeme whose Major: "that which is attributable to all the individuals is attributable to the universal which contains them," is unexpressed. But this is contrary to all probability, for so general an axiom could never be the

Major in any particular enthymeme, any more than the supreme principle of the syllogism could be the Major in any particular syllogism.

Induction is absolutely irreducible to the syllogism.

Many other modern logicians, among whom is Lachelier,[1] reduce induction to a syllogism of the third figure. But enthymeme or syllogism of the third figure, the damage remains the same; to attempt to reduce induction to the syllogism is to reduce it to *nothing*, to purely and simply destroy it. For *if* induction were a kind of syllogism, it would be no more (except in those cases in which the enumeration of parts is actually complete) than an *invalid sequence* or a *defective reasoning*, and the only thing to do would be to rule it out of Logic, as several logisticians have done.[2] For the essential law of the validity of the syllogism, namely the identity of the M in the two premisses, is obviously violated when I say:

$$\overbrace{c^1, \text{ and } c^2, \text{ and } c^3}^{M} \quad \text{is B}$$

$$\overbrace{\text{but } C^1, C^2, C^3, \text{ and all the } C^n \text{ resembling them}}^{M} \text{ together form all A.}$$

Therefore all A is B.

This is a *defective syllogism*, which has only the *material appearance* of induction and has lost its essence and all its force.[3]

[1] Cf. Lachelier, *Études sur le Syllogisme*, pp. 37–38. Having posited the two premisses of a syllogism in *Darapti:* the body A attracts iron, *but* the body A is a magnet, "we should conclude only that, *vi formae:* therefore *some* magnet attracts iron," writes Lachelier. "But since we have grounds for believing that the body A acts in virtue of a general property of magnets, we conclude, *vi materiae:* therefore *every* magnet attracts iron." This is equivalent to admitting that this so-called syllogism in *Darapti* is merely a formally invalid sequence.

[2] Cf. Louis Rougier, *La Structure des théories déductives*, pp. 16 sqq.

[3] "The matter of induction may indeed be put into a syllogism but its form may not: it is essentially opposed to the true syllogism by the absence of the middle term by which the syllogism is characterized; no *conversion* could ever obliterate this difference or cause it to disappear. *Inductio in syllogismum reducitur materialiter et non formaliter, ita quod forma inductionis reducatur in formam syllogismi*" (Alb. Magn., *Prior.*, I, II, tract. VII, Cap. IV). "Induction proves that a characteristic belongs to a common subject by producing corresponding singular phenomena. That is the logical processus proper to it. From the repetition of an occurrence under the same conditions, it concludes

The logicians of whom we are speaking have not succeeded in escaping the fascination of the syllogism and in grasping the *quid proprium* of inductive reasoning. Whether we consider its structure, the nature of inference of which it admits or its supreme principle (see below), induction in every case appears as *absolutely irreducible to the syllogism.*

*(4) It is a *fundamental* error and, in truth, destructive of all Logic, to interpret induction—as many modern authors do—from the point of view of the parts of a *collective whole* or from the point of view of a *simple collection ;* that is to regard inductive reasoning as consisting in making a predicate verified of some members of a certain collection pass either *to an entire collection of individuals* taken as such, or *to all the individuals of a collection* taken purely and simply *qua* individuals. *In the first case*, the induction would be an obviously defective process (this soldier has an immortal soul, and this one, and that one, therefore the regiment has an immortal soul).[1] *In the second case* the induction would be legitimate only on the supposition that the enumeration were *complete*, but then (and always when induction is interpreted from the point of view of a pure *collection of individuals*) there would be no more in the conclusion than there is in the enumeration itself, and the induction would be merely *useless tautology*. To say : "Joseph was sold by Reuben, Simeon, Levi, Judas, Issachar, Zabulon, Dan, Nepthali, Gad and Aser," or to say : "Joseph was sold by his brothers," to say " Peter, John, James, Andrew, Philip, Thomas, Bartholomew, Matthew, James the Minor, Simon, Jude, Matthias were in the Cenacle " or to say " All the apostles were in the Cenacle," is purely and

To interpret induction from the point of view of a pure collection of individuals is to destroy it.

to a general fact. The syllogism proceeds altogether differently ; it proves that a subject and predicate are in accordance with each other because they are both in accord with a same third term. This is why the latter is always considered as the *mean*, the instrument, used to unite, in the conclusion, the two terms that are separated in the premisses. Briefly, the middle term provides both the fact and the cause of their accord. The opposition between these two procedures could not be more complete : *syllogismo proprie dicto opponitur inductio* " (Alb. Mag., *op. cit.*, I, II, tract. VII, Cap. IV), T. Richard, *Philosophie du Raisonnement dans la Science*, pp. 298–299.—When Aristotle speaks of the *inductive syllogism* (*Anal. Pr.*, II, 23, 68 b 15), he uses the word syllogism in the *general* sense of *reasoning* (inasmuch as reasoning taken in general is divided into *induction* and the *syllogism* properly so-called).

[1] See above, No. 17.

simply to say the same thing, because in these examples, the mind remains upon the plane of facts without raising itself any higher, and consequently ends up in universal propositions which—by reason of their matter and by exception—signify absolutely nothing except a fact common to all the individuals of a collection taken as individuals.[1] We make use of the exterior appearance of induction in such cases, saying, for example: "Peter, John, James, etc. . . . were in the Cenacle, *therefore* all the apostles were in the Cenacle," *to make evident*, as by counting on one's fingers, a particular truth which is exactly the same in both propositions. But (as in the expository syllogism) there is no inference, no true reasoning here. And yet this is what several modern logicians term *formal induction;* this is the purely verbal and sterile form which they have the naïveté to regard as the only induction known to the ancients, although the latter never even thought of considering it in their theory of induction.

So-called formal induction.

Induction must be interpreted from the point of view of the universal nature realized in individuals.

In truth, as we have already remarked, the essential *rôle* in the reasoning is played, not by the individuals of a collection taken *qua* individuals, but by the *universal nature* communicable to each of them (either as middle term in the syllogism, or as subject of the conclusion in the induction). It is not from the point of view of the parts of a *collective whole* nor from the point of view of a simple collection, but from the point of view of a *distributive whole* or of a *universal* properly so-called that we must consider induction if we would understand it. For induction consists in attributing to an *intelligible universal*, disengaged, so to speak, by abstraction, a predicate verified of some of the individuals or some of the parts in which this universal is realized. This operation is legitimate when the enumeration of individuals is sufficient, and it really furthers knowledge. For to know that every metal conducts electricity

[1] See above, No. 51 C. The examples used here to show what becomes of induction *when it is interpreted from the point of view of a pure collection of individuals, correspond to those particular cases* of complete induction in which, by reason of the matter, the conclusion expresses nothing except a fact common to the individuals of a collection taken as individuals (so-called "formal" induction). True complete induction is not a tautology, but valid reasoning. See below, No. 99.

is not the same thing as to know that silver, and copper, etc., are conductors of electricity ; it is to know that there is some necessary connection (even though we do not indeed perceive it in itself) between this property and the *nature* of metal—it is to possess—however obscurely and imperfectly it is nevertheless to possess—a truth *de jure*.

Induction (induction by incomplete enumeration of which we are speaking here) [1] does not make us pass from *some* to ALL (*tous*)—to all the individuals of a collection taken as individuals—but indeed from *some* to EVERY (*tout*)—to the whole object of a universal concept (which we may call the sphere of intelligible necessities) realized in each individual. For this reason, if the logician wishes to avoid ambiguity, he must formulate his examples of induction by saying : " copper, silver, etc. . . . conducts electricity, therefore *every metal* (or better still *metal*) conducts electricity " and not by saying : " all metals conduct electricity " ; for this oral expression signifies the individuals of a collection *before* signifying the universal nature of which they partake.[2] Everyday language incurs the risk of confusion in employing the expression " *all* the " rather than " every," and making it signify more or less obscurely, through the individuals which it primarily presents, the universal nature itself which contains the reason for the attribution of a same predicate to each of these individuals. (A fact which the nominalistic logicians have not the good fortune to perceive.) If, for example, I think back upon all the saints whose lives I have read, and arrive at the conclusion, " all the saints have been contemplatives," I seem to be announcing nothing but a general fact, but I am already signifying, already insinuating albeit in the most moderate and cautious manner, a certain truth *de jure* concerning some law that binds together sanctity and contemplation, and which would be much more clearly affirmed in a formula such as : " *every saint is a contemplative*."

*97. THE NATURE OF INDUCTIVE INFERENCE. In the case of induction, as in that of the syllogism, we must distinguish very carefully between inference properly so-called (*con-*

[1] For induction by complete enumeration, see below, No. 99.
[2] See above, No 51 *c*.

Induction considered as an argument ordinarily admits of a certain zone of probability.

sequentia) which is concerned solely with the *form* of the reasoning, and the argument or proof, which takes its *matter* into account as well. Induction has the double function of inference and of proof.[1] As we shall see in Major Logic, when considered as an argument or proof, induction admits of a certain zone of probability (except in some limit-cases such as those of induction by complete enumeration). For the matter of inductive reasoning is primarily constituted, not of necessary truths, as is that of the demonstrative syllogism, but of experimental and sensible data.

Considering induction now as an *inference*, that is, solely from the point of view of the logical relations and connections in virtue of which the mind passes from the Major to the Conclusion, we must say that induction is a *true argumentation* (*vera species argumentationis*), or *formal sequence* (*consequentia formalis*), but entirely distinct from the *syllogistic inference*, and *of a kind apart*. We may for this reason call it a *formal sequence properly as inductive* ("*formalis inductive* "), that is, as an *introduction and conduction to the universal*. For, since all the knowledge we can acquire supposes two progressive procedures of the mind, the one *introducing* us to intelligible truth, accordingly as we ascend to its starting from the senses, the other causing us to *demonstrate* this truth *deductively* starting from propositions already conceived in their universality, there must indeed be two distinct kinds of inference, one of which will lead or introduce us to the knowledge of universal things starting from singular facts of experience, and the other which will lead us from previously formed universal propositions to other propositions on the same universal plane.

Thus the first type of inference (induction) has not a *perfect form*, as has the syllogism, the form of which is founded upon the perfect connection of the two terms of the conclusion with a same third term, which is the mean of the argumentation and of itself absolutely necessitates the mind to

[1] " Adverto inductionem non solum importare rationem consequentiae ex parte dispositionis et formae connectendi propositiones, quae est ratio prioristica in consequentia ; sed etiam importare rationem argumenti, seu probationis, quatenus est locus arguendi et probandi aliquam propositionem universalem ex reductione ipsius ad suas singulares." John of St. Thomas, *Logica*, Ia P., *Illustr.*, q. VIII, a. 2, p. 173. See above No. 64.

affirm the connection between these two terms. But since it draws the universal proposition, to which it should first ascend, from the singular data of sense experience taken as the subjective parts of a universal whole, this first type has everything requisite for a formal inference as inductive but not as properly demonstrative.[1] The proper end to which it is of itself ordained is to *lead up to the universal*, and the necessity it imposes upon the mind is precisely concerned, *vi formae*, only with this introduction to universal propositions in virtue of the comparison and enumeration of singular data, and not with the production of a conviction perfect in every point.

(*a*) The analogy uniting *abstraction* and *induction* is thus apparent. Abstraction concerns the *first operation of the mind* and starting from singular facts of sense experience leads the mind to ideas and concepts (*universal* as objects of simple apprehension).

Induction bears upon the *third operation of the mind*, and leads the mind to universal propositions (*universal as objects of judgment*) starting either from singular data of sense experience or from previously abstracted data and universals that are less universal than the proposition in question (particular instances).

(*b*) For Aristotle the word *induction* had a much more general sense. It went far beyond—while comprising—inductive inference or induction as we have been understanding it here, and was applicable to every passage from the plane of sensible facts to that of universal propositions, even in the case in which, in a single sensible example (but transcending all sense experience and without any inductive reasoning whatsoever) the intelligence sees immediately from its very terms, a self-evident truth such as the principle of identity or of causality. Thus understood induction is neither an inference properly so-called, nor an argument nor proof: it merely leads the mind to a connection of terms whose intelligible necessity it perceives immediately, without

[1] "In ratione inductivi, non simpliciter et evidenter probativi." John of St. Thomas, *loc. cit.*, p. 175.

reasoning. It is in this sense that Aristotle says that only by induction may we attain to universal truths : ἡ μὲν δὴ ἐπαγωγὴ ἀρχῆς ἐστι καὶ τοῦ καθόλου (*Ethic. Nic.*, VI, 3, 1139 b 28); ἀδύνατον δὲ τὰ καθόλου θεωρῆσαι μὴ δι' ἐπαγωγῆς (*Anal. Post*,. I, 18, 81 a 40, lect. 30, St. Thomas). Cf. John of St. Thomas, *loc. cit.*, p. 175.

If a predicate is true of many sufficiently enumerated parts of a universal subject (that is, of several parts which this universal really represents in relation to this predicate) it is true of this universal subject.

98. THE SUPREME PRINCIPLE OF INDUCTION. (1) From what has been said it is evident that induction considered formally as an inference is founded upon a supreme principle which is altogether different from that of the syllogism, and which may be formulated as follows :

> *What is true*
> *of many* SUFFICIENTLY ENUMERATED *parts*
> *of a certain universal subject*
> *is true of this universal subject.*

By the very fact that it supposes a pre-requisite condition which may in reality be lacking, namely that the parts be sufficiently enumerated, this principle does not guarantee the entire certitude of the conclusions resulting from the application of the inductive process ; but it constitutes the force and the legitimacy of this process taken in its formal function of inference.

Like the supreme principle of the syllogism, this principle is self-evident or self-known. We say that the parts of a certain universal whole, taken as subjects having such and such a predicate, are *sufficiently* enumerated when we have reviewed a sufficient number to know (in a certain or at least probable manner) that they really are, in relation to this predicate, the parts of this universal and not of another more restricted universal—that is, to know that *the universal which represents them in relation to this predicate is really the universal which we are considering.*

Insufficient enumeration.

If we enumerated the parts of the universal man *insufficiently* in relation to a predicate, such as " yellow skinned " or " white skinned," considering only Chinamen, for example, we might believe that the latter are represented, in relation to the predicate " yellow skinned " by this universal man. (Lao-Tsen is yellow skinned, and Whong-fu

Tsen likewise and Tchou-hi likewise . . . , therefore man is yellow skinned.) But if we *sufficiently* enumerate the parts of this universal, we see that this is not so (for this Frenchman is also a man, and this negro is too), and that Lao-Tsen, Whong-fu Tsen, Tchou-hi, etc., are but (in relation to the predicate " yellow skinned ") the parts of a more restricted universal, such as " man of the yellow race."

In other words, although the universal man is indeed realized in Lao-Tsen, Whong-fu Tsen, Tchou-hi, etc., it is not the universal that represents these individuals *in relation to the predicate* " yellow skinned." The one to do this would be the more restricted universal " man of the yellow race."

Therefore, in saying " the *sufficiently enumerated parts* of a universal whole," we suppose by hypothesis that, in relation to this predicate, the parts in question are really represented by the universal which we are considering. This universal is indeed *their* universal whole. From this it is evident that the Pr. which is true of all the enumerated parts is also true of this universal whole, since in virtue of the very definition of the universal (that which is *one in many*) every predicate *common* to many subjects belongs to the universal which represents these subjects (which is *one in them*) in relation to this predicate.

(*a*) It is apparent, then, that *when the enumeration of parts is taken as sufficient* the mind can and must conclude from the parts to the whole. For in supposing that the enumeration is " sufficient " we are in fact supposing that we know that the enumerated parts are really represented in relation to the predicate in question by the universal which we are considering and not by another. (For this reason the ancients considered induction by sufficient enumeration as induction by *virtually complete* enumeration.)

*(*b*) Only by reason of this presupposed condition is inductive inference a true inference (*consequentia formalis inductive*, as we said above). In order to be a *formal sequence* (see above, No. 63) induction presupposes a certain condition on the side of the matter. An induction such as " Peter is mortal, therefore every man is mortal "

is a *material sequence* if we do not know from some other source that mortality is of itself a characteristic which depends upon the essence ; it is a *formal* sequence if we do know this fact.

(2) But *how* can the condition presupposed here be realized ? How can the enumeration of parts be *sufficient* ? How can we be sure that it is ? This question is the central question of induction and concerns, not the logical principle, but the metaphysical foundation of induction. Thus it does not belong to Minor Logic, which considers only the form of reasoning. We shall study it in Major Logic.

The conditions for a sufficient enumeration vary according to the case

We shall only take note here that the conditions for a " sufficient " enumeration vary according to the case. For instance, in relation to an essential predicate such as *mortal* it would, strictly speaking, be sufficient to cite *one single case :* " Peter is mortal, therefore man is mortal " (if we know through some other source that this is a question of an essential predicate, and that the fact that a living being is mortal or immortal depends upon the inmost constitution of its nature). On the contrary, in relation to a non-essential predicate, such as the colour of the skin, a very long enumeration of various subjects would be necessary in order to enable us to conclude : " men are white or yellow or black or red."

We should note, too, before everything else that the enumeration is *sufficient* when we have considered a sufficient number of parts to know *in a certain or in a merely probable manner* that the universal which represents them in relation to the predicate in question is indeed the universal under consideration. What is true of the enumerated parts will then be *certainly* or *probably* true of this universal whole.

and of itself induction concludes in a merely probable manner.

It is obvious, in considering induction in itself, abstracting from certain particular conditions or limit-cases (as those of *complete* enumeration of which we shall speak below) that, in itself, it admits of a certain zone of probability. For example, when we said : " Iron and copper and gold and silver . . . conduct electricity," it is certain that, in relation to the Pr. " conductor of electricity," iron, copper, gold, silver and their like, are the constitutive parts of a certain universal whole *X*. But is this universal whole really the subject *metal* itself, or is it not a more restricted universal: " metal answering to such and such determined physical or chemical conditions," so that a metal might be found which did not answer to these conditions and therefore did not conduct electricity? We cannot affirm this with absolute certitude, and the inductive minor: " The universal which represents iron, copper, gold, silver, etc., in relation to the predicate conductor of electricity is the universal metal," is but a *probable* proposition.

The reason for this is that, in virtue of the very structure of induction, the mind in this reasoning does not identify two concepts by means of a third, a procedure which produces perfect certitude—it identifies two concepts (S. and Pr. of the Conclusion) by means of an enumeration of singular or particular subjects each of which it identifies with the predicate-concept, and from which it ascends to a concept (the subject-concept) which represents them all in relation to the predicate under consideration. By the light of abstraction, the mind immediately seizes this universal subject as a whole realized in these singular subjects. But with the exception of certain special conditions, it seizes it neither as belonging *solely* to these singular subjects and their like, nor as being unable to comprise anything beyond them.

Thus, by its very structure, induction admits of the possibility (destroyed only in certain particular cases) of a deficiency on the side of matter. But, as we saw above, this does not prevent it from being a true and formal inference (*as inductive*). Let us keep in mind that *inductive* inference is other, and has another end than *syllogistic* inference, and that the mind does not *see* the same way in induction as it does in the syllogism. In showing to the mind, in the middle term, the *reason* for the identity of the extremes, the syllogism compels it to see this identity, by the light of the premisses. In showing to the mind, in the enumeration of parts, the *matter* wherein the extremes are identified, induction compels it to see, by the light of abstraction, the universal subject to which the predicate belongs (perhaps on the condition that it restrict this subject). Thus it *authorizes* rather than *necessitates* the mind to posit the conclusion.

The Rules of Inductive Reasoning. Among the particular rules that may be assigned to induction from the point of view of Minor Logic, that is, from the point of view of the form or the correctness of reasoning, we shall signalize only the following two :

(1) The enumeration must be sufficient, if not, the inference will not be formal. The argumentation : " Peter and Paul and James . . . is French, therefore every man is French " would be a defective reasoning.

(2) When a singular or particular term is related to a subject whose *suppositio* is particular (*determinate*) we do not have the right to make this term universal by an inductive *ascensus*, even if the enumeration is sufficient. For example, do not say : " Some saint did not display this type of heroism, and some saint did not display this other type of heroism, nor some other this type, nor some other that type . . . , therefore some saint did not display any type of heroism." Nor again : " Someone ignorant of Logic can avoid this mistake, and someone ignorant of Logic can avoid this mistake, and someone else this one, and some other that one, therefore someone ignorant of Logic can avoid every mistake."

The precepts (the rules of Bacon and Stuart Mill) concerning the use of inductive reasoning in the natural sciences are often called " rules of induction." The study of these precepts belongs to Critique (a propos of the Methods of the Sciences).

B. THE DIVISION OF INDUCTION

Induction is complete or incomplete accordingly as the parts of the subject of the conclusion have or have not been completely enumerated.

99. DIVISION OF INDUCTION. Induction is COMPLETE OR INCOMPLETE, accordingly as the parts of the universal whole which is the subject of the conclusion have or have not been *completely* enumerated. Obviously, *incomplete* induction is by far the more frequently used. When the parts in question are the singular data of sense experience, as they usually are in the natural sciences, it is impossible to enumerate them completely, since the human mind cannot pass in review the indefinitude of individual cases.

All the examples of induction given hitherto were examples of *incomplete* induction. Do not allow this expression " incomplete induction " to be misleading ; it in no way signifies unfinished or badly finished induction ; it is but an abbreviation of " induction *by incomplete enumeration.*" Now the enumeration of parts therein may be

The most frequently used induction is *incomplete* induction (wherein the enumeration may be sufficient or insufficient).

INCOMPLETE

and nevertheless

SUFFICIENT,

and whenever the enumeration is sufficient it is valid and formal. True, as we shall see in Major Logic, that it is often difficult to know whether or not a particular incomplete enumeration is sufficient, or at least to arrive at this conclusion with certitude.

On the contrary, when the enumeration is

COMPLETE

it is obviously *sufficient.* Since we have enumerated *all* the parts of the universal whole, the latter is evidently the subject which represents them in relation to the predicate. For example, given the following examples of complete induction :

In *complete* induction the enumeration is always *sufficient.*

> Plants and beasts and men breathe,
> and the universal that represents plants and beasts and men is : *living body,*
> therefore every living body breathes.

Or again :

> Sight, and touch, and hearing, and taste, and smell, has a corporeal organ.
> And the universal that represents sight, and touch, and hearing, and taste, and smell, is *sense.*
> Therefore every sense has a corporeal organ.

From these examples we see that the nature of complete induction, its structure and manner of inference, are the same as those of incomplete induction, so that the division into complete induction and incomplete induction is not an "essential" one. Complete induction is rather a *limit-case* of induction. If we consider induction from the point of view of Minor Logic, as an *inference*, we find its purest (that is, its clearest and simplest) type in complete induction. For the enumeration of parts, which must be *sufficient* in order to meet the demands of the form of inductive reasoning, is manifestly so in complete induction, and every sufficient enumeration is, in truth, a *virtually* complete enumeration. But if we consider induction from the point of view of Major Logic, as an *argument* or *proof*, another *means of proof* (*locus arguendi*) is added to induction properly so-called. For here, indeed, we pass from the antecedent to the consequent, not only in virtue of the induction itself (*in vi inductionis*), but also in virtue of a reasoning founded upon the equivalence of two terms (*ab aequivalenti ad aequivalens*).[1]

Incomplete sufficient induction is a virtually complete induction.

*Thus the two (complete) inductions given as examples above have their counterpart in a reasoning with the following formulation :

(1) Every plant and every beast, and every man, breathes,
but " every plant and every beast and every man " is equivalent to " every living body,"[2]
therefore every living body breathes.

(2) Sight, touch, hearing, taste and smell have a corporeal organ,
but " sight, touch, hearing, taste and smell " is equivalent to " every sense,"[3]
therefore every sense has a corporeal organ.

This reasoning is a syllogism in which the enumerated parts properly constitute a middle TERM. (Such is not the case in induction as such, wherein the enumeration of parts *is* not a *term*, which is one and the same in the Major and the Minor, but *leads* to a term, a universal subject which figures as such only in the Minor : " sight, and

[1] Cf. John of St. Thomas, *Log.*, p. 174.

[2] Or again, according to the normal formulation of the syllogism : " but every living body is plant or beast or man."

[3] Or again, using the normal formulation of the syllogism : " but every sense is sight, touch, hearing, taste or smell."

touch, and hearing, and taste, and smell, has a corporeal organ, and *the universal which represents* sight and touch and hearing and taste and smell is sense. . . ." " Peter, and Paul, and James, is endowed with speech, and the *universal which represents* Peter and Paul and John, and James, etc., is man. . . .")

A reasoning of this kind, founded upon the equivalence of two terms, is to be found with every complete induction, but must not be confounded with the inductive inference itself. On the contrary, it masks this inference, whose structure is different and whose mean is not a term but the enumeration of parts itself in so far as it introduces the mind to a universal. Undoubtedly there is an equivalence at the foundation of induction, but it is not the equivalence of one term with another term, it is the equivalence of a plurality of parts with a universal term which represents them. Induction as such is always founded upon the supreme principle : what is true of many sufficiently enumerated parts of a universal subject is true of this universal subject.

Complete induction is a true inference, a true argumentation, by which the mind acquires new knowledge. If many modern authors have denied this it is, 1. because, as the result of nominalistic prejudice, they have failed to recognize the nature and value of the universal,[1] and thereby the entire processus of human knowledge, and 2. because they have understood induction only from the point of view of the parts of a *collective whole*, that is by completely destroying it. It is *one thing* to know that each of the five senses has a corporeal organ and another to know that *the sense*, this nature which I call the sensitive faculty, has a corporeal organ ; just as it is *one thing* to know that Peter and Paul are mortals and another to know that *man* is mortal. By the universal truth which concerns the nature or quiddity common to the enumerated parts, we implicitly possess the

Complete induction is a true and legitimate inference.

[1] Again, we are sometimes misled by the *over obvious* examples which logicians ordinarily use in order to more clearly elucidate the form of argumentation. From this point of view the traditional example of the syllogism : " Every man is mortal, but Peter is a man, etc.," would also lead us to think that the syllogism does not further knowledge.

raison d'être of the considered property (and we can sometimes disengage it explicitly later on). We said above that incomplete induction passes not from *some* to *all*, but from *some* to *every*, which is a passage from the sensible to the intelligible. Complete induction passes from *each* to *every*, from all the parts to the universal, to the sphere of intelligible necessities which is realized in each part ; and this is also to rise from the plane of the sensible to the plane of the intelligible.

(*a*) Complete induction is often called *Aristotelian induction*, and incomplete induction *Baconian induction*, and it is sometimes maintained that Aristotle and the ancients knew only the former, the latter having awaited the advent of Francis Bacon [1] or John Stuart Mill [2] to be revealed to man. In reality the ancients placed principal emphasis upon complete induction because, as we have indicated in the text, they found in it the type of induction which, by its extreme simplicity, offered the maximum advantage from the point of view of logical elucidation as well as from the point of view of pedagogical exposition, and because, understanding the word " complete " not only of that which is *formally* complete, but also of that which is *virtually* complete, every legitimate induction is " complete." Nevertheless, they were thoroughly acquainted with incomplete induction as the use which they made of it abundantly testifies, and they did not lose sight of it in their Logic. Far from having a narrower notion of induction than ours Aristotle, as we remarked above (No. 97 *b*), had, on the contrary, a *broader* and more comprehensive notion of it.

Aristotle treats of the logical mechanism of induction in the *Prior Analytics* (*I, 2, Chap. XXIII*) ; he also speaks of it in the *Topics* (*I, 12*, wherein he is obviously thinking

[1] Bacon, the Chancellor of England (1561–1626), who was never more than an amateur scientist, exerted a profound influence upon the trend of modern ideas by his *Novum Organum* (1620) and his *De Dignitate et Augmentis Scientiarum* (1623), wherein he used the inductive method and the natural sciences as a weapon against ancient philosophy.

[2] In his *System of Logic* (1843), John Stuart Mill (1806–1873) undertook to construct on nominalistic principles, a logic in which induction holds the preponderant position.

of incomplete induction), and in the *Posterior Analytics* (*I, Chap. XVIII*). He teaches that, in order for the induction to be valid, the parts contained under the universal in question [1] must be enumerated *in their entirety*, because he understands thereby, as Averroes has explained, that these parts must be enumerated in their entirety either *formally* (complete induction) or *virtually* (incomplete induction). It follows from the foregoing that a *sufficient* enumeration is, in fact, *virtually complete* enumeration, since it informs us that the universal in question does indeed represent the enumerated parts in relation to the considered predicate, and consequently contains no other parts except these and parts similar to them.

That this is the true thought of Aristotle is apparent to anyone who has read with care the twenty-third chapter of the *Prior Analytics*. It follows from the very illustration which he uses (man, the horse and the mule are long-lived, therefore every animal without bile is long-lived), which in his eyes precisely constitutes a sufficient but *incomplete* induction ; for in the *Historia Animalium* (*II, 15, 506 a 20*) and in the *De Partibus Animalium* (*II, 676 b 26, sqq., 77 a 15—b 1*), he names many other animals—roe, fallow-deer, seals, dolphins, etc., as being animals without bile.[2] The sentence : " we must apprehend C (the mean of induction) as made up of all the particulars, for induction proceeds through an enumeration of cases " (*68 b 27, Pr. Anal.*, Oxford, 1928) signifies exactly that the enumeration can be taken *as if* it were complete, that is, it is *virtually complete*.

Among the scholastics, the theory of incomplete induction was treated especially in the thirteenth century, by Albert the Great (Commentary on the *Prior Analytics*, *1. II, tract VII, Cap. 4*, and on the *Topics*, *1. I, tract III, Cap. 4 ;* etc.) and in the seventeenth century by John of St. Thomas (*Log., Ia Pars, Sum., 1. II, Cap. VI, p. 16 ; 1. III, Chap. II, p. 52 sqq. ; Illustr. q. VIII, a. 2, p. 172 sqq.*).

[1] St. Thomas expresses himself similarly, *in Analyt. Post.*, II, lect. 4, and he is obviously speaking there of *either virtually or formally* complete enumeration. Cf. also Artistotle, *Anal. Pr.*, I, 30, 46 a 18.

[2] Cf. Hamelin, *le Système d'Aristote*, p. 257.

(*b*) *General Schema of the Division of Induction. Legitimate* induction, that is, induction by *sufficient* enumeration, is divided into *complete* and *incomplete*. Taking into account induction by insufficient enumeration (illegitimate induction, wherein the sequence is not valid) and " formal induction " which is not true induction,[1] we have the following table :

DIVISION OF INDUCTIVE REASONING

INDUCTIVE REASONING	real	by sufficient enumeration	complete	LEGITIMATE INDUCTION
			incomplete	
		by insufficient enumeration		Illegitimate induction
	[apparent	. . . .		" Formal induction "]

C. REASONING BY RESEMBLANCE

100. REASONING BY RESEMBLANCE OR BY ANALOGY. (1) A reasoning by resemblance or by analogy (*exemplum*) is a *partial* or imperfect *induction* in which the mind passes from one or several singular facts (or from a particular enunciation) not to a universal conclusion, but to another singular or particular enunciation [2] which it infers in virtue of a resemblance :

> Paul was cured of his headaches by this medicine,
> therefore John will be cured of his headaches by this same medicine.
> The monkey is cured of tuberculosis by this particular serum,
> therefore man will be cured of tuberculosis by the same serum.

A reasoning by analogy is an imperfect induction which concludes from the particular to the particular in virtue of a resemblance.

This reasoning does not constitute an irreducible type of argumentation, it may be reduced to induction as the imperfect to perfect.

(*a*) Undoubtedly a reasoning by resemblance may be resolved into a complex reasoning : induction (by insufficient enumeration) + a syllogism.

[1] Cf. above, No. 96, 4.
[2] Cf. Aristotle, *Anal. Post.*, I, Chap. I, 71 a, 10 ; St. Thomas, lect. 1, 1, n. 12.

INDUCTION:
Paul was cured of his headaches by this medicine,
therefore everyone suffering from headaches will be cured by this medicine,

SYLLOGISM:
therefore everyone suffering from headaches will be cured by this medicine,
but John suffers from headaches,
therefore John will be cured by this medicine.

In reality, however, in a reasoning by resemblance the mind concludes from the particular to the particular not by means of a universal law but by means of the *resemblance* between the two cases in question :

> Paul was cured of his headaches by this medicine,
> and the case is similar for John as for Paul,
> therefore John will be cured of his headaches by this medicine.

It is as a rough draft of induction, an induction which stops mid-way, and which, instead of terminating in the universal of which the particular case stated in the Major is a subjective part, terminates in another particular case, because in the Minor the mind did not ascend to this universal itself but only to something much more general and much less determinate. That is, it ascended to that which is in truth less *proper* and most *common* as a reason of argument—to the *resemblance* which unites the particular case under consideration to another particular case, without being able to say if the one and the other are, in regard to the predicate, both contained under a same universal " reason."

(*b*) The fact that the reasoning by resemblance goes from the particular to the particular does not in any way constitute it as an example of what Stuart Mill and the nominalistic logicians call an *inference from the particular to the particular. There is no inference from the particular to the particular*. We never find a direct union of the particular to the particular in the reasoning but only in the order of images and of sense knowledge (" the association of images" and by these images "the association of ideas" in man). In reasoning by resemblance, as in every reasoning, there is a universal concept (precisely that of the *resemblance* between two cases). The reasoning of the learned man, who thinks that a particular law of the reflection of sound is no doubt applicable to the reflection of radiating heat because the two cases resemble each other, or that dew must have the same cause as the vapour which appears upon a pitcher of cold water in the summertime because the two cases resemble each other, is altogether different from the association of images in virtue of which a scalded cat fears cold water or a watch-dog barks at every beggar.

Do not confuse *reasoning by analogy* with *analogical knowledge.*

(*c*) Reasoning by resemblance is ordinarily called *reasoning* by analogy. But we must be careful not to confuse it with what is called *analogical knowledge. Reasoning by analogy* and *analogical knowledge* are two entirely different things. In a *reasoning by analogy*, the analogy, which designates a more or less accidental resemblance, refers to the manner of establishing a conclusion, to an *inference* of which it constitutes all the force (and the insufficiency). In *analogical knowledge*, the analogy refers to a *concept* and to the things in which it is realized ; it is, at least in the analogy of proper proportionality,[1] a property intrinsic to the concept itself. Consequently, if one of the things signified by an analogous concept (for example, created being) is within our immediate range, and the other is not (for example, uncreated being) we can know the second by the first as "by a mirror." This knowledge is undoubtedly inadequate, but it may be absolutely certain.

(2) It is evident that reasoning by resemblance can furnish only probable knowledge, not certainty. It plays an immense *rôle* in discovery or invention. But recourse to the more perfect types of reasoning (the syllogism, or induction by sufficient enumeration) is necessary in order to stabilize scientific judgment.

(3) What is ordinarily called an *example* or *comparison* is scarcely more than a rough draft of a reasoning by resem-

[1] The question of analogy will be treated in Major Logic and Metaphysics.

blance, whose object is not to express a more or less probable conclusion, but only to illustrate a proposition and to make it more sensibly manifest.

This is the reason for which the truth of the thoughts we express is absolutely independent of the comparisons which we use in order to make them more clear. The illustrations we choose may be false in themselves, but they are good if they serve in the manifestation of a truth. Thus it is in so many of the charming comparisons which St. Francis of Sales borrows from the *natural history* of the ancients : " And even as the rainbow touching the thorny aspalathus renders it more fragrant than the lily, so the redemption of Our Lord touching our sorrows, renders them more profitable and lovable than original innocence could ever have been." [1]

[1] St. Francis of Sales, *Traité de l'Amour de Dieu*, Bk. II, Chap. V.

APPENDIX

PRACTICAL SUGGESTIONS

I

LOGICAL ALGEBRA. As we shall see in Major Logic, the system which is currently called the *algebra of Logic* refers to a certain art of substituting, for the work of reason, the methodical use of ideographic (logistic) signs. The foundations of this discipline are in themselves absolutely foreign to true logic or the art of reasoning, and, among most logisticians, spring from a general conception (" Logic of Relation ") which is destructive of a sound philosophy of reasoning.

Nevertheless, there is nothing to prevent us from imagining an altogether different and much less pretentious *logical algebra*, constituted in conformity with the principles of traditional logic, which would provide the logician with a system of artificial signs especially adapted to the reflex analysis of reasoning.

This logical algebra would certainly not pretend to displace language, which is the direct expression of the work of thought, nor to furnish the means for a logical calculus which would dispense with thinking. It would limit its aims to the facilitation of the labour of logical reflection *for the logician*, by translating verbal propositions into a system of more complete and more precise technical signs (under this special aspect of the reflex study of the processes of the reason).

It would, moreover, be extremely useful, by the very fact that it would make logical properties sensibly evident and facilitate the use of logical rules. We are convinced that it would be of particular service, from the pedagogical point of view. If the professor would, in teaching Logic, contrive to construct such a system of signs, in union with his pupils, he would find therein the best means of keeping them interested, arousing their attention, and assisting their memory.

As an example, for the sole purpose of showing the way in which we could set about to do this, let us select some elementary signs such as the following :

T to indicate the identification of the Pr. and S. in an affirmative proposition,

X their separation in a negative,

$\dot{\mathsf{T}}$ or $\dot{\mathsf{X}}$ a *suppositio* taken in relation to ideal existence,

$\underset{\bullet}{\mathsf{T}}$ or $\underset{\bullet}{\mathsf{X}}$ a *suppositio* taken in relation to real existence,

a capital letter at the beginning of a word to indicate that the term is taken universally,

a parenthesis, a term taken particularly,

brackets, a singular term,

the sign →, to indicate an inference (" therefore ").

Obviously this list could be considerably extended. But even with signs as elementary as these it is easy to elucidate a good many interesting points. Thus, in order to translate the syllogism " Every man is mortal, but Peter is a man, therefore, etc.," into this system of signs, we would say :

Man $\dot{\mathsf{T}}$ (mortal)

Peter $\underset{\bullet}{\mathsf{T}}$ (man)

→ Peter $\underset{\bullet}{\mathsf{T}}$ (mortal)

Setting forth the syllogism in this way shows forth the fact that the singular minor (and similarly the conclusion) have a *suppositio* taken in relation to real existence, and also the fact that it affirms an essential Pr. of the S.[1]

Simple conversion would be translated by the following symbols :

A X B

B X A,

or :

(a) T (b)

(b) T (a)

[1] This is regularly the case in singular propositions, as we said above (84 II, § 4) concerning some universals.

clearly showing that in such a case there is no inference properly so-called, but simply a different expression of *one and the same truth* (see above, No. 68, 1).

Partial conversion (*per accidens*) would be translated by the symbol

$$\begin{array}{c} \mathrm{A}\ \mathrm{T}\ (\mathrm{b}) \\ (\mathrm{b})\ \mathrm{T}\ (\mathrm{a}) \end{array}$$

which shows that partial conversion repeats, in an *implicitly diminished* fashion, the *same truth* as the original proposition (see above, No. 68, 2).

In translating the passage of a universal affirmative to a singular in this system of signs

$$\mathrm{A}\ \underset{\bullet}{\mathrm{T}}\ (\mathrm{b}) \rightarrow [\mathrm{a}]\ \underset{\bullet}{\mathrm{T}}\ (\mathrm{b})$$

(for example : " Every man is mortal, therefore this man is mortal ") we perceive that, in order to be able to posit the second member, we must know that [a] exists.[1] In other words, we must state the *existence* of the singular subject (*addere constantiam*), and say : " Every man is mortal, *and this man exists*, therefore this man is mortal " (see above, Chap. III, section 2, note 72).

Syllogisms in *Darapti*, such as those used as examples, p. 231, would have as their symbols :

$$\begin{array}{rcl} \mathrm{Bat} & \mathrm{T} & (\mathrm{wings}) \\ \mathrm{Bat} & \dot{\mathrm{T}} & (\mathrm{mammal}) \\ \rightarrow (\mathrm{mammal}) & \underset{\bullet}{\dot{\mathrm{T}}} & (\mathrm{wings}) \end{array}$$

$$\begin{array}{rcl} \mathrm{Poet} & \dot{\mathrm{T}} & (\mathrm{artist}) \\ \mathrm{Poet} & \dot{\mathrm{T}} & (\mathrm{man}) \\ (\mathrm{man}) & \dot{\mathrm{T}} & (\mathrm{artist}) \end{array}$$

This shows that the conclusion must be taken in the same (" existential " or " ideal ") sense as the Major—and also

[1] A fact which is not implied in the first member of the conversion, even if it be given an existential meaning, as we have done here. (Every man is mortal, and men exist.) The *suppositio* here is indeed taken in relation to real existence, but signifies only that *men* exist ; it does not signify that *this* determinate *man* exists. To pass from A to (a) it is not necessary to mention the existence of the subject ; to pass from A to [a] such mention is necessary.

makes evident the way in which *Darapti* is reduced to *Darii*, by the conversion of the Minor :

Darapti	C T (b)
	C T (a)
	→ (a) T (b)

Darii	C T (b)
	(a) T (c)
	→ (a) T (b)

We could very easily verify all the rules of the reduction of moods by this same method (see above, No. 79).

Finally Descartes' *ontological argument* (see above, pp. 63–4) would be translated in the following manner :

Absolutely perfect	$\dot{T}$	(necessarily existing)
[God]	$\dot{T}$	(absolutely perfect)
→ [God]	T	(necessarily existing)

This makes the flaw in the argument sensibly apparent (the *suppositio* is taken in relation to ideal existence in the antecedent and in relation to real existence in the consequent).

II

DIVISION OF THE COURSE. In a philosophy course of eight or nine months' duration, this treatise on *Minor Logic* could be divided into nineteen lessons, in the following manner (omitting all the nos. and paragraphs preceded by an asterisk).

I. Preliminaries (Nos. 1 to 4). . . .

II. Simple Apprehension. Notion of the concept. Extension and comprehension of the concept (Nos. 5 to 13).

III. The different kinds of concepts (Nos. 14 to 18).

IV. Notion of the oral term. The different kinds of terms (Nos. 19 to 25).

V. Language and thought. The definition. Division (Nos. 26 to 33).

VI. The Judgment. General notions about the proposition (Nos. 34 to 43).
VII. The different types of propositions : simple and compound, affirmative and negative (Nos. 44 to 48).
VIII. Propositions *de inesse* and modal propositions. The subject and predicate from the point of view of quantity (Nos. 49 to 52).
IX. The opposition of propositions (Nos. 53 to 55).
X. The conversion of propositions (Nos. 57 to 58). Review of the preceding assignments.
XI. General notions about reasoning (Nos. 60 to 65).
XII. Division of reasoning. " Immediate inferences." General notions about the categorical syllogism (Nos. 66 to 70).
XIII. General notions about the categorical syllogism (continued).
Figures and moods. Division of the syllogism by reason of its figure (Nos. 71 to 74).
XIV. Division of the syllogism by reason of its mood (No. 75).
XV. Hypothetical syllogisms. The conditional syllogism (Nos. 86 to 88).
XVI. Division of the syllogism (Nos. 90 to 94).
XVII. Inductive reasoning (Nos. 95 to 98).
XVIII. Division of Induction. Reasoning by resemblance (Nos. 99 to 100).
XIX. General review.

III

In studying each assignment given in the table above, we would advise the student to read the larger type first, and to add the study of the inset passages in a second reading.

IV

SUMMARIES. *Summaries* have been inserted in this volume to help the student in preparing his lessons and to facilitate review. The student should commit to memory that part of the summary corresponding to each lesson.

V

THEMES. After each important section of this work, *exercises* are to be found which may be varied at the pleasure of the instructor. These practical exercises are absolutely indispensable. Themes on any one of the following subjects may be added :

Show the distinction between the three operations of the mind, and the reciprocal relations existing between them.

The extension and the comprehension of concepts (Paris).

The *rôle* of quantity in the judgment and the reasoning. Is a Logic that does not take extension into account possible ?

The *rôle* and function of the verb *to be* from the point of view of the logical analysis of thought.

The opposition and conversion of propositions.

Are there immediate inferences ?

Explain the logical mechanism of the categorical syllogism. In what sense may it be said that, in the syllogism, the mind goes from the general to the particular ?

The figures and the moods of the syllogism.

Comment of the words of Joseph de Maistre : "The syllogism is the man."

The conditional syllogism. Wherein does it differ from the categorical syllogism ? Is it a primary form of reasoning ?

Induction. Its logical structure. Is it reducible to the syllogism ?

Show that language serves not only in the expression, but also in the very exercise of thought (Lille).

ALPHABETIC INDEX

(The numbers refer to the pages)